Legitimacy of Power

The Permanence of Five
in the
Security Council

Legitimacy of Power

The Permanence of Five in the Security Council

Dilip Sinha

Vij Books India Pvt Ltd
New Delhi (India)

Indian Council of World Affairs
Sapru House, New Delhi

Published by

Vij Books India Pvt Ltd
(Publishers, Distributors & Importers)
2/19, Ansari Road
Delhi – 110 002
Phones: 91-11-43596460, 91-11-47340674
Fax: 91-11-47340674
e-mail: vijbooks@rediffmail.com
web : www.vijbooks.com

ISBN: 978-93-88161-06-0 (Paperback)

ISBN: 978-93-88161-05-3 (ebook)

Dedication

To my father, Amar Sinha, whose insights permeate this book and my high school teacher, Purno A. Sangma, later Speaker of India's Lok Sabha, who introduced me to the world of international relations.

Contents

List of Abbreviations

EU	European Union
ICC	International Criminal Court
ICJ	International Court of Justice
ICTR	International Criminal Tribunal for Rwanda
ICTY	International Criminal Tribunal for Yugoslavia
IFOR	Implementation Force
ILO	International Labour Organisation
INTERFET	International Force East Timor
ISAF	International Security Assistance Force
MINUSMA	Multidimensional Integrated Stabilization Mission in Mali
MISAB	Inter-African Mission to Monitor the Implementation of the Bangui Agreements
MISCA	International Support Mission to the Central African Republic
MONUC	UN Mission in the Democratic Republic of the Congo
MONUSCO	UN Stabilization Mission in the Democratic Republic of the Congo
NATO	North Atlantic Treaty Organisation
PRC	People's Republic of China

R2P	Responsibility to Protect
SFOR	Stabilization Force in Bosnia and Herzegovina
UN	United Nations
UNAMIR	UN Assistance Mission for Rwanda
UNAMSIL	UN Mission in Sierra Leone
UNCIO	UN Conference on International Organisation
UNEF	UN Emergency Force
UNGA	United Nations General Assembly
UNFCCC	United Nations Framework Convention on Climate Change
UNIFIL	UN Interim Force in Lebanon
UNITA	National Union for the Total Independence of Angola
UNMIH	UN Mission in Haiti
UNMIK	UN Mission in Kosovo
UNMOGAP	UN Good Offices Mission in Afghanistan and Pakistan
UNMOGIP	UN Observer Group in India and Pakistan
UNOSOM	UN Operation in Somalia
UNPROFOR	UN Protection Force
UNSC	United Nations Security Council
UNTAET	UN Transitional Administration in East Timor
UNTSO	UN Truce Supervision Organization
USSR	Union of Soviet Socialist Republics (Soviet Union)
US	United States of America

Introduction

Thrice in the last century - in 1919, 1945 and 1991 - the United States, Britain and France, the leaders of the Western world, emerged victorious in a major war and rebuilt the international order to provide security to the world. The United States was the driving force behind each enterprise, inspired by its unique blend of altruism and isolationism. After the First World War, it refused to join the international organisation it had created and withdrew across the Atlantic. After the Second World War, it formed the United Nations with a steely determination to keep its allies together and the enemies subjugated. After the Cold War, it decided to take charge and reshape the world in its own image. A victorious state creates an order to serve its interests but likes to "remain unbound itself, free of institutional constraints and obligations".[1] The United States tried the same. The story of the Security Council is the saga of the United States and its four allies from the Second World War, Russia, Britain, France and China - their cooperation and confrontations.

This book is a study of international security cooperation and its moorings in international law from the perspective of the countries of the South. In the process, it also presents the major events in international relations in the last two centuries from the same viewpoint. It contrasts the Security Council's aversion to change and its inability to keep pace with the other organs of the United Nations and international organisations in a globalising world. It goes into the reasons behind the dominant position assigned to the permanent five in the security structure and their performance since then.

The United Nations has grown into a universal international organisation covering all conceivable aspects of relations among countries, or States as they are referred to in international parlance, and a wide range of domestic issues, including human rights, development and the environment. The UN performs this gigantic task through its six organs and numerous subsidiary organisations and specialised agencies, many of which are independent but prefer to operate under its umbrella. The main purpose of founding the UN was to maintain international peace and security and social and economic issues were brought into its ambit primarily for their disturbing propensity to provoke and exacerbate security problems.

The Security Council is the primary organ of the United Nations charged with maintaining international peace and security. It is the only international body empowered to take military action. The founders of the UN were convinced that prompt and effective military action against an aggressor is essential for maintaining international peace and security. This book examines the evolution of the UN's security system, the Security Council's performance of its responsibility, the control of the permanent five over it and the military actions taken by them on its behalf. The practice of authorising military action is accepted by the permanent five as an essential tool in the Security Council's armoury and its legitimacy is no longer questioned by them. It has been resorted to on several occasions, though differences among them have often stymied action. I have dwelt at length on the origins of international security cooperation and the negotiations on the UN Charter to give the reader an appreciation of the intent behind its provisions. I have also looked at the other instruments available to the Security Council for evaluation and a better understanding of its working.

The book begins with the evolution of collective defence and collective security in modern times in Europe and the origins of international law to regulate the use of force by states (Chapter 1). Chapter 2 deals with the rise of international organisations, starting with the first notable attempt at sustained international cooperation - the Concert of Europe in the nineteenth century. The Concert came to an end with the rise of Germany and Italy, which led to the First World War. This time the United States helped Europe in building the first international organisation for general security, the League of Nations. Despite its tragic end, the League set the benchmark for international organisations.

The book then moves to the birth of the United Nations as a military alliance during the Second World War and the negotiations among the three main allies, the United States, the Soviet Union and Britain, to turn it into an international organisation for global security (Chapter 3). Chapter 4 looks at the negotiations at the San Francisco Conference where the Charter was finalised and adopted. Other allies joined these negotiations and I have narrated the concerns voiced by them about the Charter's security apparatus. These proceedings form part of what is referred to as the *travaux préparatoires* (preparatory works) of the United Nations.

The few early successes for the Security Council - independence for Indonesia, ceasefire and deployment of military observers in Palestine and Kashmir - are covered in the next chapter (Chapter 5). The differences that developed soon among the big powers on issues such as the selection of the first secretary-general, the rules of procedure of the Security Council, disarmament and the formation of the UN military form part of Chapter 6 which also deals with the formation of rival military alliances by them. Then comes the first military action authorised by the Security Council - in Korea. The circumstances leading to the two key innovations conjured by the Security Council during this crisis - authorising member states to take military action on its behalf and turning to the General Assembly under the 'uniting for peace' procedure - are narrated in Chapter 7. The subsequent freeze in military actions and the efforts to keep the Security Council alive and relevant by improvising peacekeeping operations take us through the Cold War and the two big operations in this period – Suez and the Congo (Chapter 8).

The end of the Cold War revived cooperation among the big powers and produced the most active phase in the Security Council's history. The Council authorised an array of military actions which are discussed in Chapter 9 – Iraq/Kuwait, Yugoslavia, Somalia, Rwanda, Haiti, the Democratic Republic of the Congo, Albania, Libya and concluding with Mali and the Central African Republic. This was also the period when the Security Council applied coercive sanctions. I have described them briefly, for they are an essential part of the UN security system, and taken up the cases of Southern Rhodesia (Zimbabwe) and South Africa in some detail to highlight the changing attitude of the three Western powers among the permanent five to sanctions (Chapter 10).

In this phase of activism, the Security Council also started acquiring new mandates by expanding the ambit of security to humanitarian issues, human rights, terrorism, democracy, climate change, sustainable development goals and women's empowerment and expounding the concept of the international community's responsibility to protect the citizens of countries whose governments were unable or unwilling to do so. The formation of international tribunals to try individuals guilty of heinous crimes in former Yugoslavia and in Rwanda and the setting up of the International Criminal Court and their relations with the Security Council are part of this scrutiny (Chapter 11).

In the next chapter, I have examined the compatibility of the authorised military actions with the UN Charter, taking up the arguments in support of such authorisations by various experts in the light of the provisions of the Charter. I have drawn upon the *travaux préparatoires* to understand the intent behind the provisions. The experts are mainly from the Western countries since it is these that have championed such actions and executed them (Chapter 12).

This brings us to the issue of the consonance of the provisions of the UN Charter on the powers of the Security Council with international law and whether Security Council resolutions and actions can be said to create international law. Permitting the Council to expand its mandate without addressing these issues is also discussed in Chapter 13.

I have then included a chapter on the approach of the permanent five to the Security Council and their management of it through the years. Here the United States looms large because, while ideas and suggestions have come from the other four, all authorised military actions originated from the West and the big ones were led by the United States (Chapter 14).

Chapter 15 looks at the major wars in which the Security Council did not act due to the exercise of the veto by a permanent member. Sometimes the threat or anticipation of it was enough to prevent the matter being taken up in the Council.

The book concludes with a chapter on Security Council reform. I have once again gone back to the San Francisco Conference to recapitulate the assurances given to the rest of the world by the permanent five on creating an organisation that would change with the times. The fruitless attempts since then form part of this chapter (Chapter 16).

The United Nations has built a strong global reputation through the activities of its specialised agencies, such as the World Health Organisation, UN AIDS, UNESCO and the Office of the High Commissioner for Refugees. But the main repository of power in it is the Security Council whose performance as the guardian of international peace and security has been abysmal. During the Cold War when it was deadlocked by the veto, it was the General Assembly that blazed a trail for the United Nations. It took the lead with new ideas coming from the countries of Asia, Africa and

Latin America. After the Cold War, the Security Council took over many of these new ideas by linking them to international security.

The Security Council is based on the legitimacy of power. The Charter confers special powers on the permanent five to enable them to perform the responsibility they have undertaken of maintaining international peace and security through the Security Council. The permanent five based their claim to this authority on their military power, not their commitment to democracy, the rule of law, human rights and other values that the United Nations now seeks to promote. However, lack of cooperation among them has frequently led to inaction and their refusal to provide troops to the Security Council has compelled it to resort to outsourcing military action. The Security Council started providing collective legitimisation to member states to exercise their military force due to "the Organisation's incapacity for decisive intervention in and control of international relations" reducing it to "verbal rather than the executive functioning".[2]

Even though the UN Charter confers the power of the veto on the permanent members of the Security Council, it does not place any special power or responsibility on them for maintaining international peace and security. This responsibility is assigned to the Council and the permanent five are required to work through it. The idea of a special responsibility for them found expression in later resolutions like the one adopted soon after the nuclear non-proliferation treaty (NPT) was opened for signature. The resolution sought to reassure non-nuclear weapon states against aggression by a nuclear-weapon state by declaring that this would create a situation in which the Security Council, "and above all its nuclear weapon State permanent members" would have to take immediate action.[3]

Decentralised enforcement is dependent on the goodwill of the big powers who are not interested in sending their forces to all trouble spots in the world. Member states not in their good books must depend on their own resources for their defence. Such a system can neither be called collective nor universal – it can at best be described as selective hegemonic security.

This book is about the franchising of military action by the Security Council to powerful member states. The terminology used is inevitably subjective. It is difficult to remain neutral. Military invasion no longer exists in the lexicon of governments and the selection of the term to describe it is itself an indicator of the commentator's stand on it. Countries do not invade others anymore. They send their troops to other countries at the invitation of their governments to liberate them or assist them in self-defence. Wars are fought without being declared. Countries use terms like liberation, action, operation and intervention when sending their military into another country. But some military actions do genuinely fall in these categories and it would not be fair to call all of them invasions. Using neutral terms becomes difficult in these circumstances and a value judgment must be made. I have used 'military action' for the use of force authorised by the Security Council and 'invasion' where it is not. This, however, is not always possible because several other instances of the use of force by countries deserved Security Council authorisation and it would be unfair to classify them as invasion.

Names are very important to countries and many of them are passionately attached to words and phrases that appear innocuous to outsiders. I have referred to countries by their popular short names rather than their formal names, for brevity, except where there are rival claimants such as in the case of the People's Republic of China and the Republic of China. But after the former became a member of the UN, I have called them by their popular names China and Taiwan. I have used Soviet Union for Russia for the period after the Second World War till its disintegration to distinguish it from its later incarnation, the Russian Federation. But for the two Koreas, I have used the popular geographical expressions, North and South, and the same for Vietnam during the period of its division. I have preferred to refer to the United Kingdom as Britain to reduce the number of similar acronyms - the UN and the US not being amenable to similar alternatives.

Thought also has to be given to the names of regional groups. At the UN, the most important group is the Western group, formally called the Western Europe and Others Group (WEOG), which comprises the countries of West Europe, the United States, Canada, Australia, New Zealand and Japan. This group is also referred to as the developed or industrialised countries. The countries of Latin America and the Caribbean, Africa and Asia (other than Japan and South Korea) form the Group of 77, named after its numerical strength when formed in 1964. They are also referred to as the developing countries and, more derisively, the Third World. Dividing the world into developed and developing betrays an inappropriate value-judgment that is best avoided. Similarly, industrialisation is no longer an exclusive privilege of the 'developed' countries. In the circumstances, using the terms North and South for the developed and developing countries, respectively, appears to me to be the most neutral. In the context of the Cold War, East and West are commonly used for the two sides and I have followed this practice.

My perceptions of the most powerful organ of the United Nations were shaped during my two stints in Geneva where member states forge issue-based alliances in diverse organisations without the absolute power of the veto. This overcomes the sharp political divides of New York and makes way for more dynamic diplomacy.

This book is based on the debates in the Security Council, the General Assembly and the San Francisco Conference, where the Charter was negotiated. For the history of the events and the people, I have used some of the vast numbers of books available on the United Nations, in the UN Libraries in New York and Geneva and in the Indian Council of World Affairs and the India International Centre. I have also used the archival material in India in the Nehru Memorial Museum and Library and in the United States in the New York Public Library. For the texts of the resolutions, I have depended on the website of the UN as I have on the website of the International Court of Justice for the cases cited. For the positions of the member states on various issues, I have used their formal statements made on the record.

Wherever possible I have given the document number of the resolution. Security Council resolutions are serially numbered since its beginning and start with S/RES/... followed by the resolution number and its year of adoption in parentheses. The full texts of the resolutions can be accessed on the UN website, www.un.org/en/sc/documents/resolutions/. General Assembly resolutions are serially numbered every year. They start with A/RES/... followed by the number of the session and then of the resolution. They are also available on the UN website.

I have frequently given the historical background of events to enable young scholars of international relations to understand the context better and not have to look up other sources. Sometimes, when referring once again to an incident or an article of the UN Charter or a resolution, I have repeated a few words on their contents. More informed readers may find these superfluous. I hope this does not detract from the main theme of the book - the political and legal analysis of the Security Council's mandate and actions. India's contribution to the debates in the Security Council during its seven terms (1950-51, 1967-68, 1972-73, 1977-78, 1984-85, 1991-92 and 2011-12) have been given prominence but the views of the other non-permanent members have also been briefly covered. The book is intended to help students of international relations and diplomats get a better understanding of the Security Council and the reasons for the morass it is in at present.

I am grateful to the Indian Council of World Affairs for sponsoring and supporting this project, in particular its directors-general, Rajiv K. Bhatia and Nalin Surie. I am also indebted to my friend, Ramu Damodaran, for going through the book at various stages of its writing and giving invaluable suggestions. Needless to say, the views expressed in it are entirely mine. I also wish to thank Ashok Chaddha for his secretarial assistance.

Endnotes

1   G. John Ikenberry, *After Victory: Institutions, Strategic Restraint, and the Rebuilding of Order after Major Wars.* (Princeton University Press, 2001), p. 51.

2   Inis Claude. *The Changing United Nations* (New York: Random House, 1969), p. 88.

3   UN Document S/RES/255(1968).

1   Collective Security

The United Nations was created as a collective defence organisation against the enemies of the Second World War. It evolved over time into a collective security organisation. Though collective security is now considered an essential element of international cooperation, it is a new concept in international relations. War has been accepted as a legitimate instrument of state policy and empire-building considered the best guarantee of security. This chapter deals with the rise of nation-states, their wars of national aggrandisement, the struggle to delegitimise war and to bring sovereign states within the purview of international law, voluntarily created by them to regulate their own sovereignty.

The fifteen members of the world's most powerful international body sit around a horseshoe-shaped table in the United Nations in New York. They sit in alphabetical order as per the name of their country in English. Seating revolves anti-clockwise every month and the country at the head of the table officiates as president. Every year, the term of five members expires but they cannot seek immediate re-election. Another five are elected by the UN General Assembly, giving each elected member a term of two years.

The remaining five get to stay there permanently, circumambulating the table without a break since 1946. These are the permanent five, the P-5, as they are called in UN jargon: the United States, the United Kingdom of Great Britain and Northern Ireland, France, the Russian Federation and the People's Republic of China.[1] They are there because they led the military alliance against Germany, Italy and Japan in the Second World War (1939 – 1945).

This is the Security Council of the United Nations, the only international body that can take or authorise the use of military force against a country, whether a member of the United Nations or not. Under the UN Charter, all member states of the United Nations have agreed to give this authority to the Security Council and to accept and carry out its decisions.

The United Nations was formed in 1945, initially by the governments of 51 countries which had fought the Second World War as allies.[2] It was the second general security international organisation attempted in the world. The first, the League of Nations, formed after the First World War, had collapsed within two decades of its formation. The United Nations has avoided that fate. Today, it has 193 member states, covering almost the entire world, except Taiwan, whose membership is blocked by the People's Republic of China. The Security Council is only one of the six organs of the United Nations but constitutes its core, its *raison d'être*.

The Second World War was the most devastating war in human history. It came barely two decades after the previous most devastating war, the First World War, and reinforced the determination of its victors not to repeat the mistakes made after the first. The preamble to the UN Charter began with a penitent remembrance of the two tragedies and set the goal of the organisation in its very first sentence, "to save succeeding generations from the scourge of war, which twice in our lifetime has brought untold sorrow to mankind". This was a much more direct and forthright statement of intent than the one expounded in the Covenant of the League of Nations. The League's preamble had given primacy to international cooperation over international peace and security. The priority for the founders of the UN was security from the enemy states and they wanted to create an organisation which could take effective military action to protect and enforce the peace. The Security Council was the organ charged with this responsibility.

International law and organisations are now recognised as the legitimate means for maintaining international security, and even states resorting to brute force invoke them to validate their actions. But this is a very recent phenomenon in international relations. War has been universally accepted through history as a lawful instrument of state policy. Annihilating the enemy was considered the best guarantee for peace. Even wars waged for the sole purpose of acquiring more territory were considered legitimate. Invading other kingdoms was the right of a king. War was glorified in ballads and epics and celebrated from generation to generation. Ambitious kings who annexed other kingdoms are still celebrated as great rulers. Empires are looked upon with awe and admiration as periods of peace and security and people still take pride in ancestors who subjugated other people. Empires were believed to provide better security than small kingdoms. The Indian political writer of the 4th century BCE, Kautilya, took a dim view of small kingdoms and extolled the virtues of empire-building.[3]

Such glorification of imperial conquest could not but lead to a perpetual state of war. In some societies, religious institutions sought to exercise restraint on the monarch by positing 'natural law' derived from god above state law. This endeavour was particularly strong in Europe where the Pope and the Roman Catholic Church, whose claim to divine authority was stronger than that of kings, exercised significant power over them in the Holy Roman Empire. This was not a derogation from the belief in the superiority of empires. But the intrusion of religion in state politics proved to be highly divisive and became a perpetual cause for strife. The persistent sectarian wars in Europe, especially the ravages of the Thirty Years' War (1618-1648), exposed the disruptive impact of religion and drove home the need for separating it from the state.

The disintegration of the Holy Roman Empire in Europe paved the way for states to be recognised as sovereign entities in international relations. Headed in the past by monarchs, most modern states are now republics. Monarchs claimed their authority as derived from their god and, therefore, absolute. They deployed political philosophers and religious leaders to sanctify their divine origins. The concept of sovereignty of the modern state, considered an essential attribute of it, is derived from similar dogmas but is now expressed in more legal terms. Abandoning god and religion as the source of state authority required a new political philosophy. The modern theory of state sovereignty, first expounded by the French jurist, Jean Bodin, in 'The Republic' in 1576, challenged the Pope's claim to divine authority. Bodin defined sovereignty as the supreme power of the monarch unrestrained by the laws.

Bodin expounded his concept of sovereignty with the intention of establishing a legal basis for order in society. He maintained that an essential attribute of sovereignty is the power to make laws which apply to all but the sovereign. This doctrine of absolute power ensured that there could be no legal challenge to the authority of the sovereign, either by the church or jurists. The same idea was expressed in 1651 in the Leviathan by the English philosopher, Thomas Hobbes, who asserted that the sovereign makes the law and not the other way around. Hobbes argued that the sovereign is not subject to the authority of any earthly power. He is only constrained by the laws of nature, by which he meant not god's laws but common sense. Thus, states would accept certain rules regarding the treatment of ambassadors or the conduct of war because they would expect similar conduct from other states. While Bodin declared that sovereignty in France was vested in the monarch, Hobbes believed that it could be in a person or a body or even a concept.

Modern international relations, at least since the Treaty of Westphalia, are based on the principle of the sovereign equality of nation-states.[4] However, it was not until the nineteenth century that Europe abandoned its dream of a single political entity ruled by god-given 'natural laws' and sought to promote international security through cooperation among countries. With this emerged the modern states system and started the evolution of international law and organisations. Nardin places the origin of the states system in the eighteenth century since the earlier system was still inspired by the ideal of a unified Christendom or a universal secular empire, "It is only in the eighteenth century that the idea of a states system whose unity is provided by its own distinctive institutions – those of diplomacy, the balance of power, and international law – really emerges as an independent and fully articulated conception of the character of European international society."[5]

The concept of sovereignty enabled nation-states to interact as equals, regardless of size, and to claim the right of non-interference in their internal affairs. This was expressed succinctly by Hall, "A state has the right to live its life in its own way, so long as it keeps itself rigidly to itself, and refrains from interfering with the equal right of other states to live their life in the manner which commends itself to them…"[6] Wolff also emphasised the equality of nations, "By nature all nations are equal the one to the other. For nations are considered as individual free persons living in a state of nature. Since by nature all men are equal, all nations too are equal."[7]

The rise of nation-states, however, opened the gates for more international wars, this time propelled by intense nationalism among people seeking to unify their nations, acquiring colonies or recovering ancient glory. Yunker noted, "Modern history also seems to suggest that the sovereign nation-state system possesses a strong propensity toward the generation of hostility, conflict and warfare among nations."[8] The need was felt for developing norms of behaviour for states to reduce the prospects of and recourse to war.

Napoleon's attempt to restore French glory after its defeat to Britain in the Seven Years' War (1756 – 1763) led to a series of wars across Europe. After defeating him in 1815 in alliance with Russia, Austria and Prussia (which expanded later to become modern Germany), Britain formulated a policy of balance of power on the continent to prevent the rise of a power that could challenge it. This came to be accepted even by the kingdoms on the continent as preferable to a single dominant power. The dreams of a Roman Empire or a Holy Roman Empire were finally shelved in favour of multiplicity of equal states maintaining peace through cooperation. Countries started interacting more frequently with each other to resolve disputes and provide security to each other. International cooperation for collective security may seem commonplace today but it presented serious legal and practical challenges till the twentieth century. It not only required new legal concepts and principles but also new terminology. Sovereignty gave the state absolute authority, both internal and external. Circumscribing it through any form of international law became a legal conundrum.

Interstate, Intergovernmental or International?

The term 'international' has gained currency now and is applied to organisations and practices relating to the intercourse among sovereign states. It was coined by the English philosopher, Jeremy Bentham, in the context of the law of nations to distinguish it from national laws, such as the Common Law of England. This was as much a correction of the term in vogue in Europe at that time, *droit des gens* (law of nations), as an improved translation of it in English. The fact that *droit des gens* was inappropriate in the sense that it was not law made by or for nations for their internal affairs but for relations between or among them had been pointed out by other writers. Bentham sought to correct this by suggesting using 'international' for this genre of laws to distinguish it more sharply from the laws for the internal affairs of nations.[9]

The term, however, rather inappropriately presupposes the inter-changeability of 'nation' and 'state', based on contemporary Europe. States, not nations, are the primary units of political organisation in the world, though there is a common notion that the two are co-terminus. Nation, derived from the Latin, *nasci* (to be born), started as a collective term for a people claiming common descent and, when organised as a sovereign territorial entity, called themselves a nation-state. It is now more expansively defined. Countries like the United States and India prefer to call their federating units states rather than provinces but regard themselves as single nations. The United Nations retained the League's terminology even though the latter was essentially a European organisation and could more appropriately call itself an association of nations.

Contemporary international law and relations are inter-state, or more appropriately inter-government, in character. They have not yet acquired the attributes of a world government. Governments represent the member state and all its citizens in international organisations. Other associations formed by the people, such as non-government organisations, commonly referred to as civil society, are allowed participation in some international organisations, primarily in those dealing with social issues, but they are distinctly subordinate to governments.

The urge for human unity transcending social and state barriers goes back to the *Upanishads* in India and the *Stoics* in Greece and the dream of evolving a transnational world government will never die. But the intergovernmental character of international organisations will not change in the foreseeable future because the level of diversity, inequality and distrust in the world is too high for countries to compromise their national sovereignty for the comfort of a global system where their citizens, companies or civil society acquire independent global identities. Some transnational corporations and civil society enjoy powers far beyond that of many countries and are keen to acquire more, but governments are not likely to cede their position to them. The transition from international organisations to world government will take time.

International Law

How does norm-setting take place among modern states? How do sovereign states undertake obligations and why do they respect them even in the absence of an enforcing authority? For norm-setting to take place there must be a states system with considerable degree of homogeneity among its members, who share a sufficient level of commonality to interact with each other on a regular basis. This has taken place on a limited scale all through history. Trade and military conquest have been its primary drivers. Religion too has been an important norm-setter and disseminator, moving on the back of both trade and military conquest, and sometimes on its own. Imperial powers have been important norm-setters and disseminators in history. Portugal, Spain, Netherlands, France, Britain, Belgium, and

Russia - spread their culture in their empires in America, Africa and Asia and imposed their norms of state behaviour.

The European states system in the nineteenth century after the Napoleonic wars offered particularly congenial conditions for the evolution of international norms. The sense of community already existed from Roman times and had been reinforced by Christianity. The rise of French as the language of the elite facilitated communication among them. The rise of a scientific temper also provided the necessary foundation for the development of a new body of laws, distinct from the god-given natural laws of medieval Europe. Natural laws had been gleaned by earlier European thinkers from divine laws enunciated by the clergy. With the Church marginalised, the newly emerging international law drew more from customary practice and treaties negotiated by sovereign states. The frequent meetings among multiple states allowed a new genre of multilateral treaties to be negotiated and become the new source of laws for international conduct.

When the Thirty Years' War was raging in Europe, the Dutch jurist, Hugo Grotius, wrote 'The Law of War and Peace' in 1625 in which he expounded the view that even states and their sovereign rulers must conform to certain universal laws and standards of behaviour in war and in peace.[10] With the rise of the modern sovereign state, the need arose for a law of nations "binding upon civilized states in their relations with one another".[11] This required a fundamental change in the concept of law as it prevailed in Europe then. Law was commonly understood, as defined by John Austin, to be a body of commands issued and enforced by a sovereign.[12] A legal order existed where there were an authority and an authoritative method to determine the law and to enforce it. The idea of natural laws was an extension of this definition since these were accepted as being divinely ordained. Kant declared that writers like Grotius who believed in a 'law of nations' were "sorry comforters" because such laws "do not and cannot have the slightest *legal* force since states as such are not subject to a common external constraint."[13]

The earliest works on international legal theory in Europe were by Spaniards in the sixteenth century. This was in line with treatises being written in countries during periods of expansion abroad and intense interaction with other countries. Francisco Vitoria (1480-1546), Francisco Suarez (1548-1617), and others wrote during Spain's invasions of America. Both Suarez and Vitoria were professors of theology and sought to bring some humaneness in the treatment of the indigenous people by the Spanish *conquistadors*. Inevitably they brought religion to bear on their legal precepts. International law thus goes back in its origins to 'god's law', or Natural Law, as its primary source. Human law, or Positive Law, was regarded as a supplement to it.[14]

Whitaker compared the two schools, "Historically, two prominent polar positions can be distinguished in the writing of the scholars. On the one hand, the Natural Law position views international law as a normative law of subordination, and, on the other hand, the Positive Law position looks upon international law as a customary law of coordination. The Natural Law view was dominant during the seventeenth and eighteenth centuries. After a period of re-thinking and transition in the nineteenth century, the Positive Law view became dominant in the early part of this century."[15]

From these early concepts evolved the idea of *jus gentium,* meaning 'law of nations', but in the sense of law applicable to nations, a concept that was later modified to *jus inter gentes,* (law among nations, or international law) to reflect more accurately its inter-state character. A law derived from a custom or an agreement among states was a conceptual leap for it lacked a sovereign law-giver and adjudicator. While international law was recognised as being *sui generis* (a class by itself), the lack of certain essential prerequisites of law raised unsettling questions. Kant provided the way out by suggesting the constitution of a league which would be committed to regulating the behaviour of states to avoid war and would ensure security. In an essay published in 1838, Jeremy Bentham propounded the idea of an international court. These are credited to be the early conceptualisations of international organisations.

The concept of international law gained acceptance and came to be recognised as originating in international customs and practices, whose principles were captured by scholars and formulated in legal terms in treatises. Many of these treatises are respected as reliable sources of international law and are also recognised by the Statute of the International Court of Justice, though left unnamed.

Multilateral treaties started developing in the nineteenth century and increased exponentially after the formation of the United Nations. They are a more precise source of international law and the sweeping codification of international conventions and practices has removed many ambiguities and uncertainties. But it is well recognised that treaties are enforceable only on countries that are parties to them. This gives rise to the question whether there are certain principles of international law that all countries are obliged to follow. Supporters of the universal applicability of such principles argue that in its absence the world would be reduced to a permanent state of anarchy.

Hersch Lauterpacht did not accept the notion that international law is nothing more than a series of contracts entered into by countries, bilaterally or multilaterally, and that there are no common practices and rules that bind all of them mandatorily. Writing in 1932, he asked rhetorically, "Shall international law aim at improvement by trying to bring its rules within the compass of the generally accepted notion of law, or shall it disintegrate it and thus deprive itself of a concrete ideal of perfection?"[16] The notion of the existence of certain basic norms of international conduct is recognised in Article 53 of the Vienna Convention on the Law of Treaties, 1969, which declares that a treaty is void if it violates certain peremptory norms, or *jus cogens,* of general international law. However, it does not illustrate this concept.

Once the concept of international law gained currency, the felt need for organisations to regulate it made the birth of international organisations a matter of time. Both Jeremy Bentham and John Stuart Mill regarded the absence of unambiguous laws and a well-defined authority to interpret and implement them as critical weaknesses of the prevailing international legal system. They believed that international public opinion could be a reasonably strong foundation for the effectiveness of international law. While the *lacuna* of an international legislative authority could be filled by negotiations which could develop international codes duly incorporated in treaties ratified by nations, a tribunal was essential for ensuring adjudication.

This desire for an international tribunal remained popular among several international law experts in the nineteenth century in Europe. Their efforts bore fruit in the Hague Conferences of 1899 and 1907 and later in the setting up of the Permanent Court of International Justice.

Multilateral conventions have a depository body for keeping track of and storing their instruments of ratification. Their implementation is often left to the states themselves, though most now provide for international organisations for this purpose. Some even mandate voluntary or mandatory dispute settlement mechanisms, though few can enforce their decisions or impose penalties for non-compliance. The older institutions created before the United Nations or in its early years are particularly deficient in this respect.

International law is framed by nation-states and only they, not their citizens, have rights and duties under it. Whitaker explains that "Individuals may sometimes be the 'objects' of the law but they are never the *subjects* of the law".[17] Charles G. Fenwick described it as a law of "community of communities" rather than a unified world community.[18] The rise of the civil society, particularly in Western countries, has led to the demand for greater participation of the people in international organisations. Many social and cultural organisations provide for it, but political and trade organisations are reluctant to change. Individual responsibility is now being fixed for certain crimes that were earlier dismissed as acts of state.

The lack of a legislator and machinery for enforcement and adjudication are not the only issues faced by international law. International relations are essentially political in nature and international law cannot remain untouched. Whitaker notes that law plays second fiddle in international relations, "There are exceptions, but it is a primary principle of international relations that politics is primary, law is secondary."[19] There is frequently a gap between law and practice in international affairs, particularly in the early stages of an evolving consensus that has not yet taken the shape of a universally ratified convention. This normative gap is frequently found in the actions of the big powers, which have the confidence of knowing that they can get away with it. The larger majority of countries can only bring moral pressure on errant countries. Another feature of international law is that a violation of it by a major power often becomes the law. But it is important to appreciate that nations still find it politically expedient to base their actions in law rather than brute power. If the law does not permit such action, legal luminaries are brought to weigh in on the matter and find a legal principle to validate it.

Lauterpacht examined the recurrent challenge of reconciling international law with national sovereignty. He wrote, "The function of law is to regulate the conduct of men by reference to rules...." But this rule of law is "constantly put in jeopardy by the conception of the sovereignty of states" which regards international law as emanating from the will of states. "It is a canon of international law that the jurisdiction of international tribunals is one voluntarily accepted by states." He maintained that the pressures of public opinion and political developments within the international community create the demand for limiting national sovereignty and concluding treaties to ensure the judicial settlement of disputes or "at any rate the appearance of effective legal obligation." It is on account of this limitation of international law that writers like Oppenheim regarded international law as "weak law" and asserted that this shortcoming is of a permanent nature. Lauterpacht accepted that international law should be regarded as incomplete but asserted that it is moving towards a "finite and attainable ideal of a society of states under the binding rule of law, as generally recognized and practised by civilized communities within their borders. . ."[20] Until the attainment of such an ideal, a system of collective security in which a few powerful countries get together to provide protection to all becomes an acceptable arrangement. Such hegemonic collective security began in Europe in the nineteenth century.

Collective Security and Collective Defence

Despite the explosive growth in international law and practice in all walks of life, collective defence and collective security remain its core objectives. Collective defence implies collective action by members against an external threat. This has always been the primary incentive for international cooperation. Alliances formed by states to protect themselves against a superior enemy were the earliest manifestations of international cooperation in collective self-defence although they cannot be regarded as precursors of modern international organisations since they were formed solely for defence against a common enemy and rarely outlasted the threat. The first instance of an alliance leading to sustained cooperation for several decades after the defeat of the enemy was the Concert of Europe in the nineteenth-century. The victory over Napoleon was not looked upon by the allies as sustainable since the revolutionary zeal unleashed by the French Revolution and the reformist ideas of the Napoleonic Code continued to threaten the old aristocracy of Europe. Monarchs and noblemen alike felt the need to hold together against these new forces.

Collective security deals with a threat emanating from an internal source against which all members accept the obligation to take joint action. Gordenker and Weiss distinguish between collective security and collective defence based on the prior identification of the threat, "Collective security does not permit the advance designation of a putative enemy, as in the case with defensive alliances."[21] A collective security organisation is based on the presumption that a security threat may arise from any of its members against which action may become necessary. An association of states, however, may have both objectives. Effective collective self-defence is contingent on a high degree of cooperation among members, which makes collective security an essential constituent of it.

The United Nations was formed as a collective defence organisation against the common enemy states of the Second World War. The term, collective security, does not figure in its Charter though it is now considered to be its essence. The Charter envisaged and catered for threats arising from disputes among states and assigned to it the responsibility of addressing the deeper social and economic causes of war to make international peace and security durable. However, once the enemy states themselves joined it and its membership became universal, it turned into a fully-fledged collective security organisation. The term was used in the statement issued after the first-ever summit meeting of the UN Security Council on 31 January 1992 in New York. The leaders declared "their commitment to the collective security system of the Charter."[22] The leaders also mandated the UN secretary-general, Boutros Boutros-Ghali, to draw up recommendations on strengthening this capacity of the UN. The resulting report, An Agenda for Peace, was released in June 1992. It did not define collective security but set out an ambitious set of proposals.

Legitimacy of Use of Force by States

All civilised societies have tried to define the circumstances in which the use of force by a state can be considered legitimate and to lay down some laws of warfare, but there are few instances until the twentieth century of attempts to outlaw war altogether. Religious leaders, political thinkers and jurists have sought to find ways to limit the right of states to resort to war. In Europe, they demanded a nobler objective or justification and sought to impose a code of conduct for their doctrine of a just war, *bellum justum*. In India, the concept of *dharma yuddha* required both the means and end to be just. But neither concept outlawed war.

As the divine origin of rulers and their kingdoms gave way to more mundane social contract theories, political thinkers and jurists tried to move away from religious constructs to reasoned tenets of international law through which the resort to war could be restrained. Grotius argued that a war can only be just when it is in response to an injury caused by the enemy. "There can be no lawful cause of making war except *injuria*," he wrote in his *De jure belli ac pacis*.[23]

All thinkers realise the practical difficulties in seeking to outlaw war. Even if international law were to prohibit the resort to war by states, it would have to carve out a set of exceptions relating to wars fought in self-defence. This would then have to be expanded to add the defence of allies and, in the modern world, of people who need protection against war crimes or mass atrocities. A carve-out as wide as this would practically legitimise all wars. The world would thus require a body or organisation to determine when a country is right to start a war. Besides, as Hall points out, "As international law is destitute of any judicial or administrative machinery, it leaves States, which think of themselves aggrieved, and which have exhausted all peaceable methods of satisfaction, to exact redress for themselves by force. It thus recognises war as a permitted mode of giving effect to its decisions."[24]

During the Second World War, the renowned British professor of international law, James L. Brierly, attempted to frame a set of operational principles to guide a collective security system. He prescribed that a state should have the most minimal participation in any collective security action. In an earlier article, he had examined the possibility of regulating the resort to armed force. Like Hall, he argued that the absence of an international system that could address the legitimate grievances of countries was a major hindrance to outlawing war, "The great difficulty of establishing any effective legal control over the resort to armed force in the past has been that international law offered no effective alternative way of securing the redress even of a legitimate grievance." This left aggrieved states with no choice but to resort to war, "War has been one of the means whereby from time to time States have revised the established international order." He pointed out that the League of Nations did not offer an "effective alternative either to war or to measures of force which do not amount to war". What was needed was a legislature in the international sphere which could address the demands for change in the international order without states having to take recourse to force, "....... we shall not have solved the problem of peace until we have devised, not indeed any servile imitation of a national legislature in the international sphere, but some substitute for it, some ordered process whereby we can satisfy the demand for change which is the mark of any living human society."[25]

The idea of expressly forbidding war graduated from the writings of political thinkers in Europe to the negotiating table of diplomats after the First World War. The devastation wrought by the war persuaded political leaders to incorporate the aspiration in international treaties. A small beginning was made in the Covenant of the League of Nations but it did not prohibit war. If the League failed to act, members could "take such action as they shall consider necessary for the maintenance of right and justice."[26] This was more clearly spelled out in the Kellogg-Briand Pact of 1928, which outlawed the use of war as an instrument of state policy.[27] States and the international community could, however, resort to war against a state that violated the Pact.

The Charter of the United Nations also does not outlaw war. It permits a country to use force to defend itself against military aggression by another country. However, it forbids members from waging war against each other and calls upon them to settle their disputes through peaceful means. The only other use of force permitted by the Charter is an 'enforcement measure' undertaken by the Security Council or by a regional organisation with its authority.

The United Nations created an international order in which member states agreed to restrict their sovereign right to wage war and to repose their faith in a small body of members of the Security Council. This was the *realpolitik* approach to securing international peace and a throwback to the traditional thinking in Europe that international peace is best preserved by the big powers. Krause explained the reason for this, "European history of the past three centuries contains ample evidence that international order can only be secured if a group of strong and responsible states work together and are ready to defend this order against actors who challenge it."[28]

Endnotes

1   The Russian Federation succeeded the Soviet Union and the PRC replaced the Republic of China. This is discussed in Chapter 14.

2   Argentina was an exception. It had remained neutral during the war but was still invited. The reason for this is mentioned in Chapter 4.

3   Kautilya was instrumental in the rise of India's first empire, the Mauryan Empire, in the 4th century BCE. His political treatise, the *Arthashāstra,* dealt with diplomacy and public administration.

4   The Treaty of Westphalia refers to three treaties signed after the Thirty Years' War in 1648 in Münster and Osnabrück in Germany, which enabled several Protestant kingdoms to break away from the fold of the Catholic Holy Roman Empire. It is looked upon as the beginning of the states system in Europe.

5   Terry Nardin. *Law Morality and the Relations of States* (Princeton University Press, 1983), p. 42.

6   William Edward Hall, *A Treatise on International Law.* 3rd ed. (Oxford: Clarendon Press, 1890), pp 43-44. Quoted in Nardin, p. 53.

7   Christian Wolff, *The Law of Nations Treated according to the Scientific Method.* Trans. Joseph H. Drake. *The Classics of International Law.* (Oxford: Clarendon Press, 1934). Quoted in Nardin, p. 54.

8   James A. Yunker. *Beyond Global Governance: Prospects for Global Government.* (International Journal on World Peace, Vol. XXVI No. 2, June 2009), p. 8.

9   Jeremy Bentham. *Introduction to the Principles of Morals and Legislation* in J.H. Burns and H.L.A. Hart (Eds.) *The Collected Works of Jeremy Bentham* (London: Athlone Press, 1970), p. 106. Quoted in Nardin. p. 118.

10 Alberico Gentili, an Italian who migrated to England and taught at Oxford strongly influenced Hugo de Groot (1583-1645). Groot wrote under his Latinized name, Hugo Grotius. His most famous work, *De jure belli ac pacis* (On the Law of War and Peace) was published in 1625 in Paris where he had taken shelter after fleeing from his native Holland. Grotius along with Gentili and the Spanish jurist, Francisco de Vitoria, are regarded as the founders of modern international law.

11 James L. Brierly. *The Law of Nations – An Introduction to the Law of Peace* (New York: Oxford University Press, 1963), p. 1.

12 John Austin. *The Province of Jurisprudence Determined* in H.L.A. Hart(ed.) (London: Weidenfeld and Nicolson, 1955). Quoted in Nardin, p. 70.

13 Immanuel Kant: *Political Writings.* Ed. Hans Reiss. Trans. H.B. Nisbet. (Cambridge University Press, 1970), p. 103. Quoted in Nardin, p. 74.

14 The leading naturalists were: Samuel von Pufendorf (1632-1694), Emmerich de Vattel (1714-1767) and James Lorimer (1818-1890). Some important positivists were: Richard Zouche (1590-1660), Johann Jakob Moser (1701-1785) and John Austin (1790-1859).

15 Urban G. Whitaker. Jr. *Politics and Power: A Text in International Law.* (New York: Harper and Row, 1964), p. 27.

16 Hersch Lauterpacht. *The Function of Law in the International Community* (Oxford: Clarendon Press, 1933), p. 407.

17 Whitaker. p. 10.

18 Charles G. Fenwick. *International Law, 3rd ed.* (New York: Appleton-Century-Crofts, 1948) p.3. Quoted in Whitaker, p. 8.

19 Whitaker, p. 14.

20 Hersch Lauterpacht, p. 432.

21 Leon Gordenker and Thomas G. Weiss. *Collective Security and World Politics.* Chapter in Thomas G. Weiss, *Collective Security in a Changing World* (Boulder, Colorado: Lynne Rienner, 1993) p. 6. This distinction is also recognised by writers like Eric Beckett. *The North Atlantic Treaty, 1950,* and Julius Stone, *Legal Controls of International Conflicts, 1959.*

22 UNSC document S/2500 of 31 Jan 1992, p.3.

23 Quoted in Falk and Mendlovitz. *The Strategy of World Order, Vol. III - The United Nations* (New York: World Law Fund, 1966), p. 455.

24 Quoted in Arnold McNair. *Collective Security (1936).* British Yearbook of International Law 17, pp.150-164. Reproduced in Tarcisio Gazzini and Nicholas Tsagourias (Eds.) *The Use of Force in International Law* (Farnham, Surrey: Ashgate, 2012), p. 80.

25 J.L. Brierly, *International Law and Resort to Armed Force,* Cambridge Law Journal 4, (1930-32), p. 308-19. Reproduced in Gazzini and Tsagourias, p. 77.

26 Covenant of the League of Nations, Article 15.7.

27 Named after the US secretary of state, Frank B. Kellogg, and the French foreign minister, Aristide Briand. It was signed initially by 15 countries.

28 Joachim Krause, *"Effectiveness of multilateralism in the field of collective security"* in Joachim Krause and Natalino Ronzitti (Eds.), *The EU, the UN and Collective Security: Making multilateralism effective* (Routledge, 2012), p. 10.

2   Birth of International Organisations

The earliest international organisations were set up in Europe in the nineteenth century. The Concert of Europe provided a forum to rulers for cooperation against the forces generated by the French Revolution. Though not an international organisation it paved the way for them. The Concert collapsed with the rise of Germany and Italy and a much more ambitious enterprise, the League of Nations, was attempted after the First World War. The League was an unprecedented experiment, well ahead of its time, and its tragic end provided some hard lessons for the victors of the Second World War. The League served both as an inspiration and as a warning to the big powers of the period.

International organisations started evolving in Europe in the mid-nineteenth century, during the extended period of peace provided by the Concert of Europe and the prosperity from the exploitation of colonies. Railways and steamships ferried delegations to meetings across the continent. The Westphalian states system had matured to create homologous nation-states. Sectarian wars had become a thing of the past. Nation-states had developed an ethos of co-existence based on a less divisive interpretation of Christianity and a new missionary zeal of civilising the rest of the planet instead of indulging in fratricidal wars at home. Britain enjoyed absolute sovereignty over the seas and no continental power could challenge it.

The expression, international society, came to be applied to the European states system during this period. Laws started evolving to regulate relations among them. The term commonly used now is international community, though it is often appropriated by Western countries to refer to themselves. There is little intrinsic difference in connotation between the two terms. Both imply a group of countries sharing common practices, customs and rules, which become the basis for regulating their intercourse.

International organisations are the outcome of conferences and many retain their congregational origins even after getting institutionalised. Conferences can be categorised by their periodicity into one-off, periodic and continuous. One-off conferences are called on a specific issue. Periodic conferences are called with a certain frequency to deal with an on-going issue that requires regular consultations among member states. The annual ministerial conferences of the World Trade Organisation and on climate change are examples of such conferences which have by now become a regular feature of international diplomacy. The United Nations and the League of Nations before it are examples of continuous conferences since they require member states to station a delegation permanently at their headquarters.[1] Many organisations expect delegations to be stationed permanently, but this does not preclude them from organising special conferences, where they seek high-level, meaning ministerial, participation.

Concert of Europe

The arrangement of state interaction that developed in Europe in the nineteenth century to maintain peace on the continent after Napoleon's defeat came to be called the Concert of Europe. The rulers of Europe who had formed an alliance to defeat him agreed that they would continue their cooperation for at least twenty years.

Austria's chancellor, Klemens von Metternich, brought the key allies, Britain, Prussia, Russia and his own country, together in a Quadruple Alliance to ensure coordinated action against republican and other revolutionary ideas that sought to redraw the boundaries of the kingdoms of medieval Europe and remove the aristocracies ruling over the melange of kingdoms and principalities that formed the kaleidoscopic map of Europe at the time. The Concert of Europe was more than just a military alliance. It was a continuous process of coordination among the old guard to suppress political change. It did not have a secretariat like modern international organisations. This requirement was filled by the government of Austria under Metternich's astute leadership. Friedrich von Gentz, one of the deputies of Metternich, wrote, "And so Europe seems really to form a grand political family, united under the auspices of a high tribunal of its own creation, whose members guarantee to themselves and to all parties concerned, the peaceful enjoyment of their respective rights."[2]

The Concert of Europe was an attempt at international cooperation to preserve a post-war arrangement enforced by the victors and to ensure that the revolutionary fervour of the French Revolution did not destabilise the ruling families of the continent. Tsar Alexander I of Russia wanted a great Christian nation to emerge "for the protection of religion, peace, and justice."[3] In 1818, France itself was made to restore the old order and join its protectors to make it a Quintuple Alliance. The leaders agreed to meet at fixed periods and discuss the measures necessary for preserving their international order.

The Concert of Europe started as a series of conferences of the foreign ministers of the big powers, at Aix-la-Chapelle in 1818, Troppau in 1820, Laibach in 1821, and Verona in 1822. Though these were *ad hoc* conferences, their regularity brought these countries together and led to a number of private and public initiatives to address problems internationally through multilateral agreements and even the setting up of rudimentary administrative machinery to facilitate their implementation.

Later, ambassadors replaced their ministers but no structure emerged nor did the meetings acquire any regularity. The three continental players of the Concert - Russia, Prussia and Austria - saw their alliance as a policeman that would ensure that any government coming to power through a revolution would be overthrown and the "legitimate" ruler restored. Britain took a more detached view of the alliance from its relative safety across the English Channel and its maritime supremacy. It developed the theory of the balance of power on the continent to ensure that no single country dominated it or threatened its maritime dominance.

The keenness of the Concert to restore the old rulers also brought it into confrontation with the United States. Napoleon's conquest of Spain had enabled many of its colonies in Latin America to declare independence. Even Brazil, Portugal's colony that gave shelter to its monarch during Napoleon's occupation, declared itself independent soon after the king's return. President James Monroe of the United States expounded his Monroe Doctrine cautioning European rulers against interference in the New World. This doctrine suited the British who wanted to preserve their dominance of international waters and gave full support to it. Without British naval support, the US would have been in no position to enforce its doctrine.

The Concert was a conservative reaction to Napoleon's revolutionary fervour. The only threat it could see came from the people. "There is only one serious matter in Europe, and that is revolution," said Metternich.[4] Not surprisingly, these rulers unleashed a wave of repression in Europe. The press was tightly censored and any demand for reform was firmly crushed. In Manchester, Britain, fifteen people were killed when they demanded parliamentary reform. The Concert was able to keep revolutionary forces in check very effectively in its early years. In 1823, France, supported by Austria and Russia, invaded Spain and replaced its revolutionary government with a monarchy. The monarchs and the ruling elite were able to suppress the revolutions of 1830 and 1848, preserve peace in Europe and secure their kingdoms through the better part of the nineteenth century. Any talk of parliamentary representation, labour rights or even national liberation was viewed with deep suspicion.

By the revolution of 1848, however, it was evident that the Concert's days were numbered. The new forces of nationalism and liberalism were too strong for the Old Guard. Metternich was forced to go into exile in England. In the Crimean War (1853-56), the Concert's members found themselves confronting each other. The Franco-Prussian War of 1870-71 finally brought the Concert to an end. The nationalism of Germany and Italy proved too strong for the aristocracies of medieval Europe and the quaint pluralistic kingdoms transcending national frontiers. The Concert was unable to deal with this threat to the existing order from within. It slowly withered away as its meetings became increasingly infrequent.

The Concert marked the beginning of collective security in modern times, going beyond defence against a common enemy to protecting the international order framed by the victors. This was also the longest period of relative peace enjoyed by Europe for several centuries. Its collapse saw Europe go through one of its worst phases in history, embroiling the whole world in two catastrophic wars. Though lacking a secretariat, it had several ingredients of present-day international organisations: regular consultations among leading members, willingness to use combined military force to enforce decisions, decision-making confined to a small coterie of large nations who dominated the organisation. Its weaknesses were attributed to its *ad hoc* character and its unwillingness to change with the times. It was looked upon as an amalgam of uncoordinated meetings dependent on the whims of leaders. Its proceedings were secret, which led to an atmosphere of Byzantine intrigue within it and distrust outside. Any scheme to improve upon it would have to put in place a more permanent structure with regular and more open meetings. Political thinkers started feeling the need for a more structured international organisation.

International Organisations

An international organisation is established by a treaty and has a secretariat to carry out routine functions, including monitoring its implementation. The member states constitute its general assembly that elects a smaller executive body. The International River Commission of Vienna, established by the Congress of Vienna of 1815, to ensure smooth navigation in international rivers in Europe, was among the first international organisations to be set up. The first postal conference was called in 1863 to rationalise postal charges. It led to the formation of the General Postal Union in 1875. Three years later, its name was changed to the Universal Postal Union. These organisations were set up to deal with specific issues of concern to countries.

By 1914, when the First World War started, there were thirty international organisations, dealing with subjects like telegraphs, sugar, the Danube River, agriculture, customs tariffs, public health, slave trade, opium, and maps.

League of Nations

The unification of Germany and Italy in the second half of the nineteenth century shattered the long period of peace in Europe and the international order of the Concert. Their urge to acquire colonies like the older colonial powers led them into the most devastating war in human history till then, the Great War, later called the First World War. The alliance of Germany, Italy and the Ottoman Empire of Turkey was defeated by Britain and France, but only with the assistance of the United States, which abandoned its long-standing policy of neutrality to enter the war. While the war was still going on, another force rose in the east, in Russia. This was the communist party, which claimed to represent the workers of the world. It overthrew the Romanov dynasty in November 1917 and withdrew from the war. It called upon workers all over Europe to overthrow their rulers instead of fighting for them. This was the most serious challenge to the ruling elite of Europe since the French Revolution more than a century ago. Russia converted its empire into a federation of *soviets*, the Union of Soviet Socialist Republics, or the Soviet Union.

After the war, the United States was expected to play a key role in establishing an arrangement that could enforce peace and security in Europe and the US president, Woodrow Wilson, was not found wanting. He gave to Europe the world's first international organisation for maintaining peace, the League of Nations. Left to themselves, European leaders would have created another conference-style forum for acting in concert, like the nineteenth-century arrangement. Britain certainly would not have backed such an elaborate structure and without its support France would not have been able to push the idea. The League marked a qualitative shift in the approach to maintaining peace. It was global in approach, not confined to Europe, even though it was Europe-centric. But more significantly, it was an attempt to substitute collective security for the older balance of power approach of the Concert of Europe.

This was a period when leaders in the United States, in their first flush of involvement in the Old World, were toying with ambitious ideas of internationalism. Charged with the strong missionary zeal of their founding fathers, they expounded fanciful ideas for ensuring peace in the world. President Theodore Roosevelt of the United States had been awarded the Nobel Peace Prize for 1906. In his Nobel Lecture on 5 May 1910 in Oslo, he had espoused a League of Peace and a network of arbitration treaties to settle international disputes, though he acknowledged that in the absence of an international police each country would have to depend on its own capacity to defend itself.[5]

President William Howard Taft, Wilson's predecessor, had proposed treaties of arbitration with Canada and Britain. The treaties were rejected by the Senate but this did not prevent him from supporting the idea of mandatory arbitration for settling disputes and joint military action against a state going to war without first having taken recourse to it. Religious fervour was an important motivator for these leaders. Taft was a Progressivist, while Wilson was the son of a Presbyterian minister.

The idea of an international organisation had been espoused by a former British civil servant, Leonard Woolf, in a report to the socialist Fabian Society during the war. Woolf's 'International Government' was published in 1916. It was taken up by the British League of Nations Society and, through it, in Whitehall. The British undersecretary of foreign affairs, Robert Cecil, became an ardent supporter. This helped in preventing British skepticism of an elaborate organisation from coming in the way of Wilson's enthusiasm.

Several suggestions had been floated during the First World War for such an organisation. One of the most comprehensive proposals came from General Jan Christian Smuts of South Africa on the eve of the Paris Conference. It picked up steam when President Wilson was converted to it and it found a place, albeit the last, in his Fourteen Points for the peace settlement, released on 8 January 1918, eight months after the US entered the war, "A general association of nations must be formed under specific covenants for the purpose of affording mutual guarantees of political independence and territorial integrity to great and small states alike." The idea of such an organisation had been on Wilson's mind for some time. A year ago, on 22 January 1917, in an address to the Senate he had expounded his vision of a world free from wars, with a league of nations to keep the peace. He even talked of the organisation upholding American principles of self-determination, freedom of the seas and an open world with no secret alliances. He was pre-empted in this by the communist revolution in Russia, whose leaders released documents on secret treaties and alliances and withdrew from the war.

The events in Russia made it imperative for the countries in the West to respond. The leaders of the Russian Revolution were calling upon workers all over the world to revolt against their capitalist rulers. Wilson's Fourteen Points made overtures to Germany and ostensibly also to the colonies. Britain was represented in the small group of people gathered by Wilson to draft the organisation's structure by Cecil and Smuts. Their draft became the basis of the agreement reached in Paris under Wilson, who himself added articles guaranteeing the rights of labour and of ethnic minorities.

Structure of the League of Nations

The League, which came into existence on 10 January 1920, had three principal organs: the Assembly, the Council and the Secretariat. The Assembly adopted a statute setting up the Permanent Court of International Justice, which came into existence the following year. The League also created the International Labour Organisation to channel the turbulence of trade unions and prevent them from going the communist way. The ILO was treated as a distinct body with its own assembly. The judges of the Permanent Court were elected by the League's Assembly and Council and shared its budget with it, as did the ILO. The Court was authorised to adjudicate disputes and give advisory opinion on issues referred to it by the Assembly or the Council.

The 26 articles that constituted the League's Covenant, along with the Preamble, were the first part of the Treaty of Versailles. They also formed part of four other treaties negotiated at that time: Saint-Germain-en-Laye, Trainon, Neuilly-sur-Seine and Sèvres. The League's founders probably felt that this would enhance the stature of the organisation, the first of its kind. Instead, this identification tainted the League in the eyes of Germany, making it as abominable as the hated treaties. This was later kept in mind by President Franklin D. Roosevelt of the United States, who ensured that the negotiations for the United Nations were not linked with the post-war treaties and trials.

All League member states were represented in the Assembly and had one vote each. The Council, on the other hand, had a limited membership of nine. Five of these, the US, the British Empire, France, Italy and Japan, were permanent members by virtue of their status as "Principal Allies and Associated Powers". All decisions of the Council were to be taken unanimously, except on procedural matters. Its meetings took place all over Europe (London, Paris, Brussels, San Sebastian and Rome) and were not open to the public.

American internationalists were greatly disappointed by the League's overweening political character. What they had in mind was an organisation dominated by an international court that would adjudicate disputes and lay down the law. They feared that the parliamentary type of structure with a small number of countries in the Council would be dominated by European disputes in which the US would be repeatedly drawn in. They apprehended another Concert of Europe, taking the world back to the nineteenth century. The isolationists in the American had their day and they rejected the Treaty of Versailles and with it membership of the League of Nations.

Henry Cabot Lodge, the US Republican Senate leader, expressed his anguish at the League's structure, "What many of us had in mind when we talked of Leagues of Peace where international law was to be developed and the great feature was to be a strong international court to interpret and lay down the law and behind which the nations were to stand. The court has already disappeared; international law, I think, is hardly mentioned; and the thing has turned into a plain political alliance."[6] Senator William E. Borah alleged that the US had got embroiled in European affairs and abandoned its policy of "no entangling alliances", which was the strength of the country since its formation. "We may have become one of the four dictators of the world but we shall no longer be masters of our own spirit," he said.[7]

In the absence of the United States, the League struggled to survive. The membership of the Council was increased frequently. In 1922, the non-permanent members were increased from four to six. In 1926, it went up to nine, in 1933 to ten and in 1936 to eleven. Initially, there was no set period for their term. In 1926, it was fixed at three years. The same elasticity was maintained for permanent membership. The number of permanent members was reduced to four when the US refused to join the League. In 1926, Germany was admitted to the League and given a permanent seat. This led to a clamour by Poland, Spain and Brazil. Spain and Brazil served notice to exit the League. Spain relented, but Brazil made good its threat in 1928. In 1934, the Soviet Union was given a similar honour, raising the permanent members to six. But by this time the League was already in decline. Japan walked out of it in 1935 as did Germany later in the same year. Italy left after four years, shortly before the war broke out, while the Soviet Union was expelled for its invasion of Finland. France and Britain were the only two permanent members left when the Second World War broke out.

The League was formed in the name of defending democracy and making the world safe for liberty. Wilson had declared that he was against annexations. However, when it came to dealing with the colonies of the defeated powers, the victors went into a land-grabbing frenzy. The scramble for Africa that had started before the war and was one of its underlying causes started all over again. It spread to the territories in the Middle East that fell in the hands of European powers after the collapse of the Ottoman Empire of Turkey. One of the secret treaties released by Russia after the communist revolution was the Sykes-Picot Agreement[8] among Britain, France and Russia to divide the Ottoman Empire among them. Britain and France went ahead with the deal, declaring that the "Mohammedan" regions were in no position to govern themselves and would have to be brought under international control. The League invented the system of mandates, under which members were assigned territories taken from the Axis Powers for administering without formal annexation. The stated objective of governing for the benefit of the ruled was altruistic enough to meet the high principles of the League, but in practice the mandates renewed colonial rule.

Wilson was able to get a Permanent Mandates Commission set up to supervise the work of the mandatory powers, but this was largely notional. The colonial powers treated the mandates as colonies. France got Syria as a Class A Mandate, which meant provisional recognition of its independence, but when a nationalist uprising broke out in 1925 it carried out aerial bombing in Damascus. Winston Churchill urged the use of mustard gas against the "uncivilised" tribes of Mesopotamia (in modern Iraq), which had been given to Britain as a League Mandate. He was candid enough to acknowledge, "There were to be no annexations but Mandates were to be granted to the Principal Powers which would give them necessary excuse for control."[9]

Both the League and the Concert incorporated elements of collective security and collective self-defence. The Concert was the reaction of the old aristocracy in Europe to the French Revolution. In this sense, it was for the collective defence of the rulers against their people. The League was formed by the victors of the First World War for collective defence against an external threat. The principal vanquished adversary in this war was Germany and stringent terms were imposed on it. However, events in distant Russia were also sending shivers through the victors. The Russian Revolution was drawing new battle lines across the continent between the *bourgeoisie* and the *proletariat*. Russia had formed the Communist International which claimed to speak not only for the oppressed working class in Europe but also the exploited people of the colonies of the imperial powers.

Wilson sought to deal with the communist challenge by addressing some of its allegations. He countered the denunciation of secret treaties by the leader of the Russian revolution, Vladimir Lenin, by including in his Fourteen Points a requirement that all agreements would be openly arrived at, "Open covenants of peace, openly arrived at, after which there shall be no private international understandings of any kind…"[10] He included a reference to labour rights in the Covenant of the League [Article 23] and promoted the setting up of the International Labour Organisation. To counter the charge that the war was a fight over colonial possessions he insisted that there would be no acquisition of the colonies of the defeated countries. Europeans had to be content with mandates. He was also able to keep the League untainted by colonialism by getting its headquarters stationed in Geneva, a small town in neutral Switzerland. Wilson's idealism was able to prevent the League from looking like the reactionary alliance of the Concert a century ago.

Although several international organisations had been formed before it and several were functioning well by the time of its formation, the

League of Nations was a new and revolutionary idea. This was the first time the world had a general security organisation dealing with the totality of inter-state relations.

Though the League's existence was brief and it is considered a monumental failure it had a few successes in its early years. It managed to stop a Greek invasion of Bulgaria in 1925. The signing of the Locarno Pact in 1926 brought Germany into the League. The Kellogg-Briand Pact two years later was another laurel. Some of its efforts in the field of workers' rights, health and economic development were to become the foundations of the achievements of the United Nations later in the century. The concept of a peacekeeping force was invented by the League. In 1935, the League sent a peacekeeping force to the Saar to supervise a plebiscite to decide its future. It voted for reunion with Germany, one of the first steps in Adolf Hitler's national aggrandisement.

By 1929 the international political and economic situation had started deteriorating rapidly. The Great Depression of 1929, the election of several National Socialists to the German parliament, and the Japanese invasion of Manchuria presaged the impending catastrophe of the Second World War. Both Germany and Japan left the League in 1935, the year Italy invaded and annexed Ethiopia. The Soviet Union's entry a year earlier could do little to dispel the gloom in the League. The exodus had begun. Paraguay and Nicaragua gave notice for quitting in 1935, followed by Guatemala and Honduras in 1936. El Salvador and Italy did the same the following year. Venezuela in 1938 and Hungary and Spain in 1939 completed the abandonment of the League.

The League failed because its members were not willing to place their commitment to collective security above their mutual rivalries and power games. The big powers persisted with the pre-war culture of secret diplomacy and bilateral negotiations. They themselves indulged in aggression and remained indifferent to that of other members. Japan's invasion of Manchuria and Italy's of Ethiopia went without a response from the League. Events in Asia were too remote for European powers to get worked up over and a country in Africa was not worth annoying Italy. Britain and France saw Italy as a potential ally against Germany. Even the rise of Hitler did not raise alarm bells in Britain since it hoped to divert him eastwards against the hated Bolsheviks in Russia.

The League's powerlessness had been exposed well before the Second World War began. It had even ceased to make any effort to prevent invasions or make peace. The few such efforts were made outside it. Even when the war began in 1939 the only significant action of the League was to expel the Soviet Union.

The League's failure is commonly attributed to the unwillingness of the United States to join it. US intervention had been the determining factor in the First World War. Europe had demonstrated its inability to overcome its animosities, whether through peaceful or violent means. A strong external presence was essential for this. The rise of nation-states had aroused primal passions which were manifested in claims of racial superiority and a wild rush for colonies across the world. There was no desire to make any effort for peaceful co-existence. The provisions in the League's Covenant on the reduction of armaments and peaceful settlement of disputes were never invoked or seriously pursued. Military invasion was the first course of action and racial superiority was considered adequate justification for resorting to military conquest. While Nazi Germany was demonised for its aggressive racialism, the rest of Europe kept abreast with it. The League failed because there was not enough support for it among its members. Europe did not yet fully appreciate the virtues of peace.

C. V. Narasimhan, who served as the *chef de cabinet* of three secretaries-general of the UN, maintained that one of the main shortcomings of the League was that it was designed to preserve the status quo, a failing it shared with the Concert of Europe. It came into existence as part of the Treaty of Versailles for protecting the international arrangement created by it. It was and remained a European club, despite a sprinkling of African and Asian countries like Ethiopia, Liberia, China, Japan and India.

The League was expected to rise above petty national considerations and acquire an international character. Some of its members may have entertained hopes of it emerging as a world association rather than an association of states, but their desire to punish Germany and prevent it from rising again soon overtook such noble sentiments. Germany was kept out of the League and crippling financial penalties were imposed on it. E.H. Carr attributed the failure of the League to the faith the big powers had in their commonality of interests, but they did not reckon with the dissatisfaction raging in Germany and Italy against the post-war arrangement.[11]

The Soviet objection to the League of Nations was more pronounced. They refused to join it, dubbing it a league of capitalist countries, a "Robbers' League". In 1925, the Soviet Foreign Commissar, Georgy Chicherin, in an interview to a German communist paper, *Rote Fahne*, declared, "Never under any circumstances will Russia join the League of Nations [which is] an instrument of capitalist machinations against weak countries and the colonial peoples."[12] The Soviet Union set up a rival international organisation, the Communist International, or the Comintern. Taking advantage of the reaction against the bombing of Syrian nationalists in Damascus by the French it organised a Congress of Oppressed Nationalities in Brussels in 1927. Representatives of a dozen Asian and African countries participated in it, including the Indian National Congress.

However, the failure of the workers in Western Europe to revolt against their rulers and the rise instead of militarist Japan and Nazi Germany softened the Russians. By 1933, the Russian leader, Joseph Stalin, had realised the necessity of reaching out to West Europe to counter the threat of a resurgent Germany. He signed treaties of mutual assistance with France and Czechoslovakia. In September 1934, the Soviet Union joined the League. Joining it, however, neither increased its security nor alleviated its fears. Its cooperation with the West proved fruitless in the Spanish civil war and it became suspicious of their motives as Germany annexed Austria and Czechoslovakia, both with the consent of the West European powers. When Britain agreed to Hitler's plan to annex Czechoslovakia, Stalin reached out to him and struck a deal of his own. In August 1939, the two countries signed a non-aggression agreement, the Molotov-Ribbentrop Pact,[13] dividing eastern Europe between them, leaving Hitler free to turn back west. After signing the pact, the Soviet Union invaded Finland. The League expelled it.

Hitler, however, went back on his word and attacked the Soviet Union in June 1941 forcing it to join hands with the Allies. Stalin dissolved the Comintern in 1943, bringing to a close his country's foray into an alternative global system.

The League lay in coma in Geneva during the war. Its last act was to terminate itself in April 1946 and transfer its assets to the United Nations.

Endnotes

1   Hence the term Permanent Mission and Permanent Representative for the ambassador to the UN.

2   Mazower, Mark: *Governing the World – The History of an Idea* (London: Allen Lane, 2012), p. 5.

3   Mazower, p. 7.

4   Mazower, p. 6

5   Theodore Roosevelt, *Nobel Lecture,* Oslo, 5 May 1910. [www.nobelprize. org].

6   Mazower, p. 138.

7   Mazower, p. 139.

8   An agreement negotiated between Britain and France in 1916, named after the diplomats who negotiated it, Mark Sykes of Britain and François Georges-Picot of France. Russia was minor beneficiary of the secret deal.

9   Mazower, p. 169.

10 Woodrow Wilson's 14 Points, *Message to the US Congress, 8 January 1918. [US National Archives, https://archives.gov].*

11 E. H. Carr, *Twenty Years' Crisis (1919-1939): An Introduction to the Study of International Relations* (London: Macmillan, 1946).

12 Quoted in Alexander Dallin, *Soviet Union at the United Nations.* (London: Methuen & Co, 1962), p. 15.

13 Named after the foreign minister of the Soviet Union, Vyacheslav Molotov, and of Germany, Joachim von Ribbentrop.

3   The Idea of the United Nations

The United Nations was formed as a military alliance during the Second World War. After the war, its three main allies – the United States, the Soviet Union and Britain – converted it into an international organisation for continued collective defence against the enemy States, Germany and Japan. The principal features of the military alliance were incorporated in the security structure of the new organisation. China and France were included as permanent members of the Security Council. These became the five policemen who promised to provide security to the rest of the world through a military force to be placed at the disposal of the Security Council. They agreed to stay united and take all decisions unanimously.

The idea of creating an organisation to replace the League of Nations had started engaging the minds of the Allied Powers even before the Second World War had come to an end. President Franklin D. Roosevelt of the United States had been Woodrow Wilson's assistant secretary of the navy. He was determined to avoid Wilson's mistakes and the weaknesses of the League. In 1923, he had written an article giving his ideas on resolving world peace. He regarded the requirement of unanimity in the Council as the biggest weakness of the League. He carried this idea into the United Nations by limiting this requirement to the Big Powers. "On the basis of his political instinct and his own direct experience, Roosevelt accordingly approached the problem of securing peace and stability after World War II as a thoroughly disenchanted Wilsonian idealist. He had become an advocate and exponent of realpolitik," wrote his biographers, Hoopes and Brinkley.[1]

Churchill met Roosevelt in a secret rendezvous on a ship at Placentia Bay in 14 August 1941, during the darkest period of the war for Britain. Germany was persistently bombing it and Churchill was desperate for American support. He also wanted it to commit to setting up an international organisation in which both would police the world. The United States had not yet decided on entering the war and Roosevelt was unwilling to make a commitment on an international organisation. Just a few years ago, the United States had adopted a law strengthening its neutrality and reaffirming its unwillingness to get entangled in wars outside the Americas.

The two leaders issued a carefully drafted statement, which came to be called the Atlantic Charter. The Charter did not go into the issue of an international organisation but talked of a "permanent system of general security", implicitly committing the US to a new international arrangement for global security, distinct from the ailing League of Nations. Churchill came back and told his cabinet that the US would "join with us in policing the world until the establishment of a better order."[2]

Later in the year, Japan attacked Pearl Harbour and the US entered the war. Churchill came once again to Washington, this time on an open visit, to form an Anglo-American military alliance. Roosevelt suggested calling themselves the United Nations, instead of Associated Powers, as they were referred to at that time. The United Nations thus began as a military alliance. Four nations, the US, Britain, the Soviet Union and China issued the Washington Declaration of 1 January 1942 in which they declared that they would join hands to fight Germany, Italy and Japan. Twenty-two other countries joined it the next day and another twenty-one over the next three years. The term, United Nations, was used once again in the Four-Nation Moscow Declaration of 30 October 1943 for the alliance. This declaration also contained the first commitment of the four powers to set up an international organisation. It said, "That they recognise the necessity of establishing at the earliest practicable date a general international organisation, based on the principle of the sovereign equality of all peace-loving states, and open to membership of all such states, large and small, for the maintenance of international peace and security."[3] From there to San Francisco in June 1945 the journey was interspersed with meetings in Cairo, Tehran, Dumbarton Oaks and Yalta.

The United Nations was an American idea. Churchill was not keen on a global organisation. His preference was for regional alliances, such as a West European-American alliance, because for him the chief adversary was the Soviet Union and he "was more concerned with moulding a West European-American alliance to balance the power of the Soviet Union."[4] This view coincided with Stalin's post-war security strategy, though in his case the primary threat continued to emanate from Germany. Churchill also did not want an international organisation snooping in Britain's colonies. While giving in to Roosevelt, he ensured that the UN Charter recognised the legitimacy of regional alliances. The Latin American countries also decided to put their trust in a regional alliance of their own.

Churchill did not like the idea of the Soviet Union being included in the arrangement, but he realised that it was needed to defeat Germany. The Soviet Union distrusted the West as much as it feared it, but the rise of Nazi Germany had created the need for allies and it went along with Roosevelt on the United Nations. France, which was under German occupation, had sporadic participation by its resistance leaders.

Churchill also opposed China's inclusion, calling it a puppet of the US. China was included in the core group but not in the meetings of the big three, Roosevelt, Churchill and Stalin, at Tehran and Yalta. Roosevelt was in the thrall of the ruling family of China, led by Chiang Kai-shek, whose brother-in-law, T.V. Soong, was the ambassador to Washington. Roosevelt saw a vast market of five hundred million people opening up for America once the war was over and the country industrialised and Christianised. Chiang Kai-shek had married the daughter of a rich publisher of Christian missionary books in Shanghai and himself became a Southern Methodist Christian. Churchill was to write later, "I told the president how much I felt American public opinion overestimated the contribution which China could make to the general war."[5] But in 1941, Time magazine saw the possibility of millions of Chinese converting to Christianity out of gratitude to their allies in the war.[6]

As for China's fighting capacity, Winston Churchill wrote in his history of the war, "At Washington, I found the extraordinary significance of China in American minds, even at the top, strangely out of proportion. I was conscious of a standard of values which accorded China almost an equal fighting power with the British Empire and rated the Chinese army as the factor to be mentioned in the same breath as the armies of Russia."[7]

Roosevelt's trusted envoy, W. Averell Harriman, also did not share his enthusiasm for China. He wrote later, "China's admission to the ranks of Great Powers had assumed overwhelming importance in [Cordell]

Hull's mind, as it had in Roosevelt's. The British government did not share this emotional commitment to Chiang Kai-shek's China." Averell felt that the efforts Hull made for getting the Soviet Union to accept China as a permanent member could have been better utilised to get concessions on Poland.[8]

The Soviet Union too did not think much of China. At the time of the signing of the Moscow Declaration in 1943, the Soviet Foreign Minister, Vyacheslav Molotov, objected to the Chinese ambassador being asked to join. He pleaded that the ambassador would not have time to get instructions from his capital. The US secretary of state, Cordell Hull, however, insisted, "My Government believes that China has been in the world picture as one of the Big Four for the prosecution of the war. For her now to be dumped out on her face by Russia, Great Britain and the United States in connection with the Declaration would create in all probability the most terrific repercussions, both political and military, in the Pacific area." Hull then asked the Chinese ambassador, Foo Ping-Sheung, to get instructions from his capital urgently, which he did.[9]

Roosevelt was also keen on including Brazil in the permanent members but Churchill was adamant on France as a counterweight to the Soviet Union in Europe. Having six permanent members would have required adding one more non-permanent member in the Security Council in order to retain their notional majority. This would take the total membership to thirteen, which Roosevelt considered an unlucky number. France's inclusion, thus, once again dashed Brazil's hopes of making it to the big league.[10]

Though Roosevelt had decided to establish an international organisation, he put his faith in what he called the 'four policemen' – the US, the Soviet Union, Britain and China. He was convinced that only the big powers could maintain peace in the world and power had to be concentrated in their hands. He shared his idea with Molotov during the latter's visit to Washington in May 1942. Roosevelt did not merely visualise the four powers as the policemen of the world but also as the exclusive holders of weapons with the capacity to enforce peace. Stalin endorsed Roosevelt's idea, but left China out of his configuration of big powers. He told Averell, "Roosevelt's thoughts on safeguarding of peace after the war are absolutely correct. There might be no doubt that without the creation of united armed forces of England, the USA and the USSR, which are capable to avert aggression, it is impossible to preserve peace in the future."[11]

Roosevelt promptly started devoting attention to the post-war arrangement. He was perhaps the only one who had the luxury of doing so, being well removed from the theatres of war. He tasked his State Department to work on it. Cordell Hull, the aging secretary of state, assigned the responsibility to Leo Pasvolsky, a Russian-born academic. Hull and Pasvolsky were determined to avoid a balance of power arrangement and argued for a global organisation on the lines of the League of Nations. In an address to Congress in 1943, Hull promised, ".... there will no longer be need for spheres of influence, for alliances, for balance of power, or any other special arrangements through which, in the unhappy past, the nations strove to safeguard their security or to promote their interests." [12]

The first outline of a new organisation had been prepared by Boris Stein, a Soviet foreign ministry official, soon after the Tehran summit. Stein's proposal was entitled 'The Main Principles of the Statute of the International Organisation on the Safeguarding of Security and Peace.' The organisation, comprising an assembly, a council and a secretariat, was to look after only security issues. Only the big four – the United States, the Soviet Union, Britain and China – were to be the members of the council and all decisions were to be taken unanimously by them.

The first American draft was prepared soon after Stein's and was very close to it. However, the Americans envisaged a larger council, of seven more members. This was not to the liking of the Soviet Union, but it was unable to devote much attention on account of its life and death struggle with Germany. The name of the new organisation was one of the first issues to resolve. Roosevelt wanted to retain the wartime name. The United States had already started using it for various activities, making it clear that it saw the alliance as continuing beyond the war. In 1943, it organised the first United Nations conference at Hot Springs, Virginia, to discuss food needs. This meeting led to the creation later of the UN Food and Agriculture Organization. It also set up a UN Relief and Rehabilitation Administration. Forty-four countries participated in the 'United Nations Monetary and Financial Conference' on the post-war financial system, at Bretton Woods in July 1944.

The Soviet Union felt that it would be inappropriate to carry a wartime name into peacetime. It proposed "World Union" or "International Security Organization". Britain also expressed reservation. However, Roosevelt was able to persuade Churchill and the two carried the day.

The United States was keen to avoid what it saw as the key causes of the failure of the League: (i) absence of a major power, the United States; (ii) futility of imposing sanctions on a major power, (iii) absence of a military force at the disposal of the Security Council; and (iv) lack of clear demarcation between the powers and responsibilities of the Assembly and the Council which it believed had weakened the League because aggressors could play one organ against the other.

The new organisation was conceived as a continuation of the wartime alliance. In a speech on 29 November 1942, Winston Churchill talked of the need for the big three playing the lead role in a new organisation which they would form with the other members of the United Nations. The Soviet Union too had visualised the new organisation as an alliance to provide security. This idea had been expressed in the Soviet-Polish Declaration of 4 December 1941 which would be "based on the unification of democratic countries in a strong alliance." The new organisation would replace the League of Nations and would have at its command an international armed force.

Roosevelt was determined not to create a toothless organisation inspired by high idealism and embroiled in endless debates. He wanted to concentrate power in the hands of the big four. The retention of the name United Nations was itself a declaration of his intent. In December 1943, he declared his determination and strategy for enforcing peace, "Britain, Russia, China and the United States and their allies represent more than three-quarters of the total population of the earth. As long as these four nations with great military power stick together in determination to keep the peace there will be no possibility of an aggressor nation arising to start another world war."[13]

Roosevelt also wanted to keep the organisation as flexible as possible. In April 1943, an American journalist, Forrest Davis, wrote a series of articles based on his interviews with President Roosevelt. He concluded that Roosevelt wanted a "simple, flexible and workable body of arrangements".[14] The big powers did not want to be burdened with commitments to provide security all over the world, nor did they want to be tied down with procedures and guidelines.

Roosevelt wanted wider membership in a general assembly, but this was essentially to increase the acceptability of the organisation by creating a forum for others to ventilate their concerns. Above all, the general understanding among the big three on non-interference in their respective spheres of influence reassured them all. The Soviet Union, which would be in a minority in the organisation, was particularly apprehensive of the Western countries using it against its interests.

All decisions were to be taken by the United States, the Soviet Union, Britain and China, who would maintain peace in the world. Roosevelt spelled out his vision of the future military arrangement in an interview in 1943 to the Saturday Evening Post in which he talked of 'Four Policemen', the idea he had shared earlier with Molotov. In the interview, he rejected the idea of reviving the League of Nations and in fact did not talk about creating another international organisation. He also believed that the other countries needed to be disarmed. Britain's foreign minister, Anthony Eden quotes Roosevelt in his book, 'The Reckoning', as saying that the small powers "should have nothing more dangerous than rifles."[15] Eichelberger also recalled that Roosevelt wanted the four powers "to police and disarm the world".[16]

Roosevelt, Churchill and Stalin met for the first time in Tehran on 1 December 1943 soon after the Moscow Declaration. They announced that the responsibility of ensuring peace rested on them and the others in the United Nations. They expressed the confidence that they would "command the goodwill of the overwhelming mass of the peoples of the world and banish the scourge and terror of war for many generations."[17]

Away from the publicity of the noble declarations, secret discussions had also started among the big three on dividing the spoils of war. The massive Russian offensive against Germany in the summer of 1944 and its swift success made Britain eager to have a settlement with it. In October, Churchill met Stalin in Moscow and came to the 'Percentages Agreement' on dividing eastern Europe between them. Greece fell in Britain's lap while the Soviet Union got Romania, Hungary and Bulgaria. They decided to split Yugoslavia between them.

This arrangement was confirmed in February 1945 when Roosevelt joined the other two for their meeting at Yalta on the Black Sea. Here the main discussion was on the sharing of Poland. Britain was hosting a provisional Polish government-in-exile as was the Soviet Union and both wanted to install their protégés in Warsaw. They finally agreed to have a provisional government of national unity in which representatives from both factions would be included.

The Soviet Union's main objective was to create a deep buffer in East Europe with Germany. It tried to guarantee non-interference in the region by proposing the division of the General Assembly into four regional sections: European, American, African and Asian. This would forestall a repeat of the League of Nations, in which the Latin American countries joined hands with Britain and outnumbered the East Europeans.

Despite their differences, there was a clear understanding among the big three on the role and structure of the new organisation. All of them wanted the council to be the main organ with all executive powers and the exclusive responsibility of maintaining global peace. The American idea of including some other countries in an expanded council did not dilute the control of the big powers. The American and British idea of including economic and social issues in the responsibilities of the new organisation also did not affect the primacy of security in it.

The United Nations was not conceived as a universal organisation nor did decolonisation figure in its goals. The big powers wanted to limit its membership to like-minded countries. This was an organisation of the victors and the enemy states had no place in it. For the Soviet Union, territories and their demarcation were more important than the text of the Charter. Britain and France permitted fleeting references to self-determination in the Charter but they were firm in their resolve to recover the colonies they had lost to Germany and Japan during the war.

The UN Charter contains three references (Articles 53, 77 and 107) to possible action against "enemy States." There was no such reference in the League's Covenant. Even after the entry of Germany and Japan in the UN, the three articles remain unamended. This is despite a provision in the Outcome Document of the World Summit in December 2005 to work towards deleting the references.

Roosevelt's big concern was the US Congress, which had blocked the country's entry in the League of Nations. He came to the conclusion that the objections of the American Congress could be taken care of by creating an organisation that was under US control and would serve as an instrument of US policy. Joining such an organisation would not compromise US sovereignty. He also kept the Congress closely engaged in the process. In 1943, the US Congress adopted two resolutions which outlined the ideas of the American parliamentarians on the post-war international arrangement. In the first resolution, the House of

Representatives, with the Senate concurring, talked of favouring "...the creation of appropriate international machinery with power adequate to establish and to maintain a just and lasting peace, among the nations of the world, and as favouring participation by the United States therein through its constitutional processes."[18] Soon the Senate adopted its own resolution expressing the intent of the United States to join an international authority with the "power to prevent aggression and to preserve the peace of the world."[19] Quite significantly, the resolution reproduced the text from the Moscow Declaration on the need for setting up a general international organisation.

Dumbarton Oaks

The charter of the new organisation was drafted during the so-called Dumbarton Oaks Conversations held in Washington from August to October 1944. It was attended by the US, the Soviet Union and Britain. China joined the talks after six weeks when the Soviet Union withdrew. The Soviet Union was not at war with Japan and did want to be part of those talks. China was only active in the war against Japan. The Chinese leg of the talks was "relegated in advance to a status that was little more than ceremonial or, as the Foreign Office put it, 'informative'."[20]

The meeting agreed smoothly on the five organs of the organisation – the General Assembly, Security Council, Secretariat, World Court and the Economic & Social Council. One of the proposals at Dumbarton Oaks was to have a committee of the big four and a council in which some others would be included. These two were later merged into one council by Leo Pasvolsky.[21] The Dumbarton Oaks proposals for the setting up of a "General International Organisation" were published on 9 October 1944. Some of the key issues left unresolved at these talks were – applicability of the veto, inclusion of social and economic issues in the scope of the organisation, composition of the military advisory council and voting by a Council member, particularly a permanent member, on a dispute in which it was a party.

While the big three were united in their resolve that no decision could be taken by the Council without their consent, the United States and Britain, which were confident of their majority, were prepared to show some flexibility to pre-empt criticism of the veto. The outnumbered Soviet Union, however, was not prepared to brook any exception. The US made a compromise proposal under which a great power would not have the power to veto discussion on an issue but would retain the right to do so on enforcement action. This formula was put forward before the Yalta summit of the Big Three and accepted by Stalin. At Yalta, Stalin also accepted France as a permanent member of the Council with the veto.

On membership, the Soviets bargained for more seats for their sixteen Republics to reduce the overwhelming majority of the West supported by Latin America. Stalin pointed to the six votes enjoyed by Britain through its Commonwealth. Britain had acquired five additional votes in the League of Nations through its colonies, Australia, Canada, India, New Zealand and South Africa and continued to do so in the United Nations. Stalin eventually succeeded in getting seats for Ukraine and Byelorussia (later, Belarus).

The dominance of the permanent members was maintained even in the provision on voting in a dispute in which they were a party. They agreed to refrain from doing so, but only on decisions relating to the pacific settlement of disputes. This ensured that they could veto any decision on enforcement action against them. Britain had initially taken the high moral ground that a great power should not be permitted to vote in a dispute in which it was itself involved, but it soon modified its position.

The three leaders also decided to hold the conference on the new organisation in the United States. All members of the United Nations and the Associated Nations who had declared war on the common enemy would be invited to attend. The US chose San Francisco as the venue of the conference, which was officially sponsored by the US, Soviet Union, Britain and China. France still had a provisional government and was not part of this quartet. The four co-sponsors would co-chair the conference. Armed with this pre-cooked deal, the big three proceeded to San Francisco for its ceremonial adoption.

Roosevelt decided to avoid the fate of Woodrow Wilson by including some Congressmen from both parties in the US delegation to San Francisco. He also wanted to give the conference a constitution-building character rather than the ambience of a conference of the victors imposing terms on the vanquished. This meant that some importance was attached to issues like the rights of the General Assembly, the commitment to human rights and the plight of colonial peoples. Unfortunately, Roosevelt passed away on 12 April 1945, with a little over a month to go for the conference. This removed the main force behind the proposed organisation, leaving

Vice President Harry S. Truman to step into his big shoes. The United Nations was born a posthumous child.

Endnotes

1   Towsend Hoopes and Douglas Brinkley, *FDR and the Creation of the UN* (Yale University Press, 1997), p. 11.

2   E.J. Hughes, *"Churchill and the Formation of the United Nations Organization",* Journal of Contemporary History, vol. 9 (October 1974), p. 181.

3   Para 4 of the Moscow Declaration. Quoted in Clark M. Eichelberger, *Organising for Peace – A Personal History of the Founding of the United Nations* (New York: Harper & Row, 1977), p. 221.

4   Stanley Meisler, *United Nations: The First Fifty Years* (New York: The Atlantic Monthly Press, 1995), p. 3.

5   Winston Churchill, *The Second World War, Vol. IV: The Hinge of Fate* (New York: Houghton Mifflin, 1950), p. 133.

6   'Christianity in China' *Time,* 28 April 1941. Quoted in James Bradley, *The China Mirage* (New York: Little, Brown and Company, 2015), p. 285.

7   Churchill, p. 133.

8   W. Averell Harriman and Elie Abel, *Special Envoy to Churchill and Stalin, 1941-1946* (New York: Random House, 1975), p. 236.

9   Cordell Hull, *The Memoirs of Cordell Hull* (New York: MacMillan, 1948), pp. 1282-1307.

10 Robert C. Hilderbrand, *Dumbarton Oaks: The Origins of the United Nations and the Search for Post-war Security.* (University of North Carolina Press, 1990), p. 125.

11 Ilya V. Gaiduk *Divided Together – The United States and the Soviet Union in the United Nations.* (Stanford University Press, 2012), p. 12.

12 US State Department, Foreign Relations of the United States, 1943. Quoted in David L. Bosco, *Five to Rule Them All* (New York: Oxford University Press, 2009), p.14.

13 New York Times, 25 December 1943. Quoted in Edward C. Luck, *UN Security Council,* (Routledge, 2006), p. 11.

14 Quoted in Lowe, Roberts, Welsh & Zaum, *The United Nations Security Council and War,* (Oxford University Press, 2008), p. 64.

15 Quoted in Bosco, p. 15.

16 Eichelberger, p. 236.

17 Teheran Declaration, 1 December 1943, paragraph 6, [www.gettyimages.in].

18 House Concurrent Resolution 25, 78th Congress, 21 September 1943. [www.avalon.law.yale.edu].

19 US Senate Resolution 192, 78th Congress, 5 November 1943. [www.avalon.law.yale.edu].

20 Hilderbrand, p. 229.

21 Hilderbrand, p. 31.

4 San Francisco Conference: The UN Charter

The principal features of the UN Charter had been drafted by the big three – the United States, the Soviet Union and Britain – before the San Francisco Conference. The 46 other participants invited to the conference were not expected to make any substantive changes in the draft. There were vigorous debates on issues like the veto and judicial review, but the amendments proposed were rejected. The Security Council's powers on peaceful settlement of disputes, sanctions and military action and the veto power of the permanent five remained unchanged. However, the permanent five could not finalise the composition and command structure of the UN military force and left it to the Military Staff Committee to resolve later.

The invitations to the San Francisco Conference went out in March 1945 to 45 countries. Another five were invited later. The Axis powers – Germany, Japan and Italy, were not invited. The United Nations Conference on International Organisation, as it was called, opened in San Francisco on 25 April 1945 with 50 participants. Argentina, though formally neutral, had collaborated with Germany during the war and was not among the initial invitees. The Soviet Union wanted to keep it out but the Latin American countries rallied behind it and were supported by the American millionaire, Nelson Rockefeller, and Senator Arthur Vandenberg. It became the 51st invitee.

The Soviet Union was uncertain about the level of its participation. It was planning to send its ambassador to the US, Andrei Gromyko, who had attended the Dumbarton Oaks meeting. However, Roosevelt's death mellowed Stalin and he sent Foreign Minister Vyacheslav Molotov on the request of the US ambassador.

The Dumbarton Oaks draft became the working document of the conference. The idea of holding the conference while the war was still going on was Roosevelt's. He wanted the Charter to be drafted while there was still a high degree of cooperation among the allies. He possibly foresaw the coming East-West divide. His ill-health could also have prompted him to speed up the conference.

France agreed to join the core group of the big four of Dumbarton Oaks with some hesitation, unsure of the security commitments it would be required to make. The big five met separately before the conference to decide on further amendments to the draft and continued to do so during the conference. As for the other participants, they were asked to submit their amendments within nine days. One of the principles agreed upon at the conference was that the big five could veto the amendments moved by the other members, though they gave an informal assurance that they would not do so if it enjoyed two-thirds support. The lesser countries optimistically proposed a slew of amendments.

Roosevelt's death came as a serious blow to the preparations for the conference. Truman had the unenviable task of negotiating the new international organisation by convincing not merely its two other proponents, Churchill and Stalin, neither of whom was particularly enthusiastic about it, but also a skeptical US Congress, suspicious of an international body encroaching on American sovereignty. He also had to deal with Churchill's hostility to Stalin. Not having been present at Yalta he was not privy to the deals struck there among the three leaders and had to rely on Churchill's version of the events and deals there.

The Preamble

The Charter had been drafted as a treaty among the governments of the participating countries. It was in this spirit that Smuts of South Africa, now Field Marshal, drafted the Preamble. Smuts had attended the Versailles conference on the League of Nations and had contributed to the drafting of the League's Covenant. He was a celebrated invitee at San Francisco. He opened his draft of the Preamble with the conventional phrase, "The high contracting parties", on the lines of a treaty. However, a member of the US delegation, Virginia Gildersleeve, a professor of literature, gave a rhetorical flourish to it by changing the opening phrase to, "We the peoples of the United Nations." This phrase was retained in the final Preamble and was cited years later as a visionary idea that foresaw the rise of people's power in the organisation. This, however, could barely camouflage the stranglehold of governments on the conference, where there was no representation from non-government bodies or organisations, nor could many participating governments call themselves democracies. A delegation of India League led by Vijaya Lakshmi Pandit and claiming to represent the Indian people had gone to San Francisco optimistically hoping to participate but was not allowed entry.[1] It was the government of British India that represented the country, giving it the privilege of becoming a founder member of the organisation.

The Charter

The structure of the new organisation was not significantly different from that of the much-reviled League of Nations. The General Assembly, the Secretariat and the International Court of Justice were carry-forwards from the League. All members were to be represented as equals in the General Assembly. The Charter, however, made the General Assembly distinctly subordinate to the Security Council. It was to elect only six (increased to ten in 1965) members of the Council. The permanent members, who wielded the veto, were not elected and could not be removed by it. It was given a very broad but diffused mandate. It could discuss and make recommendations on any issue within the scope of the Charter but could only draw the attention of the Council to situations which were likely to endanger international peace and security. It could not make recommendations on an issue under discussion there. It was not given legislative powers since its resolutions were not binding.

The International Court of Justice was patterned on the Permanent Court of Justice of the League of Nations. It could adjudicate disputes brought to it by states and give advisory opinion when sought by the organs or specialised agencies of the UN. As with the Permanent Court, its jurisdiction was not made compulsory. The Charter provided that "legal disputes should as a general rule be referred by the parties to the International Court of Justice" [Article 36(3)]. This was in the nature of a recommendation to member states, not an injunction on the Security Council.

The UN was given an Economic and Social Council to address the underlying problems of economic development and deprivation which were believed to be the root cause of the Second World War. It was also given a Trusteeship Council to administer territories recovered from the Axis powers and the residual mandate territories of the League of Nations. All these territories have since been given independence and the Trusteeship Council, which completed its work in 1994, awaits amendment to the Charter for its abolition. The Charter also provided for a Secretariat with a secretary–general at its head. UN officials were debarred from seeking or receiving instructions from any government or external organisation. They were required to be recruited with due regard for wide geographical representation.

Security Council's Powers

The key change between the League's Covenant and the UN Charter was in the greater concentration of power in the hands of the five permanent members and the primacy of the Security Council in the UN system. The Council was not made responsible to any other organ for its actions. It was merely required to submit an annual report to the General Assembly. Its decisions were also not subject to judicial review by the ICJ nor was it obligated to submit disputes to it for adjudication.

In the League's Council, decisions had to be taken unanimously by all members, permanent and non-permanent. In the UN Security Council, unanimity was required only among the permanent five and only procedural resolutions were exempt. Another departure from the League's Covenant was the provision for an armed force at the disposal of the Security Council and the creation of a Military Staff Committee to advise and assist it.

Article 24(1) of the Charter gave the Security Council the "primary" responsibility for the maintenance of international peace and security. The addition of the appellation 'Security' to the Council reflected the determination of the framers to keep its focus on its primary task of maintaining international peace and security. Both members and non-members of the UN could bring disputes to the Security Council. The Council was also empowered to take *suo motu* cognisance of a dispute that might endanger international peace and security and decide whether to resort to enforcement measures or to recommend peaceful settlement. While performing this responsibility the Security Council would act on behalf of all members of the United Nations. The Charter divided the Council's outcomes into 'recommendations' and 'decisions'. 'Recommendations' were to be made in peaceful settlements while 'decisions' referred to sanctions or the use of armed force. All members were obliged "to accept and carry out the decisions of the Security Council in accordance with the present Charter" (Article 25). This obligation did not extend to its 'recommendations'.

Under Article 2 of the UN Charter members undertook to settle their disputes peacefully and to refrain from the threat or use of force "against the territorial integrity or political independence of any state, or in any other manner inconsistent with the purposes of the United Nations." In this, the UN Charter made a distinct advance on the League's Covenant which had imposed a more ambivalent requirement on members. They were merely required not to resort to war against a country that had complied with the League Council's recommendations.

The collective security arrangement created by the UN Charter was remarkable for its simplicity and clarity. It began by prohibiting the "use of force" by members, except in self-defence. The injunction was unambiguous and comprehensive. It avoided the use of the term 'war' since that would trigger a debate on its definition and previous attempts had been fruitless. The framers of the Charter wanted to ensure that they vested the power to use force only in the Security Council. A Canadian proposal stipulating that military action could be taken under Article 42 only after other means had been found exhausted was rejected. The Security Council was given absolute powers to use military force but only in the case of a threat to international peace and security. This limitation was the pivot of the security structure of the United Nations balancing international security with national sovereignty.

The only concession made to states on the use of force without Security Council authorisation was on self-defence. This provision was not there in the Dumbarton Oaks draft and was successfully extracted by the other members at the conference. A new article, Article 51, was introduced in Chapter VII acknowledging that member states had the inherent right to self-defence if an armed attack occurred against them. However, the right was qualified by the caveat, "until the Security Council has taken measures necessary to maintain international peace and security". The member was required to inform the Security Council immediately and the Council retained the power to take such action as it deemed necessary to restore and maintain international peace and security. The aim of the framers was quite evident. They wanted the Security Council to be the policeman of the world and the sole body authorised to use force. Brownlie summarised this arrangement of the Charter, "The whole object of the Charter was to render unilateral use of force, even in self-defence, subject to control by the Organization..."[2]

The Security Council was the only organ empowered to enforce its decision on a member state against its will. Even the International Court of Justice was denied this authority. A member seeking enforcement of its judgment would have to turn to the Security Council. The Charter also mandated the Security Council to promote the regulation of armaments in an effort to reduce the capacity of member states to use force.

An Australian proposal that if the Security Council failed to take action to maintain international peace and security or failed to authorise a regional organisation to do so, member states would have the right to take such action as they deemed necessary, was not accepted.[3] The framers insisted that giving such a right to members would undermine the Security Council and would run the risk of war. The United Nations could not allow members to take military action other than in self defence. In 1949, when Herbert V. Evatt, who had originally made the proposal became president of the General Assembly, recognised the sagacity of not having made such a provision, "The League of Nations failed to prevent the Second World War solely because some of the Governments which belonged to it let down the League of Nations and preferred to resume the great game of power politics. This must not happen to the United Nations.... Nothing else is a substitute for it; nothing else can be a substitute for it."[4]

Peaceful Settlement of Disputes

The measures for peaceful settlement of disputes by the Security Council were spelled out in Chapter VI. The Security Council was required to get involved only in disputes that were likely to endanger international peace and security. A dispute could be brought before the Council by the General Assembly, a member state or even a non-member state that accepted in advance the obligations of peaceful settlement as provided in the UN Charter. The Council could also take cognisance of a dispute *suo motu* if it felt that it was likely to endanger international peace and security.

The Charter did not envisage the Security Council as a dispute settlement body. It provided for the Council to attempt the peaceful settlement of disputes but prescribed few obligations or procedures. Member states were advised to settle their international disputes by negotiations, enquiry, mediation, conciliation, arbitration, judicial settlement, resort to regional organisations, or other peaceful means and to refer legal disputes to the ICJ. The Security Council was empowered to investigate a dispute and even though its power in this is recommendatory some experts maintain that members are obliged to accept them. This obligation to settle disputes by peaceful means was an improvement on the League's Covenant which did not contain such a provision. The Charter gave the Security Council full discretion in recommending whatever means or terms of settlement it considered appropriate. Even referring a legal dispute to the ICJ was not made mandatory.

The Coercive Powers

The enforcement powers of the Security Council were placed in Chapter VII. Article 39 mandated it to determine if there was a threat to the peace, breach of the peace, or act of aggression and decide what measures to take. Article 40 authorised it to prescribe provisional measures to prevent the situation from escalating. The Council was given a free hand to decide what these provisional measures would be. The Council usually calls upon the parties to accept a ceasefire, withdraw their armed forces and seek a peaceful settlement.

The Charter empowered the Council with two sets of coercive powers. Article 41 empowered it to impose sanctions, including complete or partial interruption of economic relations, transport and communications links and diplomatic relations. Sanctions have been the most common measure used by the Security Council against countries under Chapter VII. Its powers in this respect were much broader than of the League's Council.

The second power given to the Security Council was its authority to take military action against a country under Article 42. This article authorised it to "take such action by air, sea or land forces as may be necessary to maintain or restore international peace and security." To enable it to exercise this authority the Charter provided for armed forces for the Security Council and a Military Staff Committee, comprising the chiefs of staff of the permanent five and such other representatives of countries as they invited. The arrangement envisaged was for member states to make troops available to the Security Council under special agreements to be signed with it under Article 43. The Charter also provided for an air force to be made available to the Security Council by member states to enable the UN to take urgent military measures. The Military Staff Committee was to assist the Security Council in operating these troops and decide on questions relating to their command.

The enforcement powers given to the Council were sweeping and unfettered. It could decide to take coercive action without any enquiry or investigation. There was no specified procedure to be followed, nor any preconditions to be met. There was no requirement for peaceful means to be exhausted before military action was taken. This issue was discussed at San Francisco but attempts to circumscribe this authority were strongly resisted by the permanent five. The argument given by them was that they did not want to shackle the Security Council like the League's Council.

However, at San Francisco the details of the command structure of the forces could not be finalised and were left to "be worked out subsequently". The framers anticipated the possibility of delay in agreements on providing troops to the Security Council and setting up its command structure for the military force. The Charter provided for this contingency by authorising the permanent five to consult each and take joint action on behalf of the UN.[5] This provision was a carry-forward from the wartime alliance. Even the text of Article 106 was similar to paragraph 5 of the Four Power Declaration the United States, the United Kingdom, the Soviet Union and China, which had declared, "That for the purpose of maintaining international peace and security pending the re-establishment of law and order and the inauguration of a system of general security, they will consult with one another and as occasion requires with other Members of the United Nations with a view to joint action on behalf of the community of nations."

Definition of Aggression

Unlike the League's Covenant, the UN Charter does not make a reference to war. The only references to war in it are to the ongoing World War II. The framers decided to prohibit 'the use of force' by a state in order to keep the injunction as wide as possible. They avoided creating complications for the Security Council by not defining or illustrating 'aggression'. Suggestions to define 'acts of aggression' were turned down at San Francisco. It was decided to leave it to the discretion of the Security Council.

There had been considerable debate on the definition of aggression in the League and in the various treaty negotiations that took place in the 1920s and 1930s. The UN General Assembly and the International Law Commission have also discussed it extensively. The nature of the aggression, whether direct or indirect and the juridical nature of the aggressor, whether state or non-state, make the question a complicated one.

In the 1950s, the General Assembly set up a Committee on Defining Aggression but it failed to come to any conclusion and the UN has been dealing with armed conflicts without a definition of the term. Both the General Assembly and the Security Council have used the phrases "breach of the peace" and "threat to the peace" in their resolutions. In its resolutions on the Korean operation in June 1950, the Security Council deemed that the armed attack of forces from North Korea constituted a "breach of the peace". Later, in February 1951, the General Assembly adopted a resolution declaring that the People's Republic of China had committed an act of aggression in Korea.[6]

The UN Charter went well beyond merely prohibiting the use of force in international relations. It even forbade the "threat" of force. Article 2(4) was quite categorical in this, "All Members shall refrain in their international relations from the threat of use of force against the territorial integrity or political independence of any state, or in any manner inconsistent with the Purposes of the United Nations." The UN Charter also made it obligatory for members to offer facilities and other assistance in case of an aggression, whereas in the League this was merely a recommendation.

The Veto

The veto became the most debated issue at the San Francisco Conference. The draft text proposed at the conference provided that all decisions of the Security Council would be taken by six (out of eleven) concurring votes, including the "concurring" votes of the permanent five. The big five argued that only they had the military and economic power to enforce peace and security in the world and unity among them was essential for this. The British permanent under-secretary for foreign affairs, Alexander Cadogan, argued that the permanent five constituted half the world's population and an equal percentage of its military might.[7] The head of the US delegation, Secretary of State Edward Stettinius, in a radio address assured the American people, "It is not a question of privilege but of using the present distribution of military and industrial power in the world for the maintenance of peace."[8] He too claimed that only the big powers had the military might to enforce the decisions of the Security Council. In his report to the US Senate in July 1945, he declared that the veto would not confer any privilege on any great power since unanimity among them was essential for maintaining and enforcing peace in the world. Lack of unanimity among them would itself be a threat to peace.

The challenge to the veto was led by Australia's foreign minister, Herbert Vere Evatt, and a motley group of small countries - Mexico, Belgium, El Salvador, Chile, Colombia, Peru and New Zealand. They questioned the compatibility of the veto with the principle of sovereign equality promised by the Charter and moved amendments regulating its use. Evatt alleged that the proposed Security Council "had grave defects and showed obvious signs of having drawn up in the exclusive interests of major powers, pre-occupied with problems of military security, and inclined to ensure for themselves special privileges to which they deemed themselves entitled by reason of their contribution to victory in World War-II."[9]

The big five, especially the US and the Soviet Union, remained firm and united. The veto was presented by them as a *condicio sine qua non,* a condition without which there would be no Charter. They issued a declaration on 7 June 1945, midway through the conference, "In view of the primary responsibilities of the permanent members, they could not be expected, in the present condition of the world, to assume the obligation to act in so serious a matter as the maintenance of international peace and security in consequence of a decision in which they had not concurred. Therefore, if a majority voting in the Security Council is to be made possible, the only practical method is to provide, in respect of non-procedural decisions, for unanimity of the permanent members plus the concurring votes of at least two of the non-permanent members."[10]

They insisted that any concession on this issue could result in their privileged position being taken away from them. The US refusal to budge was theatrically demonstrated by Senator Tom Connally who declared that without the veto there would be no UN and tore up his copy of the Charter. The Soviet Union supported the US whole-heartedly on this. It wanted to ensure that the veto was applicable to all matters of international peace and security, admission of new members, appointment of the UN secretary-general, Charter amendment and to all non-procedural matters.

A British delegate presented the veto as the key to the survival of the proposed organisation, *"Ex-hypothesi* a great Power has challenged the world organization....... Surely then the World Organisation has broken down and that very war which it is designed to prevent if possible, takes place."[11] An American delegate also made the veto the pivot of the proposed security system, "[I]f a major power became the aggressor the

Council had no power to prevent war. In such case the inherent right of self-defence applied, and the nations of the world must decide whether or not they would go to war."[12]

The representative of India, or more correctly, British India, Sir R.M. Mudaliar, proposed that the veto should be applicable only for the first ten years and then reviewed at the review conference. He said, "[I]f this unanimity rule were not to be applied at the end of ten years to any proposal regarding the amendment of the Charter, we could safely, and with good conscience and with complete trust and confidence in the five great powers in the Yalta formula during the intervening period of ten years."[13] Australia proposed that the veto should not be applied to decisions by the Security Council on the peaceful settlement of disputes.[14] The debate, however, had little effect on the outcome of the meeting. The Indian motion was rejected in the committee by 13 votes to 14.

The United States proposed a compromise that the veto be restricted to substantive issues, not procedural matters, which would allow a discussion to take place. Senator Vandenberg explained, "I agree that there must be this veto on the use of force; but I do *not* agree that it should apply up to and including the point where an aggressor is identified." [Emphasis in original].[15] This change required Stalin's consent which took some time coming. Stalin gave his consent but extracted a concession in Poland as the price. Britain had wanted its Polish government-in-exile to be included in a government to be installed in Warsaw. Stalin sacrificed the veto on procedural issues for a free hand in Poland.

Though the big five were keen on the veto there is a degree of confusion about its originator and an eagerness to pass the blame. President Truman believed that it was Churchill's idea. Ferrell writes that the Americans conjured it to protect the Monroe Doctrine.[16] It was widely believed in the United States that the Soviet Union had insisted on it. This had to be repeatedly refuted by American leaders to retain support for the UN in Congress. Secretary of State Cordell Hull told a Senator, "The veto power is in the document primarily on account of the United States. It is a necessary safeguard in dealing with a new and untried world arrangement."[17]

To counter Evatt's criticism that the League for all its flaws was much more flexible on amendments to its Covenant, the big five offered to provide for a general review conference when called by a majority of the Security Council or two-thirds of the General Assembly. This was strengthened further with a provision that a review conference would take place after ten years if so decided by the General Assembly and the Security Council by a simple majority.

The permanent five made another condescending concession in Article 27(3) on the issue of a party to a dispute voting on a resolution. The article provided that on decisions under Chapter VI and under Article 52(3) a party to a dispute would refrain from voting. These articles dealt with peaceful settlements of disputes in which the Security Council makes non-binding recommendations. The veto would continue to apply to coercive measures under Chapter VII.

The collective security arrangement of the United Nations is different in approach and content to that of the League. The League's arrangement was much more collective in nature while that of the United Nations is hegemonic and more of a 'delegated' system. Article 10 of the League's Covenant required all members to "respect and preserve" the territorial integrity and political independence of all members against external aggression. In the UN Charter there is no such obligation nor has any such authority been given to members. Besides, the obligation of members to accept and carry out the decisions of the Security Council was not present in the League's Covenant. On the contrary, Article 15 of the Covenant permitted members to take such action as they considered necessary "for the maintenance of right and justice" in case the Council was unable to reach agreement on a dispute referred to it. The UN Charter only permits members to protect themselves against an armed attack.

The League's Covenant also obligated members to submit their disputes to arbitration, judicial settlement or enquiry by the Council (Article 12). The UN Charter makes a similar recommendation by calling upon members to refer a dispute to the Security Council in case they are unable to settle it themselves by peaceful means but there is no obligation on them to do so.

Article 11 of the League's Covenant declared a war or the threat of war to be "a matter of concern to the whole League." In contrast to this, the UN Charter gives the primary responsibility of maintaining international peace and security to the Security Council. It states that the Security Council acts on behalf of members when carrying out this responsibility. In case a member resorted to war the League's Council was authorised to seek military forces from members. The framers of the UN Charter were convinced that the failure of the League was due to the weaknesses inherent in this arrangement - diffusing its authority by vesting it in the entire membership of the League and the absence of a standing armed force at the disposal of the Council.

At the San Francisco Conference, the Indian delegate sounded a prophetic alarm, "the Committee should not delude itself with the thought that the proposed Organization could prevent wars between the great nations or even between small nations, if the great powers were divided in their sympathies." He, however, said that it was better to have an imperfect organisation than to have none at all.[18]

Regional alliances and self-defence

The Soviet Union's approach to the United Nations during the negotiations was determined by its experience during the war. It looked upon the UN as an alliance against Nazism and was keen to ensure that it retained the right to defend itself against it, alone or in alliance with other countries. Soon after the war broke out, it started the process of forging alliances with countries in East Europe to counter any future threat from Germany. These alliances ran against the philosophy of the United Nations, itself an alliance against such threats. The Soviet Union, however, was not prepared to abandon its security cordon and it extracted the consent of the United States and Britain to this at Yalta. Its alliances in East Europe were given specific exemption. This ran afoul of Latin American states which demanded a similar carve-out for their Latin American alliance. They raised the bogey of communism, accusing the Soviets of funding communism in their countries, an argument that caught the attention of the Americans. They were once again supported by Nelson Rockefeller and Senator Arthur Vandenberg, who invoked the venerated Monroe Doctrine as a parallel.[19]

The US reopened the issue of the Soviet alliances at the conference and extracted a concession. Three more articles were added (Articles 52-54) permitting member states to form regional associations, provided that they were "consistent with the Purposes and Principles of the United Nations." The Charter also provided for the Security Council to use regional associations for enforcement action and permitted them to take enforcement action, but only with Security Council authorisation. There was, however, one critical exception made in order to address the chief concern of the Soviets. The requirement of obtaining Security Council authorisation would not apply if the action was against any of the 'enemy states' of the Second World War.

Trusteeship of Colonies

Before the Cold War, the US had pursued a strong anti-colonial policy. During the drafting of the UN Charter it had wanted all colonies to be placed under UN administration. This was vehemently opposed by Winston Churchill whose view prevailed. Decolonisation found no place in the brave new world created after trouncing Nazism and fascism. Even the colonial territories of the Axis powers, which were placed under the Trusteeship Council, were not promised independence. Article 76, which laid down the Trusteeship Council's mandate, did not set independence as the goal for the colonies, but "their progressive development toward self-government or independence as may be appropriate to the particular circumstances of each territory and its peoples and to the freely expressed wishes of the peoples concerned."

The US decided to use some of the islands in the Pacific - the Marshalls, the Marianas and the Carolines - as military bases. It was allowed to treat them as 'strategic areas' and was exempted from the requirement of submitting periodic governance reports to the General Assembly's Trusteeship Council. It was permitted to send its reports to the Security Council instead.

UN Military

The absence was a military force at its command was believed to be one of the key weaknesses of the League for it left it at the mercy of the big powers for enforcing its decisions. When its Covenant was being drafted, France had proposed the creation of a permanent international police force. This suggestion was not accepted and instead the League Council was authorised to recommend member states to contribute military forces when sought by it. This made the League dependent on the big powers for enforcement action. The idea of creating a force was considered again in the Geneva Protocol of 1924 but was not accepted. The inability of the League to take action against Italy for its invasion of Ethiopia and Japan of Manchuria became important reasons for its collapse.

This weakness of the League was addressed in the UN Charter in Article 43 which placed an obligation on all members to assist the Security Council by contributing towards its military requirements for enforcement action under Chapter VII. At Dumbarton Oaks three forms of a military under the command of the Security Council were considered: "(i) a permanent army of an international nature over and above the national armies, or even replacing them; (ii) national contingents under international command, which pre-supposed control by a permanent international military staff; (iii) national contingents at the disposal of an international body but remaining under the command of their national army."[20]

Roosevelt rejected the idea of a super-state with its own police force and supported the second proposal of national contingents under an international command. Agreements would be signed by member states with the Security Council for placing forces at its disposal. The US administration was deeply concerned about rejection by the Senate and did not wish to incorporate any provision that might give it a reason to do so. Placing American military personnel under UN command was one such cause for concern, even though a Gallup Poll in June 1943 had concluded that 74 percent of Americans supported an international police force.[21]

The New York Times reported that delegates in San Francisco viewed Article 43 as "the most important single paragraph" in the UN Charter.[22] On Britain's suggestion, the Charter also provided for a Military Staff Committee, comprising representatives of the military forces of the permanent five, to advise and assist the Security Council on its military requirements. This arrangement would be a continuation of the wartime joint campaign of the big powers. Until agreements for this were reached, Article 106 provided for interim arrangements on the lines of the wartime security apparatus.[23] Some members wanted more specific and immediate commitments on the creation of a United Nations force. France wanted a full-time standing international force. Uruguay wanted more details of the Military Staff Committee to be enumerated. However, delegates agreed that these details would be worked out in the Military Staff Committee later.

The importance the US attached to the idea of a military force being provided to the Security Council can be appreciated from the report submitted by Stettinius to the President and to the Committee on Foreign Relations of the US Senate soon after the conference was over. In the report, Stettinius affirmed that the Security Council would be given the use and the support of diplomatic, economic and military tools and weapons, "The whole scheme of the Charter is based on this conception of collective forces made available to the Organization for the maintenance of international peace and security." The report noted that the League of

Nations did not contain any provision requiring member states to provide forces to the League to execute military sanctions and this provision in the Dumbarton Oaks text thus represented "a long step forward."[24]

Exiting the UN

There is no provision in the UN Charter on the procedure for a member to relinquish its membership of the UN. A member of the League could leave the organisation under Article 1(3) after giving two years' notice and fulfilling all its obligations under the Covenant. The absence of such a provision can be construed to imply that the obligation of a member state to abide by its commitments under the Charter is in perpetuity. This issue has not yet been put to the test. In 1965, Indonesia announced its decision to withdraw following its inability to get its support for its claim to Sarawak. The UN, however, took no action and Indonesia changed its mind soon.

Despite the simplicity of the structure, the text of the Charter ran into 111 articles, against the Covenant's 26. Many articles were clumsily drafted and several provisions soon became outdated. There was little idealism in the atmosphere in San Francisco. It was power politics all the way. Once Germany surrendered, soon after the conference began, there was a race to seize as much of its territory as possible and the new organisation became the means to legitimise it. The Soviet Union had taken control of the eastern part, along with the capital Berlin, but it also wanted the rest of eastern Europe to be under its control as a buffer against any future invasion by Germany. Britain, France and the other West European colonial powers were keen to recover their colonies in Asia that Japan had seized during the war.

Unknown to the other delegates was the spying network that the Americans had created in San Francisco to ensure that their negotiating strategies were known to them well before they were presented at the meetings. Papers released half a century later showed that the various wings of the US government, the White House, the State Department and Congress worked in tandem during the conference to ensure a favourable outcome. They also showed the supportive role played by the media. The American delegation used the media to project its viewpoint both through private briefings and selective leaks.

The conference ended on 26 June, with all the participating countries signing the Charter. Attention then shifted to its ratification, since it could come into effect only when half the members, including all the permanent five, had done so. The most critical, after the League's experience, was the United States.

US Senate Ratification of the Charter

The Senate hearings on the ratification of the UN Charter gave further evidence, if any was still needed, of the delicate balance between the American desire to create an effective international organisation capable of preventing another war and safeguarding its national sovereignty. The State Department prepared a 50,000-word report for the Senate. Stettinius assured the Senate that the veto was there not only to ensure unanimity among the permanent five, which was essential for effective action by the UN, but also to protect US sovereignty.

The main concern for the Senate was the special agreement envisaged in Article 43 on supplying troops to the United Nations. Some senators wanted a case-by-case approval for any deployment of US troops to the UN. This was opposed by the two senators, Connally and Vandenberg, who had been part of the negotiations in San Francisco, on the plea that this would take the Security Council back to the days when the League was dependent on the whims of its Council members for military action on its behalf. Connally said, "If we have to wait to get somebody's consent, the war will be on, and we will not be able to control it." To resolve this matter, President Truman had a special law drafted for congressional approval, the United Nations Participation Act, defining his powers to provide troops to the United Nations. The Act required the President to take congressional approval for any deployment of troops beyond a certain limit set in the Act, but within that limit, the President could do so after entering into an agreement with the United Nations, subject to congressional approval of the agreement.

These preparations and gestures bore fruit. The Senate approved the UN Charter with an overwhelming majority of 89 to 2. Both Houses also passed the UN Participation Act. Roosevelt's death may have helped in getting the overwhelming endorsement of his dream project in the US Senate.

The ratifications of the other countries came equally smoothly. The required number was reached on 24 October 1945, which is since celebrated as United Nations Day.

Endnotes

1   Vijaya Lakshmi Pandit was the sister of Jawaharlal Nehru, who later became the first prime minister of India. Pandit was elected the first woman president of the General Assembly in 1953.

2   Ian Brownlie, *International Law and the Use of Force by States* (Oxford University Press, 1963), pp. 273-274.

3   UNCIO Vol. 3. Doc. 2, G/14(1), 5 May 1945, p. 552.

4   New York Times, 6 April 1949. Quoted in Subrata Roy Chowdhury. *Military Alliances and Neutrality in War and Peace.* (New Delhi: Orient Longmans, 1966), p. 68.

5   Article 106 in Chapter XVII entitled "Transitional Security Arrangements" refers to the parties to the Four-Nation Declaration, signed in Moscow on 30 October 1943 and France (thus completing the permanent five).

6   UN document A/RES/498(V) of 1 February 1951. India and Burma were the only non-communist countries to vote against the resolution, which was adopted by 44 votes for, 7 against and 8 abstentions.

7   Stephen C. Schlesinger, *Act of Creation: The Founding of the United Nations* (Cambridge, MA, USA: Perseus Books, 2003), p. 194.

8   Schlesinger, p. 201.

9   Quoted in Bosco, p. 36.

10   UNCIO Vol.11, Commission III – Security Council. Statement by the Delegations of the Four Sponsoring Governments on Voting Procedure in the Security Council, 7 June 1945. P. 711. [The Four sponsoring states were – the US, Britain, the USSR and China].

11   UNCIO Vol.11, Commission III – Security Council. 9th meeting of Committee 1, 17 May 1945 (New York: UN Information Organizations, 1945).

12   UNCIO, Commission III, Committee 1. Doc. 246. III/3/48, 14 June 1945 (New York: UN Information Organizations, 1945), p. 514.

13   UNCIO Vol.11, Commission III – Security Council. 5th meeting, 20 June 1945 (New York: UN Information Organizations, 1945), p.175.

14   UNCIO Vol.11, Commission III – Security Council. 4th meeting, 20 June 1945 (New York: UN Information Organizations, 1945), p.123.

15   Arthur H. Vandenberg, Jr. and Joe Alex Morris [Eds.] *The Private Papers of Senator Vandenberg.* (Boston: Houghton Miffin Co., 1952), p. 211.

16 Robert H. Ferrell, *Off the Record – The Private Papers of Harry S. Truman* (New York: Harper & Row, 1980), p. 24.

17 Hull, p. 1662.

18 UNCIO, Commission III, Committee 3 – Enforcement Measures. Doc. 246. III/3/10, 12 May 1945 (New York: UN Information Organizations, 1945), pp. 307-308.

19 Vandenberg, Jr. p.186.

20 UNCIO Vol. 12. Commission III, Committee 3. Doc. 134. III/3/3, 9 May 1945, p. 574.

21 Eichelberger, *Organizing for Peace*, p. 212.

22   Quoted in Lowe, p. 73.

23 John Gerard Ruggie, *Constructing the World Polity.* (London: Routledge, 1998), pp. 241-242.

24 Report to the President on the Charter of the UN. Hearings before the Committee on Foreign Relations, US Senate, 2 July 1945, pp. 23 and 60.

Beginner's Luck: The Early Successes

5

> *The Security Council has gone through four phases of about two decades each - the first under Western control, the second under the Soviet Union in alliance with the South, the third led by the West with the cooperation of Russia and China and the fourth in which the East-West divide has come back. The Security Council had some initial successes. It was able to select it headquarters, elect the first secretary-general and mediate ceasefires in Palestine and Kashmir, even though it could not resolve the disputes. It was more effective in Indonesia, a Dutch colony before the Second World War. It was able to mediate Indonesia's independence when the Netherlands tried to re-conquer it after Japan's defeat.*

Having won the war and seamlessly transformed itself into a peacetime organisation, the United Nations began its journey as the guardian of global peace and security. How did the former allies fair in their new collective enterprise? Did they live up to the assurances they had given to the rest of the world in the Charter?

The Security Council was designed to be operated by the permanent members acting in unison. The state of their relations determined the nature and level of its activity. The frequency of use of the veto is a useful indicator of the prevailing balance of power in the Council. It reveals four distinct phases in its history, the first two coinciding with the 44-years of the Cold War during which the Security Council was deadlocked by the veto, first of the Soviet Union and then the United States:

1. **1945-1969:** This phase was dominated by the US. The Soviet Union used the veto 80 times against none by the US. Until 1956 the Soviet Union was the only permanent member to exercise the

veto. It blocked 27 applications of new membership, including of countries like Ceylon (later, Sri Lanka), Nepal, Ireland, Japan and Italy. Britain and France used their veto for the first time in 1956 on resolutions against them for invading Egypt. During this period the Security Council was marginalised in international affairs. It adopted on an average only 11 resolutions a year. Two military actions were, however, authorised in this phase - the Korean operation and the authorisation to Britain to stop the delivery of oil to Southern Rhodesia.

2. **1970-1990:** The second phase can be taken to start from 17 March 1970 when the US exercised its first veto to block sanctions against Southern Rhodesia. It then had to do so repeatedly because the Soviet Union had gained the upper hand with the support of non-aligned countries. The US used the veto 64 times to protect its interests in Vietnam, the Middle East, southern Africa and Latin America. The number of resolutions adopted annually crept up to 18, but no military action was authorised in this period.

3. **1991-2011:** The third phase coincided with the disintegration of the Soviet Union. The permanent five started acting in unison and there was an explosion of peacekeeping operations, sanctions and military actions. The use of the veto declined in this phase, with the US using it 14 times and Russia 6 times. China used it 4 times, while Britain and France did not do so at all.[1] Resolutions exploded to 63 a year. This cooperation ended abruptly after the invasion of Libya in 2011.

4. **October 2011-to date:** In the current phase, the West has retained control over the Council with the support of several countries of the South, though the US can still get out-voted on Palestine. The frequency of resolutions remains high, 61 a year, and vetoes have also gone up slightly from the third phase, most of them by Russia and China on Syria. Two minor military actions were authorised - in Mali and the Central African Republic by French forces.

Selecting the Headquarters

After the San Francisco Conference, a Preparatory Commission was set up to get the United Nations started and to select its headquarters. The Commission started work in London and that is where the Security Council held its first meeting on 17 January 1946 with Australia, Brazil, Egypt,

Mexico, Netherlands and Poland as the first elected members. Britain opposed Geneva as the headquarters of the UN on account of its unhappy association with the League. The Swiss sealed their own fate by declaring that any decision of the UN Security Council to use force would have to be taken outside Switzerland on account of its policy of neutrality.

Andrei Gromyko, the Soviet ambassador to the US, supported locating the UN in the United States as a compromise between Asia and Europe. The Preparatory Commission agreed to this. President Truman suggested Chicago and San Francisco, but the Europeans ruled them out as being too far. The choice then fell on New York and was clinched when John D. Rockefeller Jr. offered $ 8.5 million to buy a slum area in Turtle Bay.

The UN moved to New York from London in two months. It operated from Hunter College in Bronx for a few months and then for a few weeks from Henry Hudson Hotel. Then it found a factory at Long Island's Lake Success where it stayed till it occupied its newly constructed headquarters in 1952.

First Secretary-General

The selection of the first secretary-general was another important task for the Preparatory Commission in London. An early confirmation of the origins of the UN as a military alliance for collective self-defence came from Britain in its proposal for this office. It proposed General Dwight Eisenhower, the US army chief. This was in line with its approach in the League of Nations, where it had provided the first secretary-general, followed by France. Trygve Lie, foreign minister of Norway, advocated Britain's Anthony Eden for the post.

The US did not want an American to be the secretary-general since it expected the seat of the UN to be located on its soil and wished to avoid making it a one-nation organisation. It favoured Lester Pearson, Canada's ambassador to the US, but Russia opposed him because of his country's proximity to the US. Some West Europeans wanted Paul Henry Spaak, Belgium's foreign minister. The Soviet Union opposed him as being too West European. It then proposed Trygve Lie, who had been Norway's foreign minister in exile. It was able to persuade the US to support him and on 29 January 1946, the UN Security Council elected him unanimously. In the General Assembly, Lie got 28 votes to Spaak's 23.

The Security Council had some early successes in arranging a truce in the conflicts in Palestine and in Kashmir and in securing the independence of Indonesia from the Netherlands. In Palestine and Kashmir, it was able to mediate ceasefires and persuade the parties to accept monitoring by its military observers. These observers were unarmed and few in number, but otherwise similar to the peacekeeping forces the UN became known for later.

The going, however, was far from easy. The very first case brought before it became a victim of the rift among the permanent five, who seemed keener on scoring points over each other than addressing the security concerns of members. Iran complained to the Council that the Soviet Union was refusing to withdraw its troops from its soil. These troops had been stationed there under an agreement during World War II, along with US and British forces. All three had agreed to withdraw by March 1946. The United States and Britain did so and decided to support Iran's demand. The Security Council asked Iran and the Soviet Union to resolve the matter through consultations. When Iran came back with a renewed complaint, the Soviet Union refused to participate in the discussions. The Security Council now found itself unable to take any action and the matter was resolved only when the Soviet Union withdrew its troops on its own. The Council had been found to be incapable of taking action against the highhandedness of a permanent member. This would become a recurrent pattern in the Council.

The Soviet Union decided to put counter pressure upon Britain. Two days after the Iranian complaint against it, it accused Britain of interfering in Greece and of supporting fascist forces there. This prompted Greece to accuse its Balkan neighbours, Yugoslavia, Albania and Bulgaria, of instigating guerrilla warfare against it. This was disputed by them and the Soviet Union. The Greek war became the first proxy armed conflict between the former allies. The Security Council investigated and debated the matter inconclusively until the conflict itself fizzled out.

The Soviet Union also took up the issue of withdrawal of British and French troops from Syria and Lebanon. On 16 February 1946, the US introduced a mild resolution in Security Council expressing the hope that Britain and France would withdraw their troops "as soon as practicable". The Soviets exercised the first veto in the Security Council, amidst an amusing procedural confusion, on this resolution on the ground that it was very mild and that their amendment seeking to strengthen the text had been voted down.[2] There were seven votes in favour and the Australian ambassador, N.J.O. Makin, who was chairing the meeting, declared the resolution adopted. The Soviet ambassador protested and quoted Article 27(3) to assert that his negative vote constituted a veto. After some discussion, Makin relented and reversed his ruling.

The Iran issue left a deep imprint on Stalin and set the tone of his interaction with the Security Council. Stalin believed that the issue was being kept on its agenda under US pressure. He felt humiliated over being dragged into the Council and was angry with the United States and Britain for diluting the principle of big power solidarity. When Secretary-General Trygve Lie visited Moscow in July 1946 Stalin told him, "Of course, one should not abuse the right to veto. Any good weapon loses its efficiency, its moral strength if it is used too often. However, if England and the United States were to collude with each other, they could always put the Soviet Union in such a position that it would have to resort to the right to veto."[3] The Soviet Union was so incensed with the issue of being on the UN agenda, that in 1948 when Iran proposed normalisation of relations, its first demand was the withdrawal of the Iran question from the Council's agenda.

Indonesia

The Security Council had better luck in its early cases outside Europe. In Indonesia, it was able to ensure that the efforts of the Netherlands to re-conquer the country after Japan's defeat were stymied and its independence secured. The Council benefitted from the fact that this happened in the early years of the Cold War when the US had not yet abandoned its policy of supporting the independence of European colonies in Asia and Africa. The matter was brought to the Security Council initially by Ukraine and taken up, thereafter, by India. The Security Council set up a Committee of Good Offices in 1947, comprising representatives of Australia, Belgium and the United States. UN intervention and efforts by India ensured that the Dutch withdrew, albeit reluctantly, and Indonesia became the 60th member of the UN in 1949.

Palestine

All three European members of the Security Council and the United States were supportive of the idea of relocating European Jews in Palestine. Palestine was part of the Turkish Empire until the First World War and had been taken by Britain as a mandate territory under the League of Nations. In 1917, during the war, it declared its intention to create a homeland for Jews there and European countries directed the flow of their Jews to it. During Hitler's rule in Germany the flow became an exodus.

After the Second World War, Britain brought the issue of its mandate before the General Assembly, which set up a high-level committee to decide its future. In August 1947, the committee recommended the division of the territory into separate Jewish and Arab states. The Arab countries opposed the recommendation but the General Assembly adopted a resolution on partition on 29 November 1947 with 33 votes for and 13 against. All European countries, including the Soviet Union, supported it. India voted against the resolution.

Fighting broke out immediately in Palestine and the Security Council adopted a weak resolution in March 1948 calling for peace. It also set up a Truce Commission. On 15 May 1948, a day after the expiry of Britain's mandate, the Jewish authorities in Palestine declared independence, which the US recognised immediately. The Arab neighbours, however, refused to do so and declared war. This was the first declaration of war since formation of the United Nations. However, it did not go well for the Arab countries and they were relieved to settle for a UN-sponsored ceasefire. The permanent five designated the head of the Swedish Red Cross, Count Folke Bernadotte, as UN Mediator on Trygve Lie's suggestion. He was also given some unarmed military observers from the three countries that were members of the Security Council's Truce Commission – Belgium, France, and the United States.

Bernadotte soon asked for guards to protect the military observers, who found themselves vulnerable to attack from splinter groups. The secretary-general sent volunteers from the guards posted at the UN headquarters in New York. The UN Guard, as they were called, were non-military in character and comprised three hundred men and a reserve of five hundred. The authority for sending them was drawn from Chapter XV of the Charter on the Secretariat, although the resolution did not identify any provision. The secretary-general said that he was sending them under the General Assembly's Resolution 186 of 14 May 1948 which authorised him to provide such staff to the UN Mediator as was required by him to perform his duties. He said that the guards would not use force except under the orders of the Mediator. The Soviet Union objected to their deployment on the ground that the Security Council could only use the armed forces provided to it under Article 43, which no country had done; but it did not veto the resolution. Tragically, Bernadotte was killed on 17 September by Israeli right-wing extremists.

India-Pakistan War, 1947-48

In the war between India and Pakistan over the state of Jammu and Kashmir in 1947, the Security Council mediated a ceasefire when India took the matter to it. Both countries accepted UN military observers to monitor it.[4] This was a significant early success for the Council, though, as in the case of Palestine, its inability to resolve the underlying dispute left both countries dissatisfied.

These successes, however, remained flashes in the pan. The Soviet Union blocked the Security Council from taking action against its invasion of Czechoslovakia. It had instigated a communist coup there in February 1948 and sent in troops to enforce it. No action was taken despite a complaint against the Soviet intervention. Later, when the Soviet Union blockaded Berlin in September 1948, its veto again ensured that no action was taken against it.

Endnotes

1   China used its veto within a year of joining the United Nations, in 1972, to block the membership application of Bangladesh because Pakistan opposed it.

2   UN Document, S/PV.23, 16 February 1946.

3   Gaiduk, p. 71.

4   UN Military Observers for India and Pakistan (UNMOGIP).

6   Divided Nations

*The unity of the principal allies started unravelling soon
after the United Nations turned itself into an international
organisation. The rules of procedure of the Security Council
could not be finalised and the permanent five were unable to
reach agreement in the Military Staff Committee on the UN
military force. The aspirations of post-war disarmament gave
way to an arms race and rival military alliances were formed
by the West - comprising the US, Britain and France – and by
the East – comprising the Soviet Union and its East European
allies. The Communist party seized control in China and the
issue of its membership in the United Nations to replace the
government of Nationalist China became the most divisive in
the Security Council for two decades.*

In the early years there were few challenges to the permanent five from the
other members of the UN and among them the West held sway. With 20
states, Latin America constituted the largest bloc in the General Assembly
and was firmly with the West. The eight countries from Asia – India, Iran,
Iraq, Lebanon, the Philippines, Saudi Arabia, Syria and Turkey – and four
from Africa – Egypt, Ethiopia, Liberia and South Africa - were too weak
to challenge the permanent five. Many of them were still colonies or in
semi-colonial state. The Soviet Union, with its five satellite states from
East Europe was badly outnumbered both in the General Assembly and the
Security Council. Dissenting voices were rare and came from within the
Western camp. In January 1947, Australia questioned the authority of the
Council to create an interim administration for the disputed Adriatic city
of Trieste and declare it the Free State of Trieste when there had been no
breach of the peace. But the five had agreed and the rest fell in line.

The division in the UN started from within the permanent five. Their unity, and more critically the collaboration between the United States and the Soviet Union, had weakened with the passing away of Roosevelt, who had assiduously worked to keep the lines open to Stalin. Truman's advisors, like George Kennan and undersecretary of state, Dean Acheson, on the other hand, were convinced that the US was the natural inheritor of the mantle of the British Empire and should pull its weight in world affairs behind it. Differences developed fast with the Soviet Union. After admitting a few new members, they could not agree on any for several years. They were divided on disarmament, particularly on the nuclear issue, and soon started forming separate military alliances. The overthrow of the Kuomintang party in China by the Soviet-backed communist party in 1949 completed the bifurcation of the permanent five. The US refused to let the communist regime take the China seat. The Soviet Union boycotted the Security Council for seven months in 1950 and declared that it considered all decisions taken in its absence illegal.

Provisional Rules of Procedure

This divide among the permanent five impacted the functioning of the Security Council from the very beginning. At its first meeting in London in January 1946, it had adopted some provisional rules of procedure. It later set up a committee to frame the rules of procedure but the committee's recommendations remained on paper and the Council has been functioning since on the basis of the provisional rules. These rules have been amended a few times but merely on issues like official and working languages.

A serious *lacuna* in the rules of procedure is the absence of any reference to quorum. In principle, the Security Council can take a decision with only one or a few members sitting. This principle was applied in 1950 during the Soviet boycott of the Council. UN experts interpreted the principle of unanimity among the permanent five to mean those present and voting, even though Article 27(3), which deals with voting in the Security Council, states that decisions of the Security Council must have "the concurring votes of the permanent members". The legal experts in the UN, whose opinion was sought by the US, declared that the absence of a permanent member could not be construed as inability of the permanent five to reach consensus and upheld the resolutions on Korea taken during the Soviet boycott. The Soviet Union did not boycott the Security Council ever again.

Another flaw in the provisional rules of procedure is the absence of any automaticity in convening a meeting of the Council when asked for by a member. Though the provisional rules of procedure state that the president "shall" call a meeting when sought by a member, no time limit is prescribed. This leaves room for the president to play around and procrastinate summoning a meeting when he is unwilling to do so. In 1990, when Iraq invaded Kuwait, the permanent members, especially the Western countries, were unwilling to have the Council interfere with their plans to take military action against it. It took the president, the ambassador of Zimbabwe, five weeks to convene a meeting, which was held behind closed doors.

In 1997, Chile, Costa Rica, Egypt, Guinea-Bissau, Japan, Kenya, Poland, Portugal, South Korea and Sweden tried to get regular rules of procedure adopted but this was refused by the permanent five. Singapore's ambassador, Kishore Mahbubani, recalled that he had made several procedural suggestions to improve the functioning of the Security Council but the permanent five resisted them. He wrote later, "We were initially puzzled until we heard the private comments of a P-5 permanent representative who expressed surprise that the 'tourists' were trying to change the arrangements of the Council." Mahbubani also noted that the Secretariat does not keep "an institutional memory of the proceedings of the informal consultations".[1]

The Military Staff Committee and the UN Military

In the negotiations leading up to the formation of the UN and in its early years there was considerable enthusiasm for an effective standing force to be placed at the disposal of the UN Security Council to enable it to perform its primary function. This became the first issue to be taken up by the Council. Its first president, Australia's N.J.O. Makin, said that this was so that "the Security Council may have available at its call as soon as possible the armed forces, assistance and facilities necessary to maintain peace."[2]

The Military Staff Committee was tasked to negotiate the formation of a standing force for the UN. The proceedings of the Committee were not made public but in April 1947 it gave its report to the Security Council. The report, titled "General Principles governing the organisation of the armed forces made available to the Security Council by Member Nations of the United Nation", noted that of the forty-one articles contained in the report there was agreement on only twenty-five. The Council discussed the report and was able to provisionally adopt the first ten articles but the discussion on Article 11 was divisive and the debate remained inconclusive. The remaining articles were never discussed.

The articles on which there was agreement dealt with the objectives of the armed forces which were drafted on the lines of Article 39 of the Charter, the overall strength of the armed forces which was to be decided by the Council on the advice of the Military Staff Committee, and the principle that while all members could contribute the forces would mainly come from the permanent members. The size of the contribution of each nation was to be decided by the Security Council as also their deployment. The troops would be stationed on the member state's territory until asked for by the Security Council, upon which they would come under its command and control. The contributing state would be responsible for logistical support and maintenance of reserves.

The major disagreement was on the size and location of the forces. The US suggested a force of around 300,000 men which was more than double the 125,000 suggested by the Soviet Union. The Soviet Union insisted on equality in the contribution of forces by the permanent members.[3] This was opposed by the West because the size of the troops would then be determined by China's capacity which was the lowest in ships and aircraft.[4] The Soviet Union suspected that the US wanted a large UN military in order to be able to dominate it by its contribution, which the Soviet Union would not be able to match.[5]

In the discussions in the Security Council on the report of the Military Staff Committee the US deputy permanent representative, Herschel V. Johnson, acknowledged that the setting up of the UN military force was an important part of the UN Charter that remained to be completed, "One vital organizational task remains undone. Article 43 of the Charter imposes upon the Security Council the responsibility for negotiating 'as soon as possible' special agreements under which the Member States will make available to the Security Council on its call, 'armed forces, assistance, and facilities, including rights of passage, necessary for the purpose of maintaining international peace and security.' Until those agreements have been concluded and put into force, the Security Council will be unable to fulfil its responsibilities as the enforcement agency of the United Nations. Chapter VII of the Charter, insofar as it relates to military enforcement measures, will remain inoperative."

However, instead of stating how the US intended to go about fulfilling this obligation, Johnson put forward the idea of member states constructing military bases around the world and making them available to the UN when needed, "We, therefore, recognize that if the United Nations armed forces are to be effective at all the member nations must make available to the Security Council a system of bases in various parts of the world from which they can operate." He then revealed his government's rethink on the idea of a UN force but without clarity, "The United Nations is not a world government. It is based on the principle of the sovereign equality of all its members. Therefore, it could not have a permanent standing armed force of its own in the sense that individual nations possess such forces....... On the other hand, the founders of the United Nations decided at San Francisco that the United Nations should not repeat the experience of the League of Nations, which relied solely upon the individual action of member states to carry out the sanctions provided in the League Covenant. It was, therefore, decided that each nation should agree in advance to provide forces and facilities upon which the Security Council could call to prevent or suppress any act of aggression or breach of the peace. Those national contingents are to be under the strategic direction of the Military Staff Committee whenever they are called into action by the Security Council." Johnson proposed that the permanent members which possessed forces capable of enforcing the peace should provide the bulk of the military forces required by the United Nations, "The interests of the United Nations as a whole must take precedence over the desires or ambitions of any single nation... The mere existence of such forces will be a powerful deterrent to any nation contemplating an act of aggression. Prompt establishment of such forces will be a demonstration to the peoples of the world of the intention of the member nations to carry out their obligations to uphold the law of the Charter."[6]

The Soviet delegate, Andrei Gromyko, wanted all five permanent members to make available forces of equal overall strength with the same composition in equal numbers of land, sea and air forces. He said that the UN Charter had placed a special responsibility on the permanent members, "Their special position consists in the fact that they are charged with the special responsibility, both for the activities of the Security Council in respect of the maintenance of international peace as well as for the activities of the United Nations in general." Gromyko concluded that this special position of the permanent members was also based on the principle of equality in the contribution that they were to make to the UN military force. He vehemently opposed the American idea of the permanent five setting up military, naval and air bases to be made available to the Security Council, on the ground that they were not provided for in Article 43, or elsewhere in the UN Charter. He argued that if bases were included in the agreements to be signed by the permanent members with the Security Council they would get legitimised and stationed permanently on the territories of other member states, "The acceptance of the proposal on bases would be utilised by some states as a means of exerting political pressure on other nations which provided such bases."[7] He argued that the armed forces to be made available to the Security Council would have to be stationed within the frontiers of the contributing member and be used outside only as envisaged in the Charter. Any other practice would violate the territorial sovereignty of states.

The Belgian delegate, Van Langenhove, was critical of the Committee for its inability to reach agreement on the setting up of a UN military force. He expressed concern over the conclusion of the Military Staff Committee that, taking into account the decision-making process under the Charter in the Security Council, the forces to be placed at the Security Council's disposal would not be used in the event of a war involving the great powers, "In our opinion such a conclusion cannot be unreservedly accepted."[8]

The Australian delegate, Lt. Col. William R. Hodgson, complained that the proceedings of the Military Staff Committee had been secret and the non-permanent members did not have any information on what had transpired in it. He emphasised the importance of a UN military force, "It is vital to the whole security system established by the Charter and essential to the growth of confidence in the United Nations." He also drew a link between disarmament and the UN military, "It must be evident to any reasonable observer that until the United Nations has developed effective instruments by which it can, in the last resort, compel observance of the law of the Charter; national governments will inevitably be reluctant to agree to any special measures of disarmament."[9] They would continue to depend on bilateral and regional arrangements for such defence thus undermining the system of collective security.

The failure of the permanent five to come to an agreement on a UN military was castigated by Brazil's ambassador, João Carlos Muniz, in 1947, "The international armed force, which should be the keystone of the system of security, has not yet been organized, nor has an agreement been reached between the Powers in regard to making the disarmament a reality."[10] Claude maintains that the failure to conclude agreements under Article 43 for a UN military implied the collapse of the security arrangement promised by the permanent five, "Even the limited collective security function that the Charter had envisaged for the Organisation was now eliminated. Not only was the application of collective security *against* great powers to be excluded, but there was to be no application of it *by* the great powers; the partnership of the giants was dissolved."[11]

Secretary-General Trygve Lie tried to revive the idea when the first Israel-Arab war broke out. He suggested the formation of a small UN Guard Force to be recruited internationally by the UN rather than contributed to it by member states. In a memorandum in 1950, Lie proposed the creation of a UN Legion of 50,000 volunteers. He said in his memorandum, "The mere existence of such a force would greatly enhance the ability of the Security Council to bring about peaceful settlements in most of the cases which are likely to come before it." He called for a new approach to be made to resolve the differences relating to the size, location and composition of the forces under Article 43.[12] These proposals did not find favour with the US which did not wish to place its own troops under UN command or permit the UN to recruit its own force. Its response to one of the proposals was that "it encroached somewhat on the military theme."[13]

The first Uniting for Peace resolution adopted by the General Assembly in 1950 during the Korean War, recommended to member states that they should have forces available for United Nations service on the recommendation of either the Security Council or the General Assembly. But as affirmed by the UN secretary-general in his report to the General Assembly, it had explicitly recognised that "this did not diminish the need for and desirability of new efforts to establish the United Nations forces that, under Article 43 of the Charter, should be made available to the Security Council."[14]

The idea of a standing UN military under the command of the Security Council refused to die. It kept coming up and even the US occasionally made supportive noises. In November 1958, the US secretary of state, John Foster Dulles, wrote to Secretary-General Dag Hammarskjöld in response to one of his proposals, "As you know, the United States.... has a strong interest in the early establishment of standby arrangements for a United Nations Peace Force."[15]

In 1970, the General Assembly adopted a resolution recommending that "the Security Council take steps to facilitate the conclusion of the agreements envisaged in Article 43 of the Charter in order fully to develop its capacity for enforcement action as provided for under Chapter VII of the Charter...."[16]

After the Cold War, hopes were aroused again of the possibility of a UN force. When Iraq invaded Kuwait, the Soviet President Mikhail Gorbachev proposed activating the Military Staff Committee to manage any possible action of the Security Council. Even the US suggested exploring the possibility of the Military Staff Committee coordinating the blockade of Iraq. But nothing came of it.[17]

In his report, *Agenda for Peace*, to the Security Council in June 1992, Secretary-General Boutros-Ghali revived the idea of "bringing into being, through negotiations, the special agreements foreseen in Article 43 of the UN Charter." He was realistic enough to appreciate that such a force would never be large enough to meet a military threat from a major power, but he hoped that it would be able to deal with small threats. As expected, the suggestion did not find favour with the big powers.

Proposals for creating a UN force continued to be made. In 1993, Brian Urquhart drew upon his long UN experience to propose the creation of a 5000-strong force costing about US$ 380 million to deal with situations like Bosnia. The mass killings in Rwanda in 1994 once again triggered a clamour for a UN force. Boutros-Ghali proposed a UN rapid reaction force in January 1995. A force akin to this was created in the summer of 1995 in Bosnia at the initiative of Britain and France in the framework of the UN Protection Force (UNPROFOR).

Later in the year, the Netherlands proposed a UN Rapid Deployment Brigade. It envisaged a force of between 2000 and 3000, costing around US$ 300 million. Canada and Denmark also carried out some tentative studies. In November 1995, a UN Joint Inspection Unit report on the military component of UN peacekeeping operations recognised the difficulties in the "financing, training, command and control, location of the force, transportation, and the geographical distribution of soldiers."[18] Enthusiasm for the proposal waned after this.

In 2000, a panel on UN peacekeeping operations headed by Lakhdar Brahimi, former foreign minister of Algeria, examined the idea of a rapid deployment force for the UN but concluded that it was not possible in the prevailing conditions. Finally, Secretary-General Kofi Annan, in his report to the General Assembly in 2005, decided to put an end to this infructuous discussion and hopeless aspiration by recommending the abolition of the Military Staff Committee.[19] The world leaders meeting at New York to mark the 60th anniversary of the UN, however, balked at the idea of such blatant admission of failure and rejected it. In true UN tradition they requested the Security Council to consider the composition, mandate and working methods of the Military Staff Committee.[20] This remains to be done. The Military Staff Committee, comprising the defence attachés of the permanent five missions, continues to meet periodically at the UN over lunch.

Several writers on the UN concede the critical failing of the UN in its inability to setup a UN military. Schlesinger, despite high praise for the UN, admits, "But the UN never developed a rapid response force of its own because the Big Powers feared a loss of control over any independent UN army."[21] Bowett had reached the same conclusion several years earlier, "Yet, despite the prominence given to Chapter VII in the Charter, and despite a general agreement that the system of collective security established by the Charter can only operate upon the assumption that the United Nations is given the armed forces necessary to maintain international peace and security, the Charter scheme has not yet been implemented."[22]

Disarmament

The Charter mandates the General Assembly to make recommendations to the Security Council on "the principles of disarmament and the regulation of armaments".[23] As seen from the negotiations among the permanent five before San Francisco, they regarded disarmament as being applicable only to the other members of the UN in order to make it easier for them to police the world. To the delegates at San Francisco disarmament covered only conventional weapons since they were not aware of the development of the nuclear bomb by the US. The use of the nuclear bombs in August over Japan and the start of the Cold War dramatically changed the dynamics of the disarmament debate, apart from giving it an ominous urgency.

The Cold War replaced talk of disarmament with an arms race. Both the US and the Soviet Union started arming their allies and building military bases abroad. The US, keen to preserve its monopoly of the atomic bomb, proposed the setting up of an international atomic body to regulate the development of nuclear energy and control the proliferation of nuclear bombs. The Soviet Union countered it by proposing the complete elimination of nuclear weapons. Its position, however, changed as soon as it developed the nuclear bomb itself. The demand for nuclear disarmament now started coming from newly independent countries of Asia and Africa but nuclear proliferation continued until all the permanent five, including the People's Republic of China, which became a permanent member later, turned nuclear and then negotiated the Nuclear Non-Proliferation Treaty in 1967 to prevent its further spread. The treaty legitimised the nuclear weapons of the permanent five and forbade other countries from acquiring them. It can be said that this treaty was based on the original design of the big powers to monopolise weapons among them and keep the rest of the world disarmed. However, it could not prevent other countries from pursuing nuclear weapons programs, some successfully.[24]

The General Assembly set up successive committees from 1952 onward for disarmament negotiations on both nuclear and conventional weapons. Apart from the Nuclear Non-Proliferation Treaty, they produced treaties on the regulation of trade in conventional weapons, elimination of chemical and biological weapons and restrictions on nuclear tests. The US and the Soviet Union also conducted bilateral negotiations on restricting nuclear weapons with modest success.

Formation of regional military alliances

The provisions in the Charter permitting regional organisations had been included to assuage the Soviet Union but their complexity exposed the Charter to the charge that they would balkanise the United Nations and lead to the revival of spheres of influence. These fears were well founded. A race began soon for the formation of separate military alliances, often arraigned against each other. In fact, when Dulles became secretary of state, he thanked Nelson Rockefeller for his farsightedness in getting the provision included in the Charter, without which NATO would not have been possible.[25]

The cycle of post-war alliances had started during the war itself. Between 1943 and 1949, the Soviet bloc countries had concluded seventeen military alliances, which were directed not merely at invasion from Germany but also any other threat or aggression.[26] The West protested that the Soviet bloc had concluded these treaties without consulting it. It maintained that these treaties were directed against West Europe and had created an atmosphere of fear there.

The wave of regional alliances after the war started with the Inter-American Treaty signed in Rio in 1947, but it was in Europe that it acquired the divisive character that broke the Second World War alliance. Once Nazi Germany had been defeated, West Europe fell back on its old loathing of Soviet communism. Even in 1946, when Europe lay devastated, there was talk of reviving West Europe as a third force. The Soviet Union had occupied East Europe as part of the Yalta agreement to create a buffer zone with Germany. Churchill wanted to build an alliance with the US to protect Britain and its empire. He developed this idea by reviving the old fear of the threat to Europe from the Soviet Union. In a speech at Fulton, Missouri, on 5 March 1946 which he called 'The Sinews of Peace', he declared, "From Stettin in the Baltic to Trieste in the Adriatic an iron curtain has descended across the Continent." He warned that the Soviet Union wanted "a very high and increasing measure of control from Moscow" in central and eastern Europe through local communist parties and the fate of countries outside the region, like Italy and France, hung in the balance.[27]

Churchill was a private citizen and not the prime minister of Britain when he delivered this speech and the British Government clarified that it had not been consulted. However, President Truman was present at the gathering and there is indication that he had been shown the speech. He was immensely impressed with it. It led him to formulate his Truman Doctrine and launch the Marshall Plan for rebuilding Europe. It also sowed the seeds of the formation of NATO three years later.

It is not that voices in support of a policy of accommodation towards the Soviet Union were absent in the US. A breakaway faction of the Democratic Party under former vice president, Henry Wallace, recommended talks with the Soviet Union to ban nuclear weapons and channelling American aid to all countries in Europe through the United Nations. Wallace had been a close confidante of Roosevelt. He was secretary of commerce under Truman and was sacked for his views. His party could not survive Truman's anti-communist tirade. Thousands of federal employees were required to certify that they did not have communist sympathies. One of the questions they were required to answer was, "At one time or two, were you a strong advocate of the United Nations?"[28]

Churchill's strategy of an Anglo-American alliance did not escape Trygve Lie's attention. He wrote in his memoir, ". . .. Mr. Churchill saw Europe with no means . . .. of recovering to become a force of any kind without American help and partnership and urged instead fraternal association among the English-speaking peoples backed by a Western security arrangement."[29]

Britain and France formed the Brussels Pact in 1948 to block the spread of Soviet-led communism, since they felt that the United Nations could not be an effective safeguard for them. They also realised that without the United States they would be helpless against it. They decided accordingly to woo anti-communist Republicans, such as Dulles, who were sympathetic to the cause of an alliance with West Europe. Senator Vandenberg also became an ardent supporter of the idea of a North Atlantic pact. The problem for the North Atlanticists was the issue of the compatibility of the new alliance with the United Nations Charter. But Vandenberg saw no contradiction in this. He regarded the new alliance as a peace pact duly authorised by the UN Charter.

The North Atlantic Treaty Organisation was formed in 1949 by the US with Canada and 10 West European countries. The obvious placement of the new alliance in the rubric of the UN Charter was in the context of Chapter VIII, as a regional organisation. However, a regional organisation was required to report to the UN Security Council about its operations and this would place it on the radar of a Soviet veto. In his report to the US Congress on UN activities in 1948, President Truman had blamed the deadlock in the UN on the veto and expressed disappointment at its functioning as a security organisation. This ruled out the possibility of NATO being created as a regional organisation. It was, therefore, decided to place it in the context of Article 51, as an organisation for self-defence. The Charter of NATO was so framed as to keep it within the framework of the objectives of the Security Council with suitably deferential pronouncements to it and the United Nations. Richard Hiscock, who also served as a British diplomat, wrote, "As a result, virtually all the treaties that were concluded were based explicitly or by implication on UN members' inherent right of individual or collective self-defence under Article 51....... although some of the treaties also contained features envisaged in the regional arrangements provided for in Chapter VIII."[30]

For the US, the formation of NATO was a radical departure from its policy of non-involvement in Europe. After the First World War it had refused to join the League of Nations and had joined the Second World War only when attacked by Japan. After the war it remained cautious about getting sucked into the European quagmire. However, the Truman Doctrine on combating communism struck a chord in the isolationist Congress. Support for an alliance with West Europe soon became overwhelming in the US Congress. The North Atlantic Treaty was approved by eighty-two votes to thirteen in the Senate, a reversal of the nineteenth-century policy of non-involvement in the affairs of the Old World. The Monroe Doctrine had given way to the Truman Doctrine.

Within four years of the end of the Second World War, the Allies were split in two rival camps. One of the enemy states, Italy, became a founder member of NATO, which was provided with a standing army, a supreme commander and a defence committee, all that had been envisaged for the Security Council's military force in the UN Charter but denied to it. Its formation marked the end of cooperation among the three main founders of the United Nations, the US, Britain and the Soviet Union and the beginning of military confrontation between them.

The US justified NATO in the context of the provision in the UN Charter permitting collective self-defence but there was no denying that the formation of NATO had dealt a body blow to the UN's primary mandate of providing peace and security to the world. Once the floodgates of such alliances were opened by Truman, his successor, former military general Dwight D. Eisenhower built a veritable shield of alliances to encircle the Soviet Union and its allies.

In May 1955, West Germany, another enemy state of the Second World War, joined NATO. The Soviet Union immediately formed the Warsaw Pact with the countries of East Europe. The Second World War was now well and truly over. Germany was no longer the enemy, even though the UN Charter retained its provisions against it.

V.K. Krishna Menon, in his address to the General Assembly on 6 October 1954, examined the issue of the conformity of the formation of treaty alliances by the big powers with the UN Charter. He asserted that they were neither self-defence organisations under Article 51 nor regional organisations under Article 52. They were, he observed, "…. a proclamation of the doctrine of balance of power and of power groupings."[31] He declared them to be against the principles of collective security and the UN Charter.

The West justified its military alliances by accusing the Soviet Union of paralysing the UN Security Council with its veto. It did not concern either side that they were violating the letter and spirit of the UN Charter. Military alliances could not possibly remove the misunderstandings that had arisen between them. They exacerbated their differences, leading to further polarisation and undermining the authority of the Security Council. The founders of the United Nations were repeating the mistakes of the big powers in the League of Nations. The numerous alliances formed during that period had served to create an atmosphere of nervous tension and mutual suspicion. The web of alliances that had embroiled all of Europe in war following the shooting in Sarajevo had been recreated after the First World War. President Woodrow Wilson's warning had gone unheeded. The founders of the United Nations did not show any more sagacity than their predecessors despite the experience of an even more destructive world war.

The framers of these alliances used ingenious arguments to distinguish them from their disastrous predecessors. The US secretary of state, Dean Acheson, told the Senate Foreign Relations Committee that these alliances were not meant to embroil the US in wars to defend invaded allies but to prevent aggression. He declared that the treaty did not violate the UN Charter, "It is an arrangement entered into within the scope of Article 51 of the United Nations Charter." He characterised it as an "ancillary method" to maintain international peace and security.[32] Senator Vandenberg defended the treaty in the same vein. He declared that unlike earlier treaties, which were partnerships of power, the Atlantic Pact was a "partnership for peace".

More detailed justifications of NATO and its presumed conformity with Article 51 of the Charter came later in books published on the subject. One of these was by Eric Becket in *The North Atlantic Treaty*. Becket argued that Article 1(1) referred to the need for "collective measures" by members of the UN to suppress acts of aggression. He concluded that the "collective self-defence" in Article 51 was the same as this and, therefore, NATO was a treaty that sought to promote the objectives of the UN Charter through its provisions of collective self-defence. This argument was at variance with the position of the US delegation at San Francisco. Stettinius had maintained that such an alliance would be against the principle of collective security envisaged by the Charter. In his Report to the US President on the Results of the San Francisco Conference, Stettinius had said, "There were theoretically two alternative means of preserving this unity. The first was through the formation of a permanent alliance among the great powers. This method might have been justified on narrow strategic grounds but it would have been repugnant to our traditional policy. It also would have contained elements of danger because it might well have been interpreted as a menace by the nations not party to it. Accordingly, this method was rejected. The second method was through the establishment of a general security system based upon the principle of sovereign equality of all peace-loving states and upon the recognition of the predominant responsibility of the great powers in matters relating to peace and security."[33]

Another writer, Kelsen, argued that a collective self-defence organisation like NATO was permissible under Article 52 of the Charter, indeed, envisaged by it, as part of its collective security architecture. He maintained that the Charter did not exclude organising collecting self-defence through regional arrangements even though, "It may be not in conformity with the intention of the framers of the Charter to organise collective self-defence by a treaty."[34] This, however, is not so conclusively borne out either by the provisions of the Charter or the *travaux préparatoires*. Self-defence, individual or collective, against an armed attack permitted under Article 51 is for a limited period, till such time as the Security Council comes into action. There is no reference to it in Chapter VIII, which deals with regional organisations. Regional organisations, under Article 53, are only permitted to take enforcement action under the authority of the Security Council. A reference to the framers of the Charter will further clarify the issue. In his report on the San Francisco Conference, Stettinius had written, "The Security Council could utilize regional arrangements for enforcement action, provided that such enforcement action should be undertaken only when authorized by the Council and that the latter should be kept fully informed of all actions taken or contemplated under regional arrangements or by regional agencies. It was recognized that the Council must have a general authority over regional security machinery in order to prevent such arrangements from developing independently and thus possibly pursuing different ends. In other words, the provision was intended to coordinate the function of a regional grouping with those of a general organization and at the same time establish the final authority of the latter."[35]

Not all writers agree that NATO is compatible with the UN Charter. Chowdhury examined the Charter-compatibility of these alliances and concluded, "It seems, therefore, fairly clear that Chapter VII is concerned with the settlement of disputes amongst States of a particular region but it does not authorise regional accords for defence against violation of peace originating in an extra-regional source. While it would embrace a dispute between Peru and Colombia, it certainly will not include an armed attack on a Latin American Republic from an extra-regional source as the Rio

Pact purports to cover nor can it include an attack on a NATO member from the Soviet Union under the Atlantic Pact or an attack on Sofia by West Germany as the Warsaw Pact purports to cover."[36]

The UN Charter did not envisage fragmented alliances replacing its collective security arrangement. Article 2(5) calls upon all members to assist the UN in any action taken by it in accordance with the Charter and to refrain from giving any assistance to a country against which it is taking preventive or enforcement action. Regional security arrangements were permitted in the expectation that they would act as collective security organisations on a regional level complementing the UN's efforts. As self-defence organisations they split the UN into rival camps.

Former UN secretary general, Trygve Lie, also disagreed with the view that alliances like NATO strengthened the collective security of the UN, "If people generally began to accept alliances as substitute for genuine, world-wide collective security, then the hope of a lasting peace would be greatly endangered."[37] The president of the General Assembly, Australia's Herbert Evatt, was equally skeptical about the compatibility of the new alliance with the principles and purposes of the United Nations. He was of the view that regional alliances could not possibly be the way forward for collective security nor could they be instruments for enhancing peace and security in the world.

The Soviet Union was more forthright in its criticism of NATO. It alleged that since the new alliance provided for the creation of an armed force without authority from the Security Council it was in violation of the UN Charter. However, despite these reservations there was little opposition to the formation of NATO in the General Assembly. The Soviet Union decided not to raise the matter and the Western countries had overwhelming support of the other members. Besides, the General Assembly was more pre-occupied at this time with an Argentinean proposal for convening a general conference of the UN to address the question of the veto. Argentina declared that the Great Powers had not been able to maintain their commitment to protecting international peace and security due their internal differences and disagreements and due to the application of the veto, which till then had only been exercised by the Soviet Union.

NATO sees itself as an international organisation in its own right, founded on the "principles of democracy, individual liberty and the rule of law."[38] During the Bosnia crisis in 1995 its secretary-general, Willy

Claes, former foreign minister of Belgium, asserted that while it could be used for enforcing decisions of the Security, "NATO is more than a sub-contractor of the UN".[39]

NATO has an enigmatic relationship with the UN. In its origins it had the same motivations and objectives as the UN – an alliance against an enemy for the collective defence of its members. Its need arose from the realisation that the original enemies against which the United Nations had been formed had now become allies and one of the key allies, the Soviet Union, had become the enemy. But it was not conceived on the same grand scale as the UN, there was neither appetite nor space for another global organisation. NATO was given a more defined region to defend - West Europe - and every effort was made to pay obeisance to the global body.

In its preamble, NATO's charter affirmed the faith of its members "in the purposes and principles of the Charter of the United Nations" and in the very first article promised to abjure "the threat or use of force in any manner inconsistent with the purposes of the United Nations." Article 5 defined the placement of the organisation in the framework of the UN system. It stated that in forming the alliance the NATO members were exercising their "right of individual or collective self-defence recognized by Article 51 of the Charter of the United Nations." It also solemnly affirmed that any attack by NATO would be reported to the Security Council and terminated as soon as the latter had taken "the measures necessary to restore and maintain international peace and security."

Thus, NATO's stated purpose was to supplement the Security Council's work, performing it till only such time as it was able to get its act together, an unlikely possibility during the Cold War. NATO members never intended to subject their alliance to Security Council approval, either before or after an operation. After the disintegration of the Soviet Union, when the Western countries regained control over the Security Council, they contemplated using NATO for enforcing Security Council decisions. The final communiqué of the NATO-Atlantic Council Ministerial meeting at Istanbul on 9 June 1994 mentioned the possibility of NATO operating under the authority of the Security Council but only on a "case-by-case basis". Before NATO launched its bombing of Kosovo, Britain decided to bring a resolution to the Security Council seeking authorisation for military action. The US secretary of state, Madeleine Albright called it "well-intentioned but not well-conceived." She cautioned, "This would give Russia, not to mention China, a veto over NATO."[40]

After the terrorist attack on the twin towers in New York on 11 September 2001, NATO invoked Article 5 of its treaty on collective defence and carried out the invasion of Afghanistan to remove the Taliban from power. It submitted its report to the Security Council in October 2005, fulfilling the requirement under the article to do so "immediately".

Admission of new members

In the early years, the Soviet Union maintained that the United Nations was an association of like-minded countries seeking to protect their interests against adversaries. It insisted that only those countries that had fought against the Axis Powers and were capable of pursuing an independent foreign policy were eligible for UN membership. It opposed Portugal for maintaining close ties with Franco's Spain, Ireland for not joining the war against fascism in the Second World War and Transjordan, for being a Western creation. It supported the application of Albania and Mongolia.

By August 1946 there were nine pending applications. The US expressed willingness to allow all to join in a package deal but Britain was adamant on blocking Albania and Mongolia. The Soviet Union insisted on each application being taken up individually. It then vetoed the candidacies of Ireland, Portugal and Transjordan. Albania and Mongolia failed to get the required seven votes. Only three countries were admitted, Sweden, Iceland and Afghanistan.

The Soviet Union continued to press for the membership of Albania and Mongolia, pointing to the services they had rendered in the fight against fascism during the war. When refused, it accused the West of following pro-fascist policies.

This impasse was broken only after Stalin's death. In 1955, sixteen countries from both sides were allowed membership in a package deal. The Soviet Union was slow to recognise the advantages of getting the newly independent countries of Asia and Africa into the UN. When the sixteen new states joined, it calculated its supporters to be nine, with the addition of Albania, Bulgaria, Hungary and Romania. When Mongolia joined in 1961, it increased the list to ten. Even in the early 1960s, it assessed that there were forty-three in the western camp and only 10 in the socialist camp. But it noted that there were forty-eight "neutralists" or uncommitted countries that could be used to turn the tide in their favour. Albania, however, broke with the Soviet leader, Nikita Khrushchev, over his attempt to make up with Tito of Yugoslavia. Albania's Enver Hoxha denounced Khrushchev's attempts to break away from the Stalinist legacy and preferred to side with China.

Seat for the People's Republic of China

The first break in the Security Council came on the issue of communist regime replacing the Kuomintang regime on China's seat in the UN. In January 1950, the Soviet ambassador, Jakob Malik, demanded that China's seat be taken away from Kuomintang party's 'Republic of China' and given to the new communist party government, which called itself the 'Central People's Government of the People's Republic of China'. Ironically it was China that held the presidency of the Council that month. As a result, Ecuador presided over the discussion. The Soviet resolution was supported only by Yugoslavia and India. Norway and Britain abstained while the remaining six members China, Cuba, Ecuador, Egypt, France and the US opposed and defeated it. Malik declared that the presence of the Kuomintang representative was "undermining the prestige and authority of the Security Council and the United Nations as a whole."[41] He announced that the Soviet delegation would not sit in the Security Council as long as it was there and would not recognise any decision of the Council taken in its absence as legal.

The US Ambassador, Ernest A. Gross, regretted the Soviet boycott but maintained that its absence did not diminish the Security Council's powers or its authority to act, "Our work here in the United Nations is too important to the people of the world to be imperilled at the whim of a member motivated by malaise or a desire for propaganda." India had joined the Council for the first time in 1950, along with Ecuador and Yugoslavia. In his first intervention India's ambassador, B. Narsing Rau, addressed the issue of China's representation by pointing out that unlike in the General Assembly and the Trusteeship Council the Security Council rules did not state who would examine the credentials of a delegation. This was left to the secretary-general. He proposed that the issue of recognition of governments be decided by the Security Council on the basis of information collected by the President from all member states on which government they recognised. This proposal was referred to a committee of experts but nothing came of it.

The Soviet boycott was to prove fateful for Korea. It enabled the Security Council to decide on its first military action, which, in the absence of its own armed force, was outsourced to the United States. The US took advantage of the Soviet boycott to take an authorisation from the Security Council for military enforcement action against North Korea. This is discussed in the next chapter.

Soviet Disenchantment with the UN

By the second part of the first session of the General Assembly, in 1946, the Soviet Union had started viewing the UN as a hostile organisation. It regarded the Security Council's inability to undertake measures against Franco's regime in Spain and secure the withdrawal of British and French troops from Syria and Lebanon and British troops from Greece and Indonesia as critical failures. It was also displeased with the retention of Iran's complaint against it on the Security Council agenda and the rejection of membership applications of Albania and Mongolia.

In a debate in the Security Council on 29 August 1946, Gromyko retaliated against the Western criticism of the presence of Soviet troops in Iran, North Korea and Port Arthur in China by opposing the continued presence of Western troops in non-enemy countries of the Second World War. This was directed at Britain which had troops in other countries in Europe, the Middle East and South East Asia. The US too had troops in Czechoslovakia, France, Egypt, Morocco, China and India. It also had troops in the Pacific islands like the Marshalls, the Marianas, the Carolinas and New Caledonia, as well as in Australia. He proposed that all members submit to the UN information on the location of their troops abroad. The United States responded by declaring that it had nothing to hide and suggested that the disclosure should include troops stationed in former enemy countries as well. However, Britain shot down the idea.

The Soviet Union, nevertheless, placed this proposal formally before the General Assembly in October 1946. The United States decided not to oppose it and the General Assembly adopted a resolution requiring members to disclose information on troops abroad and calling upon them to reduce armaments. The US went ahead and did so but Britain refused.

US Disenchantment with the UN

The UN came under attack in the US as anti-communist feeling increased. Resentment grew against the Soviet Union's frequent use of the veto and there were widespread calls for its abolition. The United States, confident of its majority support, no longer found the veto attractive. While not openly advocating its abolition or dilution, it started looking for a way of breaking the Soviet blockade. There were demands in the United States for calling a general conference of the United Nations to reform the Charter and make the organisation more effective.

To right-wing Republicans effectiveness meant the ability to confront the Soviet Union. The Soviet Union had denounced the Truman Doctrine and the Marshall Plan as violations of the UN Charter. When it formed the Cominform, right-wing radicals in the US regarded it as a revival of Lenin's Communist International. Such was the seriousness of the matter that Secretary of State George Marshall had to advise the Congress in 1948 that UN reform needed to be handled with care.[42]

The United States also lost interest in the United Nations as it realised that it could not have its way in the Security Council despite its majority. By 1946, Dean Acheson had come to regard the United Nations as a "monkey house". He later declared it to be a hopelessly idealistic creation of "that little rat, Pasvolsky".[43] Kennan agreed with him. In 1948, he assessed the United Nations negatively, "Occasionally it has served a useful purpose. But by and large it has created more problems than it has solved."[44]

Even some American observers were disturbed by their country's high-handed treatment of the UN. The American Association for the United Nations wrote a letter accusing the Truman administration of treating the United Nations as "an instrument of policy - indeed an instrument of power politics to be used when convenient, and to be ignored and misused when convenient."[45] Eleanor Roosevelt, wife if the deceased president and now a US delegate to the UN on human rights, complained to Marshall that "in every possible way the US is acting to hurt the UN and to act on a unilateral basis."[46]

In September 1947, Marshall put forward a proposal to create an Interim Committee of the General Assembly, a kind of "little assembly." This was to comprise all members of the General Assembly and function between its sessions in view of the deadlock in the Security Council. All the other big powers opposed this idea. The Soviet Union said it would vote against the proposal and not participate in it. Britain expressed doubt about its viability. France was concerned about being dictated by "small and irresponsible states." The United States, however, pressed with the idea, declaring it to be experimental and short-term. The General Assembly approved it on 13 November 1947. The Interim Committee functioned for that session and the next. The Soviet Union boycotted it and the United States used it to consolidate its hold over its allies.

Europe was in dire straits after the war and in desperate need of aid. Marshall drew up an elaborate plan for providing assistance to West Europe, which came to be called the Marshall Plan after him. But this was not merely a humanitarian program of reconstruction. It was backed by the Truman Doctrine on providing aid to combat the global threat of communism. Couched in these security terms, the program was approved by the US Congress as part of the Cold War against the Soviet Union, in order to make the world safe for capitalism.

With the Cominform in East Europe and the Organisation for European Economic Coordination in the west the divide in Europe was complete and the UN Commission for Europe faded into oblivion.

From this, the progression to the United Nations being regarded as a hindrance to achieving American foreign policy goals was but a small step. Both the United States and the Soviet Union had started regarding each other as enemies and each was determined to expand its sphere of influence. The US saw the Soviet Union as bent on spreading its influence across the world through communism. It declared socialism to be antithetical to American values and decided to counter it by projecting itself as the protector of the free world, based on a democratic political order and a free market economy. The Soviet Union identified itself with the working class and other underprivileged sections of society all over the world and promoted violent movements. It championed anti-colonialism and anti-racism and slowly joined hands with countries of Asia and Africa on these issues. A divided Security Council did not have much chance of fulfilling its mandate of maintaining international peace and security. During the 44 years of the Cold War there were over 100 major conflicts in which 20 million people were killed.[47]

Endnotes

1   Kishore Mahbubani, *Permanent and Elected Council Members.* Chapter in David M. Malone (Ed.), The UN Security Council – From the Cold War to the 21st Century. (Boulder, Colorado: Lynne Rienner, 2004), p. 259-260.

2   SCOR First Meeting, 17 January 1946. p. 6.

3   D. W. Bowett. *United Nations Forces – A Legal Study* (New York: Frederick A. Praeger Publishing, 1965), pp. 14-16.

4   Richard Hiscocks. *The Security Council – A Study in Adolescence,* (New York: The Free Press, 1973), p.73.

5   Inis L. Claude, *The United States and the Use of Force.* (International Conciliation, March 1961, No. 532. Carnegie Endowment for International Peace), p. 352.

6   UN Security Council document S/361 of 4 June 1947 (138th meeting). Statement of the US deputy permanent representative, Herschel V. Johnson. UNSC Official Records, 1947. pp. 954-955.

7   UN Security Council document S/361 of 4 June 1947 (138th meeting). Statement of the Soviet delegate, Andrei Gromyko.

8   UN Security Council document S/361 of 4 June 1947 (138th meeting). Statement of the Belgian delegate, Van Langenhove.

9   UN Security Council document S/361 of 4 June 1947 (138th meeting). Statement of the Australian delegate, Lt. Colonel William R. Hodgson.

10 João Carlos Muniz, Statement at the second session of the UNGA, 16 September 1947, *The Voice of Brazil in the United Nations, 1946-1995* (Brasilia: Alexandre de Gusmão Foundation, 1995), p. 42.

11 Claude, *The Changing United Nations,* p. 31.

12 UNSG Trygve Lie's "Memorandum of Points for Consideration in the Development of a 20-Year Programme for achieving Peace through the United Nations". JN (SG) Vol.46 (I), 1950. Pp. 111-113. (New Delhi: Nehru Museum and Library).

13 Quoted in Lowe, p. 102.

14 GAOR 308th Plenary Meeting, 17 November 1950, p. 439.

15 Quoted in Lowe, p. 104

16 UNGA Resolution 2734 (XXV) of 16 December 1970. Para 9.

17 John Quigley, *The 'Privatisation' of Security Council Enforcement Action: A*

Threat to Multilateralism. Michigan Journal of International Law, Vol. 17(2), Winter 1996, pp. 256-257.

18 'Military Components of United Nations Peace-Keeping Operations' (JIU/ REP/95/11), UN doc. A/50/576 of 14 Nov. 1995, Recommendation 4(p. vii) and paragraph 32 (p. 9). Quoted in Lowe, p. 121.

19 UN Document A/59/2005 of 21 March 2005, Kofi Annan, *In Larger Freedom,* Report to the UN General Assembly. Para 219.

20 UNGA Resolution A/Res/60/1 of 24 October 2005, World Summit Outcome, 16 September 2005, para 178.

21 Schlesinger, p. 286.

22 Bowett, p. 561.

23 Article 11(1) of the UN Charter.

24 Indian and Pakistan declared themselves nuclear powers in 1998. North Korea withdrew from the NPT and tested a nuclear device in 2006. Israel is widely believed to have nuclear weapons. Argentina, Brazil and South Africa abandoned their nuclear weapons programs and joined the NPT in the 1990s.

25 John Foster Dulles. *War or Peace* (New York: MacMillan, 1950), p. 92.

26 Chowdhury, p. 2.

27 Quoted in Fraser J. Harbutt. *Iron Curtain – Churchill, America, and the Origin of the Cold War* (New York: Oxford University Press, 1986), p. 28.

28 Daniel Hellinger and Dennis R. Judd. *The Democratic Façade* (USA: Brooks/ Cole Publishing, 1991), p. 156.

29 Trygve Lie. *In the Cause of Peace: Seven Years with the United Nations* (New York: Macmillan, 1954), p. 37.

30 Hiscocks, pp. 75-76.

31 E.S. Reddy and A.K. Damodaran. *Krishna Menon at the United Nations – India and the World* (New Delhi: Sanchar Publishing House, 1994), p. 55.

32 Chowdhury, p. 6.

33 *Hearings on the United Nations Charter,* Senate Committee on Foreign Relations, 79th Cong. 1st Session, p. 72. Quoted in Chowdhury, p. 67.

34 Kelsen, Hans. *Law of the United Nations* (New York: Frederick A. Praeger, 1950), p. 922.

35 *Hearings, Senate Foreign Relations Committee, on the Charter of the United Nations, 79th Cong. 1st Sess. pp. 96-97. Quoted in* Chowdhury, p. 141.

36   Chowdhury, p. 140.

37   Quoted from NATO Committee Hearings (Part 3, p 892) in Chowdhury, p. 7.

38   Preamble to the NATO Charter.

39   Quoted in Lawrence S. Kaplan. *NATO and the UN: A Peculiar Relationship* (Columbia, Missouri: University of Missouri Press, 2010), p. 150.

40   Madeleine Albright. *Madam Secretary: A Memoir* (London: Pan Macmillan, 2004), p. 384.

41   Jakob Malik, statement at the 461st meeting of the UNSC, 13 January 1950. SCOR, p. 10.

42   Mazower, p. 234.

43   Mazower, p. 222. The reference is to Leo Pasvolsky, special assistant to US secretary of state, Cordell Hull, and one of the key drafters of the UN Charter.

44   Mazower, p. 222.

45   Quoted in Bosco, p. 50.

46   Quoted in Bosco, p. 50.

47   Report of UNSG, Boutros Boutros-Ghali to the UNSC, *An Agenda for Peace,* 17 June 1992, para 14.

7   False Start: The Korea Operation

The first major crisis for the Security Council came in 1950 when the Soviet Union boycotted its meetings to press for the membership of Communist China. North Korea invaded the South during this period and the US, taking advantage of the Soviet Union's absence, got the Security Council to authorise military action by member states. The Soviet Union challenged the validity of this decision and returned to the Council to block any further such decisions. The US, however, found a way out by taking the matter to the General Assembly under an innovative procedure, which it called 'uniting for peace'. However, the war remained inconclusive and a ceasefire was negotiated by the two sides.

Five years into its formation, the Security Council could do no more than mediate ceasefires in disputes and post observers to monitor them. Then an opportunity came its way in 1950 to show its mettle. North Korea invaded South Korea. Fortuitously for the United States, this came when the Soviet Union was boycotting the Council in protest against the Republic of China occupying the China seat. It grabbed the opportunity with a clever procedural innovation. It got the Council to authorise member states, led by it, to take military action to defend South Korea. This was the first instance of a group of member states taking a mandate from the Security Council to use military force.

The Korean War was the first major conflict between the two sides in the Cold War. Distrust had always been high among the Allied Powers during the Second World War and the old colonial struggle resumed among them as soon as it was over. In Europe, the Yalta deal on spheres of influence prevented a direct conflagration but large parts of Asia, which had been liberated from Japan, were up for grabs. The Soviet Union started funding communist parties and firing up nationalist, anti-imperialist and anti-capitalist emotions all over the world. The communists had their first big success in China, where the communist party drove the Kuomintang regime of Chiang Kai-shek out of the mainland and declared the formation of a People's Republic.

Korea had been occupied by Japan since 1910. In August 1945, the defeated Japanese forces surrendered to the Allies – to Soviet forces north of 38th parallel and south of it to American forces. It was agreed between the two new occupying powers that they would make Korea independent by 1950, but they failed to reach an agreement on its modalities even after two years of negotiations. The United States took the matter to the General Assembly, which adopted Resolution 112/11 creating a UN Temporary Commission for Korea and recommending elections under its supervision. Both parts of Korea held elections in May 1948. However, only the election in the South, in which Syngman Rhee was elected president, was supervised by the Commission. The North refused entry to it and held its elections on its own. After the elections, the Soviet Union announced the withdrawal of its forces from North Korea. The United States followed suit in the South.

The communist victory in China was a serious blow to the United States, which had backed the Kuomintang government and had gone to the extent of making it a permanent member of the Security Council. It saw in China a bulwark against both Soviet communism and Japanese militarism. Now the Kuomintang party had taken refuge on the island of Taiwan and the communists were threatening to take over Korea. The US had to make quick strategic adjustments to meet this new threat to Western dominance in Asia.

The opposition Republican Party accused President Truman, a Democrat, of being weak and incapable of dealing with the communist threat. Truman decided to counter the charge by retaliating forcefully in Korea. He declared that he had to draw the line in Korea as also in Indo-China, the Philippines and Formosa (the Japanese name of Taiwan).

On 25 June 1950, the day North Korea invaded the south, the US called an emergency meeting of the Security Council. It submitted a resolution stating that the Council had "determined" that the armed attack by North Korea constituted a "breach of the peace" and demanding North

Korea to withdraw its forces north of the 38th parallel. The resolution also "called upon" all members "to render every assistance to the United Nations in the execution of the resolution and to refrain from giving assistance to the North Korean authorities." The resolution received nine votes in favour, including those of India, which had joined the Council for the first time earlier in the year, and Egypt. Yugoslavia abstained, while the Soviet Union was absent due to its boycott.

The United States interpreted the resolution to mean that it could give military assistance directly to the South Korean government, though the text called for assistance to the United Nations. It was also unclear if a member could take military action in response to such a general call. Yugoslavia sought to promote a peaceful settlement of the dispute by introducing a resolution calling on the Council to invite North Korea to present its case. This resolution was defeated but South Korea was invited to send a delegation on the suggestion of the United States. Egypt, India and Norway abstained in the vote.

The United States soon set all ambiguities about its military intention at rest in two subsequent resolutions. Two days later, the Security Council adopted Resolution 83(1950) "recommending" that members "furnish such assistance to the Republic of Korea as may be necessary to repel the armed attack and to restore international peace and security in the area." This resolution changed the recipient of the assistance – from the UN to South Korea, making it easier for the United States to intervene in its defence. The resolution was adopted with the support of seven members – the United States, China, Cuba, Ecuador, France, Norway and Britain. Yugoslavia voted against the resolution while the Soviet Union continued to be absent. India and Egypt did not vote as they had not received instructions from their capitals.

At the next meeting, three days later, the Indian ambassador, B. Narsing Rau, who was also the President of the Council during that month, explained that the Indian government would have voted for the second resolution had instructions reached him on time. However, there seemed to be some degree of hesitation since he gave a lengthy explanation, "This decision of the Government of India does not, however, involve any modification of their foreign policy. This policy is based on the promotion of world peace and the development of friendly relations with all countries; it remains an independent policy which will continue to be determined solely by India's ideals and objectives."[1] Rau went on to explain that India continued to hope that there would be a peaceful settlement of the dispute by mediation. He also gave an account of time zones to explain why the instructions could not reach him in time.

Egypt's ambassador, Mahmoud Fawzi Bey, explained that his government had abstained because the conflict was due to the confrontation between the East and West blocs, and the United Nations had not taken any action in several other cases of aggression in which the sovereignty and unity member states of the UN had been violated. This was a reference to the continued presence of British troops in Egypt.

The British ambassador, Gladwyn Jebb, welcomed India's support and expressed regret over Egypt's abstention. He said that the argument that the UN had not acted in other cases of violations of national sovereignty was not adequate justification for not taking action in this case. Bey responded that Egypt had brought the case of the occupation of parts of Egypt by British forces before the Security Council in 1947 but it had not taken any action. He pointed out that the resolution on Korea of 27 June was merely a "recommendation" and it was for each member state to decide its course of action.

The Yugoslav delegate, Nincic, persisted in his efforts for a negotiated settlement in which the people of Korea could be brought together to find a solution to their problem. He said that the problem was "a direct consequence of the general tension of the post-world war, a tension which at recent times had assumed such forms that it had become commonly known as the 'cold war'. We believe that the source of the continued tension lies in the practice, widely applied after the Second World War of dividing certain geographical areas into spheres of influence or interest."[2] He cited his own region, the Balkans, as being an object of this division. He again proposed inviting representatives of both parts of Korea for talks in the UN and also introduced a resolution calling for direct talks between the two sides in Korea but it was turned down by the same seven who had supported the earlier resolution.

On the day the second resolution was adopted, President Truman announced that he had ordered American air and sea forces to give cover and support to South Korean government troops. He said, "The attack upon Korea makes it plain beyond all doubt that communism has passed beyond the use of subversion to conquer independent nations and will now use armed invasion and war. It has defied the orders of the Security

Council of the United Nations, issued to preserve international peace and security."[3] He ordered military assistance to Taiwan, to France in Indo-China and to the Philippines. The rivalry between the United States and the Soviet Union, which had taken the shape of a cold war in Europe, had turned into a fully fledged war in Asia and firmly aligned the United States with the European colonial powers.

The United States now took steps to ensure that there was no interference from the Security Council in its military operation. On 3 July 1950, Secretary-General Trygve Lie and his staff drafted a resolution requesting the US to assume command of the proposed multinational force, which would operate under a UN flag. The resolution also proposed a committee, comprising Australia, France, India, New Zealand, Norway, Britain, the US and other states which might contribute forces to the war, to coordinate assistance for Korea. While Britain, France and Norway supported the proposal, the US turned it down. Britain and France then proposed another resolution on the same lines but without a coordination committee. It met with the same fate.

Four days later, the Security Council adopted Resolution 84 (1950), presented by Britain and France, setting up a military command structure acceptable to the US. It welcomed the prompt offers of the assistance to South Korea and "recommended" that they form a unified command "under the United States". The Security Council also "requested" the United States to "designate" the commander of this force. The unified command could use the UN flag "at its discretion". The United States was "requested" to "provide the Security Council with reports as appropriate on the course of action taken under the unified command."

Jebb gave an imaginative justification for authorising member states to take military action. He said that since the Security Council had not been provided by members with an armed force under Article 43, it could only act under Article 39, which authorised it to "recommend" measures that could be taken to restore international peace and security. Therefore, he declared, it was not for the UN or the Security Council to appoint a UN commander. "All the Security Council can do is to recommend that one of its members should designate the commander of the forces which individual members have now made available," he said.[4] This country, he went on, could only be the United States and the unified command could only be under it. On the issue of the forces flying a common UN flag, he said that this would have to be left to the discretion of each individual force on the ground since it would be for them to decide in their "good judgment" when and where they should use the UN flag or their own national flag.

Although the sponsors of the three resolutions maintained that they had been adopted under Article 39, the resolutions themselves did not refer to any article or chapter of the Charter as the source of their authority. Article 39, in any event, provides for action to be taken by the Security Council under Articles 41 or 42. Its reference to making "recommendations" cannot be stretched to mean authorising military action since that would render meaningless the elaborate checks contained in the rest of the chapter on the use of force by the Security Council.

On the question of reports to the Security Council, the resolution proposed that the Security Council be informed as and when the United States felt it necessary to do so. There was no binding obligation or time-table. The British ambassador also declared that there was no need for the Security Council to create any further machinery to monitor the war. He consoled the Council by adding, "In any event, since we believe the Security Council is acting under Article 39 of the Charter its function is not an operative one; all it should do is to make sure that individual efforts of the members concerned are properly coordinated. If the present draft resolution is accepted the Council will, at any rate from time to time, consider such reports as are made available to it by the United States."[5] Egypt and India joined Yugoslavia in abstaining on the third resolution.[6]

The United States swiftly established a unified command under its direction for the "international force by designation". It appointed General Douglas MacArthur, Supreme Allied Commander for the Occupation of Japan, a hero of the Second World War and of American rule in the Philippines, as the head of the United Command and designated him 'UN Commander'. It did not consult the Security Council nor did it instruct him to report to it. By the end of 1950, the countries that joined this force were Britain, Australia, France, Greece, Netherlands, Philippines, Thailand and Turkey. Altogether fifteen countries provided troops during the war to this international force - a quarter million from the US and about 36,000 troops from the others, apart from those of South Korea. India and Sweden gave non-military assistance.

Trygve Lie sought to create a role for the Security Council in the operation by nominating a South African colonel as his representative to General MacArthur to keep the Security Council "in the picture". To widen the base of the troop-contributing countries, he proposed the formation of an international brigade under the Security Council. The US rejected the proposal. Nevertheless, Norway, which held the presidency of the Council in July 1950, described the Korea operation as a "UN action". Truman called it "a police action under the United Nations," as did Trygve Lie, although there was no provision for police action in the UN Charter and the forces used were from the military. President Syngman Rhee of South Korea described the force as a "joint military effort of the United Nations on behalf of the Republic of Korea." This would imply that the operation was in self-defence by South Korea which the Security Council had decided to assist through its members. However, Rhee went on to state that he had placed the Korean army under the command of General MacArthur who had been appointed as the "supreme commander of the United Nations forces."[7]

Urquhart, a senior UN official noted, "The UN had little or nothing to do with the military action."[8] Eichelberger, the American academic who had been involved in the drafting of the UN Charter, wrote that the US made no effort to use the Military Staff Committee to conduct the operation since it had the Soviet Union as a member. Instead, diplomatic representatives met at the US State Department in Washington, "Consequently, collective action was more and more directed by Washington instead of by the United Nations."[9]

The Soviet Union realised that it had made a tactical blunder in boycotting the Security Council. It returned to the Council in August, which was also its turn for the presidency. This brought back the impasse in the Security Council and put the United States in a difficult position because its military operation in Korea was already underway. The Soviet Union refused to recognise the validity of the Security Council resolutions adopted in its absence as they had only 'six valid' votes. It claimed that the Chinese vote was invalid as it had been cast by the Kuomintang regime's delegate and the resolutions did not meet the requirement of unanimity of the permanent five. As noted in Chapter 6, the Provisional Rules of Procedure do not provide for a quorum and the US view that only a negative vote constitutes a veto, not abstention or absence, was upheld by the legal experts of the UN Secretariat.

The Soviet ambassador, Jakob Malik, turned his ire on the Republic of China and declared that the China seat could not be occupied by the Kuomintang delegate. The US, Britain, France, Cuba, Ecuador and Norway criticised him severely for this stand. Yugoslavia and India supported him, but Egypt joined the West on this occasion. The President's decision was overruled by eight votes. Only three countries supported him, the Soviet Union, Yugoslavia and India. This was the first vote by India with the Soviet Union and against the US in the Security Council.

The Soviet Union introduced a number of resolutions to compel the US to stop bombing North Korea. The US was able to defeat them with the support of its Western allies and other non-permanent members of the Council. The Soviet Union occasionally succeeded in drawing support from Yugoslavia but failed to get the consistent support of India or Egypt. The US objected to the use of the term 'US Air Force' for the forces it had deployed with its allies in Korea and insisted that any resolution on the issue must refer to them as UN Forces.

The Soviet Union also accused the American forces of bombing civilian areas. The United States acknowledged that civilian targets had been attacked during the operations but blamed it on North Korea's military and its supporters for using civilian facilities to store military equipment. The US delegate quoted from a report of General MacArthur to the Council, "The enemy hides vast quantities of military equipment in civilian dwellings, resulting in the necessity to fire and destroy such dwellings when such information is firm.... The UN forces are urgently endeavouring to restrict destruction to the established military forces of the invader."[10]

India opposed the Soviet resolutions condemning the attacks on civilians on the plea that the allegations had not been confirmed through an investigation. A resolution brought by the Western countries calling on all States and authorities not to support or encourage the North Korean authorities and to withdraw their armed forces who were helping them was vetoed by the Soviet Union. India did not vote on any of these resolutions.

The Soviet Union scored a minor victory when it managed to get the support of Britain to inviting the People's Republic of China to the Security Council to hear its views. The US did not oppose it. However, two sessions were then taken up on who would speak first, the US or the People's Republic. The Soviet Union insisted that since the People's Republic had been specially invited to present its views it should be allowed to speak first. The matter was finally decided by a vote, in which the Soviet Union found itself isolated. India and Yugoslavia abstained. All the others supported the US. The delegate of the People's Republic,

General Wu Hsiu-chuan, spoke later but had the last word. He utilised the platform of the Security Council to denounce the United Nations, "I would like to remind members of the Security Council that so long as the United Nations persists in denying admittance to a permanent member of the Security Council representing 475 million people, it cannot make lawful decisions on any major issues or solve any major problem, particularly those which concern Asia." He declared that such a United Nations would not be "worthy of its name" and his government would not recognise its resolutions or decisions.[11] Wu referred to the Republic of China as the "Kuomintang reactionary remnant clique" and declared that the communist party had liberated all of China, except Taiwan and Tibet.

The US was determined not to allow the Soviet Union to use the military threat to extract any concession from it on the membership of the PRC. An Indian proposal for a ceasefire, membership to the PRC and a committee comprising the US, Britain, the Soviet Union, India, Egypt and the People's Republic to decide the future of Taiwan did not find favour either with the secretary-general or the United States. Lie did not agree with this proposal because it would be a reward to the aggressor, China. India then proposed a US-Soviet summit to resolve their differences, but neither side took up the offer. Even the British tried to persuade the US to accept the People's Republic in place of the Republic of China, but to no avail.

The US secretary of state, Dean Acheson, summed up his country's stand in a letter he wrote to Britain's foreign minister, Ernest Bevin, on 10 July 1950, "(1) We would not agree to a forced trade of Formosa to the Communists for their withdrawal from Korea. (2) Our policy aimed at as early and complete a liquidation of the Korean aggression as was militarily possible, without concessions that would whet Communist appetites and bring on other aggressions elsewhere."[12]

The Soviet Union held the US responsible for linking the Korean issue with the recognition of the People's Republic by including Formosa in the military action plan of US forces in the region. Jakob Malik said, "In ordering his armed forces to open hostilities, to launch aggressive operations against the people of Korea and to begin armed intervention in Korea's domestic affairs, the President of the United States also decided, in passing, to seize the Chinese island of Formosa by ordering the United States Seventh Fleet virtually to occupy that island."[13]

Uniting for Peace Resolution

The US and Britain decided to overcome the impasse in the Security Council by taking the matter to the General Assembly. But they were prevented by Article 12 of the Charter which forbade the General Assembly from making recommendations on matters under consideration in the Security Council. Acheson devised a way out, in what came to be known as the Acheson Plan. He took recourse to the provision in Article 24(1) of the UN Charter, which gives the Security Council "primary" and not exclusive responsibility for the maintenance of international peace and security. He decided that the matter would be taken off the Security Council agenda first and then taken up in the General Assembly. Jebb obliged by moving a proposal stating that the Security Council had not been "exercising its functions in respect of this question within the meaning of Article 12 of the Charter."[14] This was unanimously adopted. The Soviet Union supported it on the plea that the adoption of the resolutions in June-July 1950 in the absence of its delegation had been illegal.

The US and Britain then introduced a resolution in the General Assembly calling for "united action for peace". This resolution, 377A of 3 November 1950, was adopted by a two-thirds majority and came to be known as a "Uniting for Peace" resolution. Paragraph 1 of the resolution stated, "Resolves that if the Security Council, because of lack of unanimity of the permanent members, fails to exercise its primary responsibility for the maintenance of international peace and security in any case where there appears to be a threat to the peace, breach of the peace or act of aggression, the General Assembly shall consider the matter immediately with a view to making the appropriate recommendations to Members for collective measures, including in the case of a breach of the peace or act of aggression the use of armed force when necessary, to maintain or restore international peace and security. If not in session at the time, the General Assembly may meet in an emergency special session within twenty-four hours of the request therefor. Such emergency special session shall be called if requested by the Security Council on the vote of any seven members, or by a majority of the Members of the United Nations."[15]

The resolution was adopted by the First Committee of the General Assembly with 50 votes in favour, three abstentions and only the Soviet Union voting against. It provided for the General Assembly to meet in an emergency special session at 24 hours' notice if the Security Council had been prevented from acting due to a veto and invited "member states to at once create and maintain armed forces so trained, organised and equipped that they could promptly be made available for service as United Nations units."[16]

The Soviet delegate, Andrey Vyshinsky, declared the resolution to be contrary to the UN Charter because it gave enforcement powers only to the Security Council and the command over a UN military force to the Military Staff Committee. He said that under Article 10 the General Assembly could discuss any issue relating to the maintenance of peace and security but when such a matter was under consideration in the Security Council the General Assembly could not make any recommendation. He asserted that the General Assembly had no powers of enforcement action, particularly by armed means.

India supported the idea of the General Assembly taking up consideration of an issue on which the Security Council was deadlocked but wanted a notice of a week instead of 24 hours for summoning an emergency special session. This additional notice was important for the countries of Asia and Africa which had to reckon with poor communication and transport links with New York. Although countries had resident missions in New York instructions were required from national capitals. India also expressed reservation on the requirement of national forces to be kept in readiness by countries for deployment to the UN when requisitioned by the General Assembly or the Security Council. Rau said, "The national units are to be made available to the United Nations only in accordance with members' respective constitutional processes and without prejudice to their use in exercise of the right of individual or collective self-defence under Article 51 of the Charter. These are severe limitations, and hence our doubts as to the practical benefit of the recommendations."[17] Rau went on to add that India's main reservation was due to the emphasis in the resolution on strengthening the UN's military machinery instead of its peace efforts. India was also keen to allow more time for bilateral negotiations before the matter was taken up by the Security Council or the General Assembly.

The 'uniting for peace' resolution enabled the US to wriggle out of the delicate situation it was placed in due to the return of the Soviet Union to the Security Council. It was generic in character and set up an elaborate security mechanism with a 14-member Peace Observation Commission, including the permanent five, for two years (1951 and 1952). The Commission could observe and report on any situation endangering international peace and security if the Security Council was not in a position to do so. Its decisions were to be taken by a two-thirds majority. The Security Council could also utilise the Commission in accordance with its authority under the Charter.

The resolution also set up a 14-member Collective Measures Committee on the steps taken to maintain and strengthen international peace and security. The communist countries boycotted the Committee, calling it ultra vires of the UN Charter, since peace and security was the turf of the Security Council. However, despite their absence, the Committee was unable to agree on the terms a military force for the UN.

The Peace Observation Commission was in effect a parallel Security Council with wider membership. It was an early recognition of the need for its reform by making it more broad-based to increase its legitimacy and abolishing the veto to end its deadlock. It was also the "high-water mark of enthusiasm" for the UN's collective security.[18] This enthusiasm, however, only lasted till the West enjoyed a majority in the General Assembly.

Meanwhile, in the war in Korea, the North Korean forces had rapidly occupied nearly the entire peninsula. General MacArthur launched a counter-offensive and pushed them behind the 38th parallel. He then pressed ahead and reached the Chinese border. This provoked a massive counter-attack by China, which pumped in 260,000 troops and drove the US-led forces well south of the 38th parallel. There was intense outrage in the US and General MacArthur asked for atomic bombs to be placed at his disposal. This created an outcry in Asia and even Britain became concerned over the adventurism of the American general. Both MacArthur and President Truman came in for severe criticism in the US Congress for their mishandling of the war. Eventually, on 10 April 1951, Truman dismissed MacArthur and replaced him with General Matthew B. Ridgeway, who was given a more restricted mandate to hold the forces of China and North Korea on the 38th parallel.

The war soon entered a protracted grind in which neither side was able to achieve durable success. In October 1951, they agreed to direct talks in Panmunjom. A change in government in the United States, bringing another war hero, General Eisenhower, to the presidency, made it more confident of making compromises. The death of Stalin in March 1953 also brought a more mellow leadership in the Soviet Union, willing to put pressure on China to come to an agreement. An armistice treaty was signed after two years of peace talks, on 27 July 1953, which continues till now.

The North Korean invasion of South Korea confirmed the worst fears of the US about the expansionist designs of the communist parties of Russia and China, acting in collusion, to conquer all of Asia. It vindicated to it the iron curtain theory expounded by Churchill in his Fulton speech four years ago and strengthened its resolve to take on communism militarily, leaving no room for negotiation or compromise. The enemy of the Second World War, Japan, was co-opted as an ally, aligning it with South Korea, a country it had occupied for four decades. It also placed the US alongside France, the colonial ruler of Indo-China (modern, Vietnam, Laos and Cambodia). The anti-communist fever in the US made it oblivious to the anti-colonial dimension of the unrest in Asia and distorted its foreign policy goals and claims of upholding freedom and democracy. It even put it at odds with Britain, which perceived merit in making concessions to the communists in China to wean them away from the Soviet Union.

This was arguably the most critical period for the survival of the nascent United Nations. The only reason it appears to have done so was the transition of leadership in the Soviet Union. The Soviet Union was in no position, militarily or economically, to take on the West in a full-blooded conflict. The Korean War made it realise the folly of letting the US gain further advantage by getting the Security Council to endorse its actions. It returned to the United Nations with the determination that if it could not have its way in it, it would not let the US do so.

Trygve Lie regarded the Korea operation as one of his great achievements, "The aggression in Korea might also have doomed the United Nations; but here in continental Asia the United Nations passed the test and set a first precedent for armed international police action in the field . . .. I consider my stand on Korea the best-justified act of seven years in the service of peace."[19] Nearly seven decades later, Korea remains a heavily militarised and divided country and a flashpoint for a nuclear war.

The 'uniting for peace' resolution is regarded by its admirers as a useful improvisation. President Truman outlined three principles for these resolutions: "(i) to maintain the peace the UN must be able to learn the fact about any aggression; (ii) it must be able to quickly call upon the member nations to act if the threat becomes serious; and (iii) the peace-loving nations must have the military strength available, when called upon, to act decisively to put down aggression."[20] Then he went on to espouse disarmament for all nations, except the US. For other nations his prescription was swords to be beaten into ploughshares but for the US, "… the US has embarked upon the course of increasing its armed strength only for the purpose of helping keep the peace."[21]

Even some Western countries realised that the lack of unanimity among the permanent five was hampering the ability of the Security Council to function according to the Charter. However, instead of seeking a revision of the Charter they sought to validate the unilateral action taken by the United States. In the debate in the General Assembly when the First Committee of the General Assembly presented its report on the resolution, the French ambassador, Jean Chauvel, regretted that the Soviet Union had blocked the Security Council's functioning on 45 occasions by its veto. He said, "The assumption upon which the Charter was drafted at San Francisco, viz. that there would be continued cooperation and understanding among the Five Permanent members of the Security Council, has not been borne out by facts."[22]

Referring to the inability of the Security Council to set up its own military force and the deadlock due to the veto, Chauvel said, "It is unthinkable that this entire machinery, designed to safeguard the peace and security of the world, should remain inactive when there is a threat to peace and security. . . And if . . . there is a real danger of such inactivity, then we must revise our customs, our methods, our rules and our interpretations. We may even have to revise the Charter."[23]

There was little attempt by any of the permanent five to be neutral in the dispute and seek a negotiated settlement by calling the two sides for talks. Speaking against the Soviet proposal to invite a representative of North Korea to the Security Council to present its case, Jebb said, "But the North Koreans have, I believe, by their refusal to obey the injunctions of the United Nations, put themselves, as it were in a state of contumacy and, to be quite blunt they have – whatever the exact legal position may be, in fact put themselves in a state of hostility with the United Nations itself. It would really be impossible, therefore, after all that has happened, for the North Korean representative to be allowed to come to this table and to argue, as he undoubtedly would, that his authorities were quite in order to resist the injunction of the Security Council - that they were the victims of aggression, and so on."[24]

Once the US lost majority support in the General Assembly the precedent of the 'uniting for peace' resolution became an albatross around its neck. Arab countries resorted to it repeatedly in the Palestine conflict. They used it on several occasions to censure Israel in the General Assembly when the Security Council was hamstrung by the US veto. Nevertheless, in the absence of the power of enforcement, their resolutions remained on paper. They realised to their dismay that they could get the authority from the General Assembly but would have to depend on their own resources to enforce it.

The Korean War put India in a quandary and compelled it to make critical choices early in its foreign policy. India identified three priorities during the Korean conflict in its effort to avoid a world war: (i) localising the hostilities in Korea to prevent its spread to other parts of Asia, (ii) expediting entry of the People's Republic of China to the Security Council and (iii) persuading the Soviet Union to return to the Security Council. Prime Minister Nehru based his decision to support the first two American resolutions on Korea on the report of the UN Commission on Korea which had declared that North Korea had committed aggression. He noted that whatever "minor events may have taken place earlier" the use of force by North Korea to settle disputes with the South could not be condoned.[25] The reference in "minor events" was to the effort by India's high commissioner to Britain, V.K. Krishna Menon, to draw Nehru away from the United States by bringing to his attention certain press reports in Britain stating that South Korean forces had moved beyond the 38th parallel before the North Korean invasion, "thus making the position not without ambiguity."[26]

The Security Council's decision to entrust the command of the UN force to an American general also put India in a quandary. It disagreed with the decision because it diluted the authority of the United Nations. In a message to New Delhi, Rau had informed, "MacArthur is supreme commander of allied forces in Japan but he is, in effect, subject to orders of US whose officer he is." The secretary-general in the external affairs ministry, Girija Shankar Bajpai, endorsed this view, "Draft resolution practically entrusts direction of operations in Korea to USA. Since we are not rendering any military aid, it seems best for us not to take part in debate or voting. We need not oppose the resolution."[27] He told Loy W. Henderson, the US ambassador, that India did not approve of it but would refrain from opposing it. He said that India could provide armed forces to the Security Council only under special agreements but also pleaded that it had no capacity or resources.

Nehru became apprehensive of US intentions in Korea after Truman's announcement on US protection for Taiwan, Vietnam and the Philippines. He believed that this could enlarge the theatre of the Korean War and risk a third world war. He said that it was "exceedingly maladroit of the US Government to mix up the Korea issue with Formosa, Indo-China, etc". The US feared the spread of communism but "in fact, it is helping a colonial power to maintain itself against a movement for freedom," he wrote with reference to the US policy on rushing to help the French in Indo-China.

Nehru was very critical of MacArthur's eagerness to expand the war beyond Korea, "MacArthur is in supreme command and he has been directed not only to deal with Korea but also with Formosa as well as probably Indo-China. You cannot separate these, so far as his command is concerned. If we put any of our forces at his disposal we get mixed up with these other, and according to us, undesirable ventures."[28] Nehru wrote later, "UN policies are, no doubt, affected by General MacArthur's reports and advice. There can be no doubt that if MacArthur had his way there would immediately be war on a wider scale and uttermost destruction."[29] He expressed his reservations on the belligerent turn taken by the United Nations in a statement in the Indian Parliament during the Korean war, "Instead of looking upon it as a great organisation for peace, some of its members have gradually begun to think of it as an organisation through which war can be waged."[30]

The apprehension that General MacArthur was serving the US government rather than the United Nations was shared by many. An article in the New Statesman, London, on 12 August 1950, said, "In discussing military plans with Chiang Kai-shek, General MacArthur is not in any way acting for the United Nations. In seeming to countenance Chiang Kai-shek's naval and air blockade of China, in flat defiance of Truman's instructions, General MacArthur confirms the view that he is not a fit the proper person to be in charge of responsible military operations."[31]

Nehru took a dig at Britain after it changed its view on China's admission under American pressure. In a letter to Rau, Nehru wrote, "Britain follows a curious and vacillating policy, trying to influence the USA, but ultimately being influenced by it for obvious reasons."[32]

But India's position on certain issues was not without its discrepancies. India abstained on the Yugoslav resolution on inviting both Koreas on the ground that North Korea had not been recognised by the United Nations. This ignored the fact that the People's Republic of China, which India supported so vigorously, had also not been recognised by the UN. Rau also argued that North Korea had not complained of any dispute with South Korea before its invasion nor brought the matter before the Security Council. So, Article 32 of the Charter had no application at that stage and India could not support inviting North Korea to the Council meeting.

India made brief interventions in the debates on Korea but was very active behind the scenes in keeping the Security Council engaged and in drafting resolutions to bring about a ceasefire. On the question of which name to use, Taiwan or Formosa, India proposed a compromise: using the Chinese name, Taiwan, with the Japanese name, Formosa, in parentheses. This was accepted and thereafter the island was referred to as Taiwan (Formosa) in the UN. In August 1950, when the Soviet Union returned to the Security Council and the Cold War deadlock resumed, India suggested a committee of non-permanent members to help in resolving the Korean problem. Rau said that non-permanent members were to be preferred "because none of them can be accused or suspected of any expansionist ambitions."[33]

India's stand on the Korean issue was broadly in line with the Western position, closer to the British than the American. By this time, US policy had hardened and it was unwilling to give any quarter to either the People's Republic of China or to the Soviet Union. Thus, while the British were willing to invite it to the Security Council to present its views, the US was vehemently opposed to it. India was more vocal in its support for the People's Republic than even the British. However, India refused to join the Soviet Union in condemning civilian casualties in the air attacks by American forces. It maintained that no enquiry had taken place and till then such reports would have to be treated as unfounded allegations.

Korea remained one of only two instances of the Security Council authorising military action by member states till the end of the Cold War. The other was Britain which was authorised to enforce sanctions against Southern Rhodesia in 1966. The legal framework for such authorisation remained ill-defined. The resolutions did not invoke any provision of the Charter. The only "authorisation" contained in the resolutions was to the unified command to use the UN flag, concurrently with the flags of the participating nations, an instruction that did not conform to the flag code issued by the secretary-general on 19 December 1947. The rest were "calls" made to member states to take action.

The Korean War put to rest the collective security system envisaged in the UN Charter. The permanent members had by then abandoned the prospects of a military force under the Security Council but they had been unable to devise an alternative. The Korea operation was a hurried response to an emergency, made possible by the Soviet boycott, and could not become a paradigm for future action. The resolutions were too vaguely anchored in the Charter and adopted in such extraordinary circumstances that they could not but be a one-off exercise. The only take-away from them was the use of the phrase "as may be necessary" in Resolution 83(1950) with reference to the nature of assistance to South Korea.[34] This phrase was to morph later into numerous variants of "necessary" action by member states when the Cold War ended.

Endnotes

1 Intervention of B. Narsing Rau, India's delegate in the Security Council at its 475th meeting, 30 June 1950. SCOR, 475th Meeting, pp. 2-3.

2 Intervention of Nincic, the Yugoslav delegate in the Security Council at its 474th meeting, 27 June 1950. Security Council Official Records, 474th Meeting, p.6.

3 Quoted in the intervention of the US ambassador, Warren R. Austin, in the Security Council at its 474th meeting, 27 June 1950. SCOR, 474th Meeting, p. 5.

4 Intervention of Gladwyn Jebb, the British delegate in the Security Council at its 475th meeting, 30 June 1950. SCOR, 475th meeting, pp. 3-4.

5 Intervention of Gladwyn Jebb, the British delegate in the Security Council at its 475th meeting, 30 June 1950. SCOR, 475th meeting, p. 4.

6 UN Document, S/RES/ 84 (1950) of 7 July 1950.

7 Letter dated 15 July 1950 from President Syngman Rhee to General MacArthur. Circulated in UNSC as document S/1627 (1950).

8 Brian Urquhart. *A Life in War and Peace* (New York: Harper & Row Publishers, 1987), p. 120.

9   Clark M. Eichelberger. *United Nations – The First Fifteen Years* (New York: Harper and Brothers, 1960), p. 23.

10   Statement by US delegate Gross at the 508th meeting of the UNSC on 30 Sep 1950, SCOR, p. 6.

11   Statement of Gen. Wu Hsiu-chuan of the People's Republic of China, at the 527th meeting of the Security Council on 28 November 1950, SCOR, p.4.

12   Dean Acheson. *Present at the Creation: My Years in the State Department* (New York: W.W. Norton, 1969), p. 418.

13   Intervention of Jacob Malik, the Soviet ambassador in the Security Council at its 480th meeting, 1 August 1950. SCOR, 480th Meeting, p. 20.

14   Gladwyn Jebb, Statement at the 531st meeting of the UN Security Council, 31 January 1951, SCOR, 1951.

15   UN Document, A/RES/ 377(V),3 November 1950. The resolution was adopted with 52 votes for, 5 against (Czechoslovakia, Poland, USSR, Byelorussia and Ukraine) and 2 abstentions (India and Argentina).

16   John Foster Dulles, Statement at the 299th plenary meeting of the UN General Assembly on 1 November 1950. GAOR, 5th session. Para 37, p. 294.

17   B. Narsing Rau, India's ambassador the UN. Statement at the 301st plenary meeting of the UN General Assembly on 12 November 1950. GAOR, 5th session, para 164, p. 336.

18   Inis Claude Jr. *The Management of Power in the Changing United Nations.* (International Organization, Vol. 15, No.2 (Spring 1961), p. 231.

19   Lie, p. 323.

20   Harry S. Truman, US president. Statement at the 295th plenary meeting of the UN General Assembly on 24 October 1950. GAOR, 5th session, para 57, p. 246.

21   Harry S. Truman, US president. Statement at the 295th plenary meeting of the UN General Assembly on 24 October 1950. GAOR, 5th session, para 70, p. 247.

22   J. Chauvel, Statement at the 299th plenary meeting of the UN General Assembly on 1 November 1950. GAOR, 5th session, para 124, p. 300.

23   J. Chauvel, Statement at the 299th plenary meeting of the UN General Assembly on 1 November 1950. GAOR, 5th session, para 131, p. 301.

24   Gladwyn Jebb, Statement at 483rd meeting of UNSC on 4 August 1950. SCOR, p. 8.

25 J. Nehru, Telegram dated 27 June 1950 to India's High Commissioner to Britain. JN (SG) Vol.46 (I), 1950. (New Delhi: Nehru Museum and Library), p. 165.

26 V. K. Krishna Menon, Telegram dated 27 June 1950 to Prime Minister J. Nehru. JN (SG) Vol.46 (I), 1950, p. 164. (Nehru Museum and Library, New Delhi).

27 G. S. Bajpai, Telegram of 6 July 1950 to India's permanent representative to the UN. JN (SG) Vol.47 (II), 1950. P. 267 (Nehru Museum and Library, New Delhi).

28 J. Nehru's letter of 1 July 1950 to B. N. Rau. JN (SG) Vol.47 (I), 1950, pp. 50-53 (Nehru Museum and Library, New Delhi).

29 J. Nehru- Note dated 9 Nov 1950 to Secretary General of Ministry of External Affairs. JN (SG) Vol.62 (II), 1950. (New Delhi: Nehru Museum and Library,), p. 345.

30 Jawaharlal Nehru. *India's Foreign Policy – Selected Speeches, September 1946 – April 1961.* Statement in the *Lok Sabha* on 12 June 1952 (New Delhi: Publications Division, Government of India, 1961), p. 64.

31 "The Menace of General MacArthur", The New Statesman and Nation, London, 12 August 1950. JN (SG) Vol.53 (I), 1950, (New Delhi: Nehru Museum and Library), pp. 86-88.

32 J. Nehru's letter of 17 Nov 1950 to B. N. Rau. JN (SG) Vol.64 (I), 195 (New Delhi: Nehru Museum and Library), p.162

33 B. Narsing Rau, statement at the 487th meeting of the UNSC, 14 August 1950, p. 9.

34 UN Document S/RES/83 (1950), operative para 1.

8 Innovative Compromise: Peacekeeping Operations

The differences among the permanent five paralysed the Security Council after the Korean War and persisted throughout the Cold War. The UN secretary-general used his good offices to mediate in disputes where possible and was able occasionally to get the combatants to agree to a ceasefire. Dag Hammarskjöld devised the mechanism of peacekeeping operations by troops from neutral and non-aligned countries to monitor the ceasefire. He did so successfully in the Middle East and in the Congo and peacekeeping became the Security Council's most important contribution and preoccupation.

Peacekeeping, now seen as a regular function of the Security Council, does not figure in the Charter. It was improvised to enable the United Nations to help countries which were willing to take its help despite inaction by the permanent five. In doing so, the Council settled for the limited role of monitoring the peace which had been negotiated through other processes. Peacekeeping remains the main claim to fame for the Security Council as the guardian of international peace and security, but it was not its creation. The failure of the permanent five to provide troops to the Security Council for a UN military forced Dag Hammarskjöld to conjure the mechanism through the General Assembly. Its legitimacy was questioned then by France and the Soviet Union. Peacekeeping resolutions do not specify the article of the Charter they are adopted under. They are generally believed to fall under Chapter VI, on the peaceful settlement of disputes, but some later ones also have authorisations under Chapter VII.

After the Korea operation, the Security Council was grounded by the Soviet Union. The Cold War was at its peak in the 1950s when Dag Hammarskjöld was confronted with a challenge in the Congo. He drew upon the experience of the UN military observers in Palestine and Kashmir and decided that troops from neutral countries could be used in this operation. The Congo operation was designed by Hammarskjöld on the Suez pattern. Though peace remains elusive in the Congo as well as in the Middle East, peacekeeping is now established as an important responsibility of the Security Council.

The Suez and Hungary Crises 1956

The first peacekeeping operation came in 1956 after the Suez War. The Suez crisis started when Egypt, under President Gemal Abdel Nasser, nationalised the Suez Canal. Britain and France complained to the Security Council against Egypt for violating the Suez Canal Convention of 1888 by unilaterally ending the system of its 'international operation'. The next day, Egypt complained against the military actions of Britain and France, which it said constituted a threat to international peace and security. The US ambassador, Henry Cabot Lodge, welcomed the efforts of Britain and France to resolve the issue peacefully and supported placing the item on the Security Council agenda. The Soviet Union, on the other hand, demanded the inclusion of both complaints, maintaining that the Egyptian government's nationalisation of the Suez Canal Company was an internal matter of the state.

The British ambassador, Pierson Dixon, tried to turn the tables on the Soviet Union by quoting from the statement of its delegate in the Security Council in 1946 on freedom of transit in the straits of Bosporus and Dardanelles. He recalled that the Soviet Union had then opposed Turkey's blockade and sought international control of the waterway. Dixon demanded the same for the Suez Canal, "In relation to these waterways, it is, in fact, necessary to establish international control with the participants of the most interested powers."[1]

Britain and France plotted an ingenious strategy to regain control of the canal. They persuaded Israel to invade Egypt and advance to the Suez Canal. Britain then declared that navigation in the canal was threatened and called on both sides to withdraw their troops to a distance of ten miles from the canal and allow an Anglo-French force to be stationed along it "temporarily". Egypt and Israel were given twelve hours to respond, failing which "British and French forces will intervene in whatever strength may be necessary to secure compliance".[2] Israel agreed to the proposal, Egypt turned it down.

Meanwhile, the Soviet Union took the opportunity provided by the preoccupation of the Western countries with the Suez crisis to do some autumn cleaning of its own in Hungary. Its troops marched into Budapest to remove Prime Minister Imre Nagy and replace him with a more pliable, Janos Kadar. On 27 October 1956, Britain, France and the US wrote to the President of the Security Council on the situation in Hungary. The Soviet Union opposed discussion on the ground that it was an internal matter of Hungary. However, the Security Council adopted the item by vote, which being procedural, was not subject to the veto.

The US realised that opposing the Soviet Union in Hungary would require restraint by its allies, Britain and France, in Egypt. On 28 October, President Eisenhower called then for a meeting in Washington. The next day the US asked for a Security Council meeting to call upon Israel to accept a ceasefire. Earlier, the UN Troops Supervision Organization had issued an order to Israel to do so, which it had ignored.

Two days later, the US introduced a resolution in the Security Council demanding the withdrawal of Israel to the 1949 Armistice Line. It was enthusiastically supported by the Soviet Union. Britain opposed it and asserted that it had the right to protect its own nationals and national interests in case the Security Council failed to do so. Both Britain and France exercised their first vetoes, also the first other than by the Soviet Union. Ironically, they used it on a resolution introduced by their NATO ally. Two other NATO allies, Australia and Belgium, voted for it as did China, Cuba, Iran, Peru, the Soviet Union, the US and Yugoslavia.

Four days later, the Soviet Union vetoed a similar US resolution on Hungary. The United States then took both issues to the General Assembly, which took them up in emergency special sessions. The General Assembly asked the secretary-general to put together a UN emergency force to secure and supervise the ceasefire that had been negotiated with the combatants. It authorised the secretary-general to directly recruit a limited number of officers from the UN Truce Supervision Organization. Nationals of the permanent five countries could not participate in the force, which would be under the control of the UN secretary-general and would be financed from the regular UN budget. The resolution also appointed the commander of this force. Thus, the intervention of the General Assembly ensured a genuinely international force of the UN, even if its role was confined to holding a pre-negotiated peace.[3] Britain and France agreed to this arrangement under American pressure. The French representative, Louis de Guiringaud, however, cautioned against dilution of Security Council's powers, "We should also be careful to see to it that the Security Council retains its competence in all matters pertaining to the application of the measures provided for in Chapter VII of the Charter."[4]

The two crises exposed the variable standards applied by the permanent members, France, Britain and the Soviet Union, in two concurrent and parallel situations. The Soviet Union wanted the Council to act immediately in the Middle East. Its ambassador, Arkady Sobolev, said in the Council, "Events are now developing so rapidly that this is no time for long speeches in the Council. The Council must act and act swiftly."[5] But on Hungary, he asked for postponement of discussion by three or four days. Imre Nagy, the deposed prime minister of Hungary, appealed for help against the Soviet invasion. The Soviet Union accused him of joining hands with reactionary forces and claimed that its troops had gone into Hungary at the request of its government to help "put an end to the armed uprising of criminal elements of a Fascist type against the legal Government of Hungary."[6] France and Britain waxed eloquent on Hungary's struggle for freedom but on Egypt they opposed the proposal to take the issue to the General Assembly under 'uniting for peace' on the plea that the necessary "pre-condition of invoking the procedure is that a lack of unanimity of the permanent members of the Security Council should have prevented the Council from taking a decision."[7] This conveniently ignored the fact that their vetoes on two resolutions just the previous day had prevented the Security Council from taking action.

The Soviet Union challenged the legality of the United Nations Emergency Force (UNEF-I) set up by the General Assembly. It argued that this could only be done by the Security Council under Article 43 but it would accept it since Egypt had done so. It abstained in the vote. UNEF-I continued till 1967 when it was withdrawn at Egypt's request. Brazil, Canada, Colombia, Denmark, Finland, India, Indonesia, Norway, Sweden and Yugoslavia contributed troops to it, which at its peak, in 1957, had over 6000 personnel.

The Suez and Hungarian crises in 1956 defined the limitations of the Security Council in dealing with military aggression by a permanent member. Such conflicts had not been envisaged in the Charter and the Council was not designed to deal with them. Besides, now a new genre of conflicts, presaged by the Indonesian, had started spreading across Asia and Africa. These were the freedom movements in countries still under European colonial rule. Although these were wars for freedom, the involvement of one or more permanent members gave them a Cold War hue and put them beyond Security Council intervention.

The Congo Operation, 1960-1964

The general principles of UN peacekeeping adopted for the UN Emergency Force in 1956 in the Suez war were reinforced in 1960 in the Congo operation. Hammarskjöld's conception of these UN troops was the same as in the Middle East - keeping the permanent five out and using troops from neutral and non-aligned countries. However, the nature of the crisis in the Congo was different from the Middle East and its peacekeeping operation was without precedent then and remains unique. The UN entered the Congo at the request of its government for assistance in what would today be called nation-building. The UN force was sent by the Security Council and was under UN command, but the troops came from smaller and neutral countries, not the permanent five. However, the force soon got embroiled in a domestic power struggle which acquired a Cold War dimension due to the interference of the superpowers. It also had to deal with the armed rebellion of a province, aided and abetted by the former colonial ruler, Belgium.

The Congo crisis started soon after it gained independence from Belgium on 30 June 1960. The Congo joined the UN within a week and immediately asked it for technical assistance in its administration and for arranging military assistance from 'neutral' countries. President Joseph Kasavubu and Prime Minister Patrice Lumumba accused Belgian forces, several thousand of whom had stayed behind in the Congo, of continuing to interfere in its internal affairs and of engineering secession in the mineral-rich Katanga province. Hammarskjöld called a meeting of the Security Council and sought instructions on how to proceed with military assistance.

France wanted the Congo to be handled by the US, Britain and itself rather than the Security Council. The US was unwilling to interfere directly but was keen to keep the Congo from seeking the help of the Soviet Union or China against Belgium. It found the idea of a UN force a more acceptable expedient.

The Council adopted three resolutions in quick succession on the Congo. Dag Hammarskjöld drafted the first himself.[8] The resolutions authorised him to provide the Congo with the military assistance requested.

They called upon Belgium to withdraw its troops and authorised him to take "all necessary action" to this effect. The third resolution also reaffirmed that the UN force would not "be a party to or in any way intervene in or be used to influence the outcome of any internal conflict, constitutional or otherwise."[9] No specific provision of the Charter was cited. Hammarskjöld did not seek nor was given much guidance. He set up the Congo Advisory Committee comprising representatives of the countries contributing troops to the UN force and relied heavily on his advisers in the Secretariat, drawn from various countries.

At a meeting of the Security Council in July 1960 Hammarskjöld outlined three key principles of the terms of engagement of the UN troops in the Congo: (i) consent of the host State, (ii) cooperation of the UN force with the host State without becoming its instrument, and (iii) non-involvement in the internal affairs of the host State. He sourced his peacekeepers from countries not tainted by colonialism - Ethiopia, Ghana, Guinea, Morocco and Tunisia from Africa and Ireland and Sweden from outside.[10] These soon became cardinal rules for all peacekeeping operations, though the Congo operation involved far more energetic enforcement of the peace than was the case either in Palestine or subsequent peacekeeping operations.

Hammarskjöld submitted his first report to the Security Council a week after he was given the mandate to provide assistance. He reported that the UN force in the Congo was far bigger than the UN Emergency Force in the Middle East and involved many more countries. He noted, "The United Nations has embarked on its biggest single effort under United Nations' colours, organized and directed by the United Nations itself."[11] Whether intended or not, this was a dig at the much larger Korea operation, which was also called a UN force but was under US command.

Unfortunately for the Congo, the rivalry between President Kasavubu and Prime Minister Lumumba soon turned into an internal power struggle, which Belgium took advantage of. By September 1960 Lumumba had fallen out with Kasavubu and the commander of the Congolese National Army (ANC, in its French initials), Colonel Joseph-Désiré Mobutu (who later used his African name, Mobutu Sese Seko), started taking control. The conflict now got embroiled in the Cold War, with the West supporting Kasavubu and the Soviets backing Lumumba. In November 1960, two Congolese delegations came to the General Assembly, one representing Kasavubu and the other Lumumba. The General Assembly adopted a resolution supporting the Lumumba delegation. The vote was 53 for, 24 against and 19 abstentions. India, Ghana, Guinea, Indonesia, Mali, Morocco and the Russian bloc supported it. The West opposed, while Tunisia, Nigeria and Ethiopia abstained.

Lumumba wanted the UN force to help his government fight secessionism in Katanga province. When the UN turned down the request, he turned to the Soviet Union. However, Andrew Cordier, UN under-secretary for General Assembly affairs, an American, closed all airports in the Congo making it impossible for Russian help to reach Lumumba. Russia criticised the UN sharply for this. It also vetoed a Security Council resolution sponsored by Ceylon and Tunisia opposing outside interference in the Congo.

In December, Mobutu's men took Lumumba into custody. A month later, he died in mysterious circumstances. The US ambassador, Adlai Stevenson, regretted Lumumba's death and called for constructive efforts by all to keep the situation from deteriorating any further. The Soviet ambassador, Valerian Zorin, blamed the United Nations and the secretary-general for aiding the colonialists and their stooges in the Congo. India's ambassador, C.S. Jha, also maintained that the UN shared responsibility, "We consider that the failure must be laid to the United Nations as a whole, to the Cold War approaches by various powers and to wrong and inadequate decisions of the Security Council or the General Assembly."[12]

The US extended support to Prime Minister Cyrille Adoula, who had replaced Lumumba, and also backed his government's efforts to suppress the rebellions in the provinces of Katanga and Orientale. In November 1961, the General Assembly adopted a resolution supporting the UN action in suppressing the Katanga rebellion, even though the European powers, Britain, France and Belgium opposed it. This enabled the US to get the support of the Afro-Asian group. The Soviet Union became isolated in its support of Antoine Gizenga in Orientale province. The UN forces were able to suppress the rebellion in Katanga by early 1963 and were also able to persuade Gizenga to patch up with the central government in Leopoldville (now, Kinshasa).

The representative of the UN secretary-general in the Congo, Rajeshwar Dayal, reported that the activities of the Belgians in the Congo had increased the intransigence of the Congolese army and inhibited peaceful political activity and return to constitutional rule. He also said that the presence of Belgian soldiers in the Katangese armed forces had weakened the authority of the central government.

Jha, speaking as an invitee in the Security Council, criticised Belgium for not withdrawing its forces as required by Security Council resolutions and the big powers for paralysing the Security Council by their lack of unanimity. He said, "All Congolese armed personnel including ANC and private armies should be disarmed and neutralised. The United Nations should be entrusted with the functions of law and order until such time as the ANC's force, with the assistance of UN becomes a disciplined force."[13]

Sustained US pressure and the opposition of Hammarskjöld, whom the Belgians accused of being anti-Belgium, brought Belgium round to accepting Leopoldville's authority over Katanga and withdrawing its support to the secessionist violence there. Mobutu facilitated this by accepting the return of Belgian officials to Leopoldville. Lumumba's arrest had caused alienation of several countries in Asia and Africa which supported him. Guinea, UAR and Indonesia announced their decision to withdraw their forces from the UN Force. Hammarskjöld turned to India for help. Nehru felt he could not let the UN down even if it meant abandoning Lumumba. He accepted the request.

Hammarskjöld ensured that unlike in the Korean War, in the Congo both the military operation and diplomatic negotiations were under his control. When he faced problems due to frictions between Dayal and the US ambassador, Clare H. Timberlake, he removed Dayal but also insisted on both the US and Britain recalling their ambassadors. Timberlake left a month after Dayal. But Hammarskjöld's task was unenviable. It was against him that Khrushchev made his notorious dramatic gesture of thumping the desk with his shoe. Khrushchev proposed a troika of three persons to perform the task of secretary-general after his death.

The People's Republic of China, which was not a member of the UN at that time, opposed the UN mission. It supported the rebellion of Antoine Gizenga. Later, when Gizenga patched up with the central government in Leopoldville, it supported other rebel groups to carry out guerrilla warfare, including an uprising in Kwilu province in 1964. The Soviet Union, which had supported Lumumba, later recognised the government of Adoula.

As the Congo crisis dragged, Hammarskjöld complained that the continued external interference in the Congo through military assistance and such innocuous means as radio broadcast were vitiating the domestic situation. The UN Force was getting depleted and becoming ineffective in the face of growing factionalism in the Congolese forces and their infighting.

The four-year Congo operation of the UN Security Council was its first major operation in a conflict in which an internal power struggle was inflamed and aroused by external interference. In the three rounds of operations against the Katanga separatist regime, the UN Force killed 350 Katangan soldiers and lost 42 of its own. A total of around 93,000 personnel from 34 countries eventually served in the Congo operation, which lasted from July 1960 to June 1964, with about 15,000 stationed at any point in time. The operation was eventually shut down in 1964 by the General Assembly for lack of funds.

Hammarskjöld was tragically killed in an air crash in the Congo in September 1961. After his death, Belgium claimed and got $ 1.5 million as compensation from the UN for damage to the property of Belgians by the UN forces. This settlement was reached in 1965, after which Belgium agreed to pay its share of the 4-year UN operation. Both France and the Soviet Union refused to fund the UN peacekeepers in the Congo. Belgium and France challenged the authority of the General Assembly to treat the expenses on UN peacekeepers in the Congo as an expense of the United Nations under Article 17(2) of the Charter. The General Assembly referred the matter to the International Court of Justice for its advisory opinion.[14] The ICJ ruled in favour of the General Assembly. [This case is dealt with in greater detail in Chapter 13].

The UN forces in the Congo went well beyond peacekeeping and the use of force for self-defence. They took action against the armed separatist movement of Katanga and prevented its secession. The operation was regarded by some commentators as a model for future action by the UN. However, Hammarskjöld's death and the absence of similar congeniality among the superpowers in later conflicts slowed the evolution of peacekeeping.

Principles of Peacekeeping

In 1973, when the UN deployed another emergency force in the Middle East, UNEF-II, it also codified the principles of peacekeeping on the following lines: (i) peacekeeping troops could be deployed only with the consent of the parties to the dispute; (ii) peacekeepers had to be strictly impartial in their deployment and activities; (iii) peacekeepers could use force only in self-defence; (iv) peacekeepers should be mandated and supported by the Security Council in their activities; and (v) peacekeeping operations had to rely on the voluntary contributions of member states for military personnel, equipment, and logistics."[15]

Very few UN peacekeeping operations were approved during the Cold War. Its end opened new vistas for the Security Council. It became possible for the permanent five to sit together and take decisions by consensus. In the first forty-three years of the UN, between 1945 and 1988, there were only a dozen peacekeeping missions. Between 1988 and 1992, another ten peacekeeping operations were mandated by the Security Council. In 1990, the UN had 15,000 soldiers as peacekeepers, which rose to 75,000 in three years. Their cost rose from US$ 490 million to over 3 billion dollars in the same period. Most of the peacekeeping efforts from the late 1980s and till the early 1990s - Iraq/Iran, Afghanistan, Namibia, Angola, Mozambique, Nicaragua, El Salvador, and Cambodia- were relatively successful as they were linked to inter-state wars and were undertaken after a ceasefire had been negotiated.

The UN peacekeeping agenda was modified by Secretary-General Boutros Boutros-Ghali, who sought to reorient the United Nations toward human security. He presented these ideas in a report to the Security Council, 'An Agenda for Peace' in 1992 in which he expounded his view that people were more threatened by disease, poverty and internal armed conflict than by external invasions. His hypothesis was that newly independent countries were often the source of the problem due to their own weaknesses or the partisan behaviour of their rulers. International intervention was essential to provide human security and national sovereignty could not be allowed to impede it. This idea was then extended to cover nation-building activities, such as democratisation, holding elections, developing administrative and security institutions and promoting economic development.

The new peacekeeping was given attractive names like peacekeeping, peace-building and peace-making. However, Boutros-Ghali soon discovered the operational limitations of his troops. Peacekeeping had been tolerated by the big powers because it did not give the Security Council real military capacity. The permanent five were not ready to place their troops under UN command or risk their lives in inconsequential lands. UN peacekeepers were a disparate collection of soldiers taken from countries eager to earn some money. They did not have the military capacity to take on the tasks assigned by Boutros-Ghali. The expansion of peacekeeping operations "meant that the old and creaking cold war machinery of peacekeeping was being turned to situations for which it was never intended," Kofi Annan was to write later.[16] Disasters and mishaps were inevitable. Boutros-Ghali discovered that robust peacekeeping required the military support of the US, but this made it subject to the vagaries of US domestic politics. Suffering casualties in foreign lands was unacceptable even to the United States.

The Cambodia operation, conceived under Pérez de Cuéllar but executed by Boutros-Ghali, was a relative success, though the Khmer Rouge was able to keep its arms and its hold over the territory under its control. The Security Council now started sending peacekeepers to countries riven by domestic strife. Peacekeeping in Somalia, Bosnia and Rwanda required entanglement in local feuds and had to be more robust. Each of these missions had more than 20,000 UN peacekeepers but they still needed American support and both suffered casualties. The American experience in Somalia was particularly traumatic. The UN troops were bogged down and suffered casualties and so did the American troops, which withdrew in 1994. This is covered in the following chapter.

Boutros-Ghali did a re-assessment of his Agenda for Peace in 1995 when it became evident that it was at variance with perception of the key Western states. He admitted that the UN could only carry out limited peacekeeping operations with two to four thousand troops. A more active operation could only be launched by the big powers, or more precisely, the United States.

UN peacekeeping started getting scaled back after the mid-1990s. Between 1994 and 1997, only two new missions – in Tajikistan and Guatemala - were authorised. The number of UN peacekeepers declined from 53,000 in 1995 to 13,000 in 1998. The UN budget for peacekeeping fell over the same period from $ 3.3 billion to below $ 1 billion.

Under Kofi Annan there was a renewed attempt to revive robust peacekeeping. UN peacekeepers were now expected to be 'impartial' not 'neutral'. This implied the freedom to take sides in local feuds. Six missions were authorised between 1998 and 2000 – Central African Republic, Sierra Leone, Kosovo, East Timor, the Democratic Republic of the Congo and Eritrea/ Ethiopia. Then there was a lull in 2001 and 2002. Again, between 2003 and 2006, the Council authorised another six missions – Liberia, Côte d'Ivore, Burundi, Haiti, Sudan and Somalia. In East Timor and Kosovo, the mission also acted as a transitional government.

In 2000, a study prepared by Lakhdar Brahimi and Kurm, known as the Brahimi Report, emphasised the impartial and non-intrusive character of peacekeeping. "The Panel concurs that consent of the local parties, impartiality and the use of force only in self-defence should remain bedrock principles of peacekeeping." However, by the time of the Brahimi Report, there was already an urge to distinguish between the victim and the aggressor and to use force to protect the former and enforce peace instead of merely maintaining it.

In 2004, an ambitious UN report concluded that the UN had got more civil wars concluded through negotiations in the post-Cold War period than in the two previous centuries.[17] It recommended doubling the number of available peacekeepers, creating capacity for rapid deployment, setting up a Peace Building Commission and a more structured relationship between the Security Council and regional organisations. The Peace Building Commission was set up in 2006 as an advisory body to the Security Council and the General Assembly but the permanent five did not implement the recommendation to create a rapid deployment force. In this phase of peacekeeping, the UN tried its hand at introducing democracy by holding elections and building institutions of administration and judiciary. Peacekeeping was used to promote political, cultural and economic norms set by the West, which was convinced that elections and economic liberalisation would bring peace and prosperity. But the UN soon discovered that the permanent five had not abandoned their interference in satellite countries. An unfriendly government elected by the people was not safe from their machinations. Peacekeeping operations were perennially underfunded even though Western countries criticised them for financial profligacy and incompetence.

Peacekeeping operations have also been used as ancillaries to complement or supplement military enforcement action by member states or operated sequentially. In Somalia, Haiti, Rwanda and Bosnia the peacekeeping operations had to be augmented by member state forces because they were not able to handle the situation. Their simultaneous operation, however, led to serious concerns for the safety of the peacekeepers, both due to misdirected friendly fire and targeting by local combatants.

So dependent has been the Security Council on member states for the security of its peacekeepers that in September 1993 it adopted a resolution on this issue.[18] It stated that before launching a peacekeeping operation the Council should ensure that the host country will take all appropriate steps to ensure the safety of the personnel engaged in the operation. The resolution, adopted unanimously, further exposed the chasm between peacekeeping and the Council's mandate of maintaining international peace and security.

During the period of hyperactivity after the Cold War, the Security Council also authorised some of its peacekeeping forces to take enforcement action under "robust" peacekeeping. Its resolutions used phrases like "all necessary measures", "all necessary means", "all means" and "all necessary action" to authorise military action as in enforcement action resolutions. They also made references to Chapter VII provisions. The use of force was variously authorised, for self-defence by the peacekeepers, for protecting civilians, for facilitating delivery of humanitarian assistance, or generally for achieving the objectives of the mission.

These provisions were incorporated in the resolution on UN peacekeepers in the Democratic Republic of the Congo, Sierra Leone, Burundi, Côte d'Ivoire, Haiti, Sudan, the Central African Republic, East Timor and Mali. The resolutions assigned the authority either to the peacekeeping force or to the member states participating in them, without indicating if there was a distinction between the two. In Sierra Leone (UNAMSIL, 1999), the authority was given to the UN peacekeepers. In East Timor (INTERFET, 1999), the participating member states were given the authority, as were those in the Central African Republic (MISAB, 1997) and in Afghanistan (ISAF, 2001). In Côte d'Ivoire, French forces were authorised to use "all necessary means." Even the UN Interim Force in Lebanon (UNIFIL), which had been set up earlier was given the same authority to enable it to meet threats to it.

The UN has organised 71 peacekeeping missions since 1948. The largest deployment is in the United Nations Stabilisation Mission in the Democratic Republic of the Congo (MONUSCO) which has around 18,000 uniformed personnel. Among the permanent five, only China makes a worthwhile contribution.[19] In August 2018, there were about 92,000 uniformed personnel operating in 14 peacekeeping missions with a budget of US dollars 6.7 billion. Of these, the UN Truce Supervision Organisation (UNTSO) in the Middle East and the UN Military Observer Group for India and Pakistan (UNMOGIP), two of the oldest missions, are funded from the UN's regular budget.

The principal troop-supplying countries in the early years of the UN were Austria, Ghana, Fiji, Malaysia, Canada and the Scandinavian countries. Later, as the numbers of UN peacekeeping forces increased, other countries with larger armies started contributing. The leading contributors in this period were Pakistan, Bangladesh and India.

Peacekeeping is regarded by the UN as its key contribution to maintaining international peace and security and because of the generally high reputation of UN peacekeepers many supporters of military enforcement actions also try to pass them off as peacekeeping operations. But the UN remains undecided on the degree of force it should permit its peacekeepers to use. In Somalia, UNOSOM I was based on consent and not expected to use force. But this seriously incapacitated it and UNOSOM II was given a Chapter VII mandate, which did not help either and drew flak because of its casualties.

Endnotes

1   Statement of British delegate, Pierson Dixon, at the 734th meeting of the UNSC on 26 September 1956, SCOR, p. 14

2   Dixon, at the 748th meeting of the UNSC on 30 October 1956, SCOR, p. 3.

3   UN Document: Resolution 1000 (ES-1) of 5 November 1956.

4   UN Document, A/PV.567, 7 November 1956, p. 114.

5   Statement of the Soviet delegate, Sobolev, at the 746th meeting of the Security Council on 28 October 1956, SCOR, p. 4.

6   Sobolev, at the 748th meeting of the Security Council on 30 October 1956, SCOR, p. 8.

7   Dixon, at the 751st meeting of the UNSC on 31 October 1956, SCOR, p. 13.

8   UN Documents, S/RES/143(1960), 14 July 1960; S/RES/145(1960), 22 July 1960; S/RES/146(1960), 9 August 1960.

9   UN Document, S/RES/146(1960), 9 August 1960. Para 4.

10 Dag Hammarskjöld, UN Secretary-General, at the 873rd meeting of the Security Council, 13 July 1960. SCOR, 13 July 1960, para 28, p. 5.

11 Dag Hammarskjöld, UN Secretary-General, at the 877th meeting of the

Security Council, 20 July 1960, SCOR, 20 July 1960, p 4.

12 C. S. Jha, Statement at the 941st meeting of the UNSC, 20 February 1961, SCOR, para 40, p.10.

13 C. S. Jha, Statement at the 929th meeting of the UN Security Council on 2 February 1961, para 93, p. 26.

14 ICJ Advisory Opinion, *Certain Expenses of the United Nations (Article 17, paragraph 2 of the Charter),* 1961-1962.

15 Kofi Annan. *Interventions – A Life in War and Peace* (London: Allen Lane, 2012), p. 33.

16 Annan, p. 36.

17 UN High-level Panel on Threats, Challenges and Change, *A More Secure World: Our shared responsibility,* 2004, p. 13.

18 UN Document, S/RES/868(1993).

19 The uniformed personnel from the P-5 in August 2018 were as follows: China - 1968, France - 743, Russia - 75, UK - 695, and USA - 55. (UN Peacekeeping Fact Sheet at www.un.org).

9   Military Actions after the Cold War

The collapse of the Communist bloc brought the Cold War to an end and gave the Western countries full control of the Security Council. With no Soviet veto to restrain them, they decided to activate the Council, an opportunity for which was provided by Iraq's invasion of Kuwait. The United States revived the Korean model of authorised military action to enable its forces and of its allies to invade Iraq and compel it to withdraw from Kuwait. Its spectacular success led to more such operations, though with mixed results. The authorisation for the invasion of Libya in 2011 was particularly controversial. Russia blocked further military actions, except for two in Africa. The United States failed to get authorisation for coercive action in Syria despite repeated efforts.

We have seen how a divided Security Council during the Cold War let major conflicts take place around the world. What is its record after the Cold War ended and the permanent five started cooperating with each other?

The Soviet Union did not survive its defeat in the Afghan War and disintegrated in 1991. All its fourteen satellite republics broke away, leaving the rump state, the Russian Federation, as the successor. For the third time in the century, the victorious Western powers got an opportunity to reshape the global security structure. In some respects, 1990 was even more fortuitous than 1945, since the system was already in place or fully in their control. The Russian Federation was led by leaders less suspicious of the West than Stalin and Leonid Brezhnev and was willing to let the United States take the lead. China was preoccupied with its internal problems. In 1989, a confrontation between demonstrators and the army in Tiananmen

Square in Beijing had ended in a violent military crackdown, which soon spread across the country.

The non-aligned countries were also in disarray. The movement had virtually aligned itself in later years with the Soviet Union, whose collapse not merely removed the movement's relevance but also its main political and economic support. The movement lost its vitality and influence, but for the odd success. In the case of the secretary-general's mission to Nicaragua in 1989 the non-aligned members insisted that the decision be taken by the General Assembly and not the Security Council. Similarly, in 1990, when the Council proposed an election observer mission for Haiti, the Latin American members of the Council successfully got the General Assembly to authorise it, which it did the same year.

Cooperation among the permanent five started in a small way when Mikhail Gorbachev took over as the eighth and last secretary-general of the Soviet Communist Party in 1985. The brutal war raging between Iraq and Iran since 1980 gave them an opportunity to come together. Towards the end of 1986, the British ambassador to the UN, John Thomson, invited the ambassadors of the other four permanent members to an informal discussion, not in the Security Council but at his residence, to discuss cooperation among them to bring the war to an end. Both the Soviet and the Chinese ambassadors accepted the invitation, though China had some reservation.

Secretary-General Pérez de Cuéllar, recently elected to a second term, followed up on this initiative in January 1987 by inviting the ambassadors to his house. By May the ambassadors were able to reach agreement on a mild resolution calling on both sides to end the conflict and take steps towards resolving their dispute. No enforcement measures were envisaged due to China's opposition. This draft resolution was then informally shared with the non-permanent members, marking the beginning of a new era in the Security Council in which the permanent five would finalise a resolution and then present it to the non-permanent members for their endorsement. The outcome, Resolution 598 (1987), calling for a ceasefire and protection by both sides, was the first success for the Security Council in a long time.

This practice of the permanent five meeting behind closed doors soon became routine. When these secret meetings became known, the non-permanent members protested but to no avail. The practice became more frequent after the collapse of the Soviet Union and even non-permanent members found merit in it. Drifte explained the virtues for such two stage decision-making, "Council members, permanent and non-permanent, acknowledge that openness and transparency should characterize the Council's place on the international arena but they all emphasize that without the prior confidential engagements the Council would not manage to present a united front in response to any of the many disturbances landing on the Council's plate."[1]

In this changed global paradigm, Iraq's president, Saddam Hussein, invaded Kuwait and handed the West a golden opportunity to activate the Security Council. They got the Council to authorise military action just as in 1950, once again led by the United States, but this time with the consent of all five permanent members. Its swift success prompted it to activate the full range of the Council's powers under the Charter, and soon to go beyond it. There was a veritable explosion of enforcement measures, both sanctions and military action. Between 1990 and 2011, in addition to Iraq-Kuwait, the Security Council authorised military actions in former Yugoslavia (Croatia and Bosnia and Herzegovina), Somalia, Rwanda, Haiti, the Democratic Republic of the Congo, Albania and Libya. It also imposed punitive sanctions on many countries and provided Chapter VII powers of enforcement action to several peacekeeping missions.

The ground for this activism was laid soon after the Gulf war by the first-ever Security Council summit called by Britain during its presidency on 31 January 1992. Speaking at this summit Secretary-General Boutros-Ghali joined the chorus for democratising national and international institutions, "Added to its dimension of right is the dimension of responsibility, both internal and external. But its misuse also may undermine human rights and jeopardize global order. Civil wars are no longer civil, and the carnage they inflict will not let the world remain indifferent. The narrow nationalism that would oppose or disregard the norms of a stable international order and the micro-nationalism that resists healthy economic or political integration can disrupt a peaceful global existence."[2]

The Security Council summit had been called to chalk out a new and ambitious agenda to strengthen its mandated task of maintaining international peace and security. But there was also a more serious unstated motive - recognition of the Russian Federation as a permanent member in place of the former superpower. This is discussed further in Chapter 16.

Iraq/Kuwait

Kuwait had been a British protectorate from 1899 to 1961 when it became independent. In 1990, Saddam Hussein, the military ruler of neighbouring Iraq accused it of stealing its oil through clandestine drilling and decided to annex the tiny oil-rich principality. He invaded Kuwait on 2 August 1990. There was outrage in the Arab world and a palpable apprehension of further invasions by the maverick dictator. Saddam Hussein had not calculated on the outrage his invasion would evoke in the Arab world and elsewhere. Even the Soviet Union, now much weakened, refused to back him. The US seized the opportunity to build a broad coalition of conservative Islamic countries against the more secular and modernist regime of Saddam Hussein. This was not difficult for the US since it had recently used a similar alliance to defeat the Soviet Union in Afghanistan.

The Security Council condemned the invasion the same day, declared it to be a breach of international peace and security and, acting under Articles 39 and 40 of the Charter, demanded that Iraq withdraw its forces from Kuwait. A few days later, the Council imposed strong economic and arms sanctions under Chapter VII on Iraq. The US quickly formed a military alliance of Gulf Arab and several Western countries. On 12 August 1990, the US Navy imposed a naval blockade on Iraq. This was endorsed by the Security Council two weeks later.[3] The Security Council then adopted four resolutions in quick succession tightening sanctions and issuing warnings to Iraq.[4]

The Security Council finally adopted Resolution 678 on 29 November 1990, which invoked the authority of Chapter VII and authorised member states in "cooperation with the Government of Kuwait" to "use all necessary means" to uphold and implement resolution 660 (1990) and all subsequent relevant Security Council resolutions and "to restore international peace and security in the area".[5] The reference to Chapter VII was general in nature, not to any specific article. This was done deliberately to give the member states the maximum flexibility in the military action. Their authority was not confined to forcing the Iraqi troops out of Kuwait. They could take other measures necessary for peace and security. Iraq was given a deadline of 15 January to withdraw. Cuba and Yemen voted against Resolution 678, while China abstained.

The US used the 40-year old expedient of Korea selectively. Once again, instead of raising a UN force under Article 43, it resorted to getting a very broad mandate for member states to "use all means necessary" to vacate the aggression but it did not set up a unified command under its authority as in Korea. It preferred to act under Chapter VII, rather than Kuwait's right to self-defence. There was also a perfunctory attempt at a peaceful resolution. In the first resolution, the Council called upon Iraq and Kuwait to resolve their differences through negotiations and take the support of the League of Arab States for this. But Iraq showed no interest in mediation nor did the Security Council make an attempt to initiate peace talks.

The Security Council neither set up a mechanism to monitor the military action nor specified its duration. Member states were "requested" to keep it informed "regularly" of the action taken by them. The reporting request was to the member states, not the secretary-general. Although the objectives of the military action were defined by the resolutions, the addition of restoration of international peace and security in the area made it very broad.

On 17 January 1991, a coalition of 20 states attacked Iraqi troops in Kuwait and Iraq in what came to be called later the First Gulf War. This was essentially a massive air attack by the United States which continued for over a month. The ground war that followed was short. The US preference for aerial warfare ensured swift victory but all local allies who had enthusiastically joined the "coalition of the willing" were reduced to bystanders and spectators of a high-tech air show. The advent of global satellite television through the American television channel, CNN, made it the first war to be telecast live around the world.

The military action came to end on 3 March 1991 when the Iraqi forces agreed to withdraw from Kuwait. The Security Council enforced a ceasefire and imposed disarmament and compensation on Iraq for its invasion of Kuwait. It also laid down a process for demarcating the boundary between the two countries.[6] A 5-member Demarcation Commission recommended a boundary which was endorsed by the Security Council.[7]

The military coalition formed against Iraq wanted to keep open the possibility of entering the country to destroy its military capability and bring about regime change. This was hotly debated at the time. The UN under secretary-general and legal counsel, Carl-August Fleischhauer, took the position that this was not permissible under Resolution 678 since it had been adopted to implement Resolution 660, which had only called for the withdrawal of Iraqi troops from Kuwait. However, the coalition powers steadily ratcheted pressure on Iraq. Resolution 687 called upon it to dismantle its chemical weapons and the next resolution demanded that it stop the repression of its people. These were essentially within the domestic jurisdiction of the country.

Resolution 687 (1991) also prohibited nuclear, chemical and biological weapons for Iraq and the deployment of ballistic missiles within 150 kilometres of the border. Subsequently, by Resolution 707 (1991) the Security Council demanded full disclosure by Iraq of all plans to develop weapons of mass destruction and ballistic missiles. It also demanded inspection rights for teams of the Security Council or the International Atomic Energy Agency.

Secretary-General Pérez de Cuéllar was unhappy with the methods adopted by the United States and its manipulation of the Security Council. In his report on the work of the organisation to the General Assembly on 13 September 1991, he expressed reservations on the validity of the action of the United States. He characterised the US-led multinational coalition as a "type of sub-contract". He wanted action by a UN force under a UN commander with troops contributed by member states and reporting to the secretary-general. This was in line with the peacekeeping forces that had been deployed by the UN from the time of Secretary-General Dag Hammarskjöld. He said that the Gulf War "was not a United Nations war. General Schwarzkopf was not wearing a blue helmet."[8] He also felt that the mandate given to the West was very wide and open-ended. He was concerned about the US not being answerable to the UN and there being no UN participation in the decision-making process in the execution of the war.

Though the US action had Security Council backing, the manner in which the US secured it left many third world countries apprehensive. There was a perception among them that the US had manipulated the Security Council. This feeling was reinforced by a statement of President Bush to some Arab journalists in which he hinted that the US would have gone ahead with the invasion regardless of the Security Council's mandate since it was an issue of good versus evil. Bush confirmed this later in his book, "If at any point it became clear we could not succeed, we would back away from a UN mandate and cobble together an independent multinational effort built on friendly Arab allied participation."[9] Later, when Bush was unsure of the support for using US ground troops to send relief to Iraqi Kurds and impose a no-fly zone in northern Iraq he decided that he did not need Security Council approval.

Though Kuwait had been liberated, the Iraq problem continued to fester as the US increased its demands and Saddam Hussein used a mixture of deceit and bluster to evade them. In October 1998, Iraq announced that it would no longer cooperate with UN team (UNSCOM) on disarmament monitoring and inspection. This prompted the Security Council to express alarm and warn of the "severest consequences for Iraq" if did not cooperate with UN inspectors.[10] Iraq's refusal led to bombing by the US and Britain in December 1998, which continued into 1999. They claimed that Security Council Resolutions 1154 and 1205 provided a legal basis for their action. These resolutions had been adopted under Chapter VII of the Charter but neither provided for the use of force for enforcement. Other permanent members disagreed with this and deemed the air strikes illegal. The US and Britain seemed to be unconvinced themselves of the validity of this implicit authorisation. They supplemented it with allegations of violations by Iraq of the ceasefire imposed after the First Gulf War.

The decisive Security Council action to get Kuwait liberated from Iraqi occupation in 1990 is cited as the most successful example of its role as enforcer of peace and security in the world - the Council had made a determination of a breach of international peace under Article 39, called upon Iraq to withdraw and when it failed to comply, authorised member states to restore international peace and security in the area. Once the Iraqi forces had been driven out of Kuwait the Council had enforced a ceasefire, imposed disarmament on Iraq and delineated the boundary between the two countries.

The success of the strategy in Iraq opened the floodgates of intervention across the world. There was renewed confidence in the utility of the Security Council and a strong desire to use it to resolve all problems – political or economic. Democracy came to be regarded as the solution for domestic conflicts and capitalism as the panacea for economic ills. They became the declared goals of military adventurism authorised by the Security Council. The veteran UN official, Brian Urquhart, spoke on this in 1995, after his retirement, "Desert Storm.... was a huge success in the use of pre-eminent force. Particularly on the television it looked terrific. And people began to think, 'Ah, now that the UN is united once more, it can do anything by force'. They forgot that it's one thing to agree on a solution to a problem, but it's quite another to put it into effect."[11]

Two new crises erupted soon to give an opportunity to test the new order–Yugoslavia and Somalia.

Yugoslavia

Yugoslavia was formed in 1946 as a federation of six republics and two provinces by the communist party under Marshal Josip Broz Tito, who had led the struggle against Nazi Germany during the Second World War. It was a federation of the Slavic territories of the former Austro-Hungarian and Ottoman empires. The people in the provinces of Slovenia and Croatia were Roman Catholic and had been part of the Austro-Hungarian Empire, thus closer to the West than the Serbs, who belonged to the Orthodox sect and had suffered under the Ottoman Turks since their defeat in 1389 CE. Tito, though a communist, had managed to keep Yugoslavia out of Soviet tutelage by forging, with India, Egypt and Indonesia, the non-aligned movement. With his death in 1980, the federation started weakening. The election of a Serbian nationalist, Slobodan Milosevic, as president of Yugoslavia in 1987, triggered its collapse.

Slovenia and Croatia declared themselves independent on 25 June 1991, following a referendum. Both were admitted almost instantly to the UN. Serbia was not particularly concerned about Slovenia. The Serb-dominated Yugoslav National Army tried for 10 days to hold on to it and then withdrew. But it was determined to protect the Serb minority in Krajina region of Croatia. In September 1991, the UN Security Council declared that the situation in Yugoslavia constituted a threat to international peace and security and imposed an arms embargo on all factions.[12] It also appointed Cyrus Vance as the envoy of the secretary-general to Yugoslavia. Vance was able to negotiate a ceasefire by January of the following year, which gave some respite. One of the first acts of Boutros Boutros-Ghali, when he became secretary-general, was to send UN peacekeepers, the UN Protection Force (UNPROFOR).

In 1992, the province of Bosnia and Herzegovina declared independence, a declaration supported neither by the Serb nor the Croat minorities.[13] Vance worked out a partition plan, but with the defeat of President George H. W. Bush in the US, its commitment became uncertain. The Serbian army entered Bosnia to put down its secession and the Bosnian Serb leader, Radovan Karadzic, decided to carve out the contiguous Bosnian Serb territory by eliminating Bosnian Muslims from there. Brutal atrocities were committed by all sides. The Serbs laid siege to Sarajevo where there was heavy fighting throughout 1992 and 1993.

In May 1992, the Security Council declared that the conflict in Bosnia and Herzegovina and other parts of the former Yugoslavia constituted a threat to international peace and security "in the area". It imposed comprehensive sanctions on Yugoslavia and called upon NATO to enforce it through an embargo.[14] The Council steadily upped the ante. It declared that individuals would be held responsible for war crimes. It expanded the mandate of the UN peacekeepers by adding delivery of humanitarian aid, escorting aid convoys, imposing a no-fly zone, establishing a tribunal of trying guilty individuals and declaring certain areas as safe areas.

In August 1992, Security Council's Resolution 770 invoked Chapter VII to call upon all member states to take "nationally or through regional agencies or arrangements all measures necessary" to enable the United Nations to deliver humanitarian assistance.[15] This was a path-breaking resolution in two respects. It declared that the internal situation in Bosnia and Herzegovina was a threat to international peace and security and delivering humanitarian assistance there was "an important element in the Council's effort to restore peace and security in the area". The appeal to take measures was not only to member states but also to regional agencies or arrangements. This was to facilitate the entry of NATO, though no regional organisation was named. The Security Council asked member states to report to the secretary-general on the measures taken by them. There were no negative votes on this resolution. India, China and Zimbabwe abstained.

The Security Council rapidly adopted four more resolutions authorising member states to take all necessary measures to protect its peacekeeping forces, UNPROFOR, IFOR and SFOR, in Bosnia and Herzegovina and Croatia and enable them to perform their mandate.[16] They also asked member states to use of air power to protect UN peacekeepers and "safe areas" created by the UN for civilians. However, both came under attack by different factions involved in the fighting. The Security Council also started authorising its peacekeeping operations to use force under Chapter VII but to no avail. China objected to the practice but did not block it. Boutros-Ghali estimated that the UN would need 34,000 troops for this. It managed to get only 5000 to patrol the safe areas.

At the end of 1992, the Serbs controlled 70% of Bosnia while the Croats controlled 20%. The balance was held by the Muslim-dominated government led by Alija Izetbegovic. Within two years the Security Council had passed over a hundred resolutions on Yugoslavia, mostly on

Bosnia and Herzegovina. However, with no authority to enforce them it was mocked by all sides.

In August 1995, following a particularly brutal massacre of civilians in Srebrenica, the Security Council once again sought NATO military intervention against Bosnian Serbs to protect its peacekeepers and Bosnian Muslims. NATO carried out another round of aerial bombardment which finally brought the warring factions to the negotiating table. But these talks were not held under the auspices of the UN. The US took them over and held them under its assistant secretary of state, Richard Holbrooke, at a US air base in Dayton, Ohio. Holbrooke assembled President Milosevic of Serbia, President Franjo Tudjman of Croatia and President Izetbegovic of Bosnia and got them to agree to a loose Bosnian federation comprising a Muslim-Croat federation controlling 51% of the country and the Serbs controlling 49%.

While the talks yielded quick results, the manner in which the US took charge of the process, ignoring both the UN and NATO, irked even its closest ally, Britain. David Owen, former foreign secretary, who had put together a proposal earlier with Cyrus Vance, complained that the US had been unfair in its criticism of UNPROFOR and its European allies. EU's Special Envoy to the Former Yugoslavia, Carl Bildt, was also unhappy with the US ignoring the sensibilities of Europe.

The Bosnia resolutions, all sponsored by Western countries, introduced the concept of authorising military action by member states to protect UN peacekeepers and assist the United Nations in delivering humanitarian assistance. No specific threat to international peace and security was identified nor could any be inferred from the resolutions. In the absence of its own military force, the Security Council was dependent upon the goodwill of member states for the protection of its own peacekeeping forces. NATO treated itself as the military arm of the Security Council in Yugoslavia. Its ships monitored compliance of the sanctions and enforced the no-fly zone imposed by the Security Council, but it was reticent to commit ground troops for fear of casualties.

Somalia

Somalia became independent in 1960 with the merger of British and Italian colonial territories. It enjoyed parliamentary democracy till 1969 when a violent *coup d'état* plunged it into civil war. The country came under the repressive rule of General Mohamed Siad Barre who perpetuated it by promising to re-conquer all the land used by Somalis in the past – French Somaliland (Djibouti), the Northern Frontier District of Kenya and the Ogaden province of Ethiopia.

As long as Ethiopia was under Emperor Haile Selassie, the US backed it against Somalia, which was supported by the Soviet Union. When Haile Selassie was overthrown in a leftist revolution the roles reversed and the US started supplying weapons to Somalia. A civil war erupted there in the 1980s.

General Barre's misrule resulted in a rebellion in the north, which soon spread and forced him to leave Mogadishu in 1991. He eventually took refuge in Nigeria. The rebellion was taken over by the United Somali Congress, one of whose leaders was General Mohamed Farah Aideed. Barre had kept him in prison for seven years and then sent him as ambassador to India. Aideed, however, was soon challenged by a party colleague and Mogadishu businessman, Ali Mahdi Mohamed. Both controlled parts of Mogadishu. The collapse of the Barre's government in December 1990 led to a breakdown of law and order in the country. The West supported Ali Mahdi and in a conference in Djibouti in May 1991, boycotted by Aideed, had him installed as President.

The Security Council ignored Somalia during this period because of its preoccupation with Iraq and Yugoslavia. By 1992 Somalia was in the grip of a severe famine and marauding armed gangs. At this point, Boutros-Ghali pointed to the need identified in his Agenda for Peace for a multinational force that could be deployed under UN command to provide security cover to the relief program. Even the New York Times wrote, "But when will Mr. Bush gather political courage to say what this specific Somalia operation demonstrates about a larger problem – that the world needs a permanent, multination cavalry on call for just such emergencies?"[17]

Boutros-Ghali was able to get a Security Council resolution to send a small contingent of peacekeepers, 500 lightly-armed Pakistanis. The UN decided to provide humanitarian relief but in the absence of military protection, the relief could not reach those in need in the interior. In August 1992, the Security Council decided to augment its peacekeepers but they had neither the mandate nor the capacity to ensure proper distribution of the aid. The US also decided to send food aid. Boutros-Ghali appointed an Algerian diplomat, Mohamed Sahnoun, as his special representative to Somalia. Sahnoun worked on the warlords but was soon frustrated by lack of support from New York. He vented his anger and was promptly removed by Boutros-Ghali. The civil war raged and international aid agencies bore the brunt of it.

As the situation deteriorated, the US felt compelled to take action, but instead of deploying troops under the UN it opted for authorisation for its own military action by the Security Council. Security Council Resolution 794 of 3 December 1992 authorised the secretary-general and member states to facilitate in cooperation the delivery of humanitarian assistance in Somalia and the enforcement of an earlier resolution imposing an arms embargo on the country. The resolution thanked the offer of the US, without naming it, to establish an operation to create such a secure environment. The US assured that it would deploy its troops in Somalia for this humanitarian cause.

A Unified Task Force (UNITAF), a coalition of the willing spearheaded by the US, was sent to Somalia. 28,000 American troops and 17,000 more from twenty other countries reached Somalia as part of the US Operation Restore Hope. The UN's UNOSOM II had about 20,000 peacekeepers at its peak from Turkey, Malaysia, Pakistan and elsewhere but they were heavily dependent on the US-led forces for their protection against the well-armed Somali warlords. US secretary of state, Madeleine Albright, made a grand declaration on 26 March 1993 that her country had launched, "an unprecedented enterprise aimed at nothing less than the restoration of an entire country as a proud, functioning, and viable member of the community of nations."[18]

The situation took a serious turn when on 5 June 1993, 25 Pakistani peacekeepers were killed by a Somali militia. The US sent additional troops but on 3 October 1993, 18 American soldiers were killed and two of its helicopters shot down while trying to catch Mohammed Aideed. There was outrage in the US and it peremptorily withdrew its troops. Other countries in the force followed suit. The US attack on Aideed had been launched without intimation to the UN but in the ensuing uproar all its leaders, including President Bill Clinton, put the blame on it. The US withdrawal left the UN peacekeepers totally exposed to the Somali warlords. The Security Council struggled for some time to bring the Somali factions together, but eventually withdrew its peacekeepers in 2005. Somalia was left at the mercy of the warlords.

As in Bosnia and Herzegovina earlier in the year, the Somalia resolution was to facilitate the delivery of humanitarian assistance. It authorised member states to "use all necessary means" to establish a secure environment for humanitarian relief operations in Somalia. This resolution for the first time authorised the secretary-general and member states to set up a unified command of the forces. Member states were required to report to the Council on a regular basis, starting with the first report in fifteen days. It also created an *ad hoc* commission consisting of members of the Security Council to report to the Council on the implementation of the resolution. The involvement of the secretary-general in the setting up of the unified command and the specific time limit for the first report reflected an effort by Boutros-Ghali to make his office more relevant to the process. The resolution was adopted unanimously, the first such supported by India.[19]

Somalia became yet another quagmire for the Security Council. Urquhart noted that in its enthusiasm, the West had ignored the key difference between Iraq's invasion of Kuwait and the internal conflicts of Yugoslavia and Somalia with deep ethnic complexities of intertwined communities. There were no clear military goals to achieve there and few solutions acceptable to all.

The acrimonious experience of deploying two separate forces in Somalia led to a different kind of catastrophe in Rwanda – inactivity in the face of genocide.

Rwanda

Hutus and Tutsis are two tribes living in about the same proportion in Rwanda and Burundi. Both countries became independent from Belgium in 1962. The Hutus took power in Rwanda and the Tutsis in Burundi. Their mutual rivalries continued.

Paul Kagame, a Tutsi who grew up in a refugee camp in Uganda, put together a Tutsi army to seize power in Rwanda. In August 1993, Belgium and the Organization for African Unity brokered peace between him and the Hutu President of Rwanda, General Juvénal Habyarimana. The accord provided for Kagame's Rwandese Patriotic Front to share power with the Hutus till elections in 1995. The accord also enabled the Security Council to send 2500 peacekeepers.

However, the accord broke down soon and the UN Secretariat warned the Security Council of the danger of large-scale violence. The Western countries were, however, in no mood to increase their involvement. The US was more concerned about increasing financial accountability in the United Nations by appointing an inspector general. This demand was made by President Clinton to Boutros-Ghali in May 1994, when the secretary-general called on him to discuss Rwanda. This was despite the fact that a US government nominee, Joseph Conner, was the under secretary-general for administration and management and half the staff assigned to the United Nations' administration and management were Americans.

The small contingent of UN peacekeepers with instructions to use force only in self-defence was incapable of stopping the violence. In April 1994, President Juvénal Habyarimana of Rwanda and the new Hutu President of Burundi, Cyprien Ntaryamira, were killed when their aircraft was struck by a missile. Rwanda's interim president, Agathe Uwilingiyimana, took shelter in the UN compound but her guards were overpowered in an attack there and she was taken away and killed. Ten Belgian Blue Helmets were also killed. Belgium withdrew its contingent from the UN peacekeepers. The Security Council reduced the strength of its peacekeepers and tasked them to mediate a ceasefire between the parties.

Meanwhile, the Hutus, who suspected Kagame of shooting down the aircraft, went into a frenzied killing of Tutsis. In April 1994 Hutus in Rwanda killed around 800,000 Tutsis. The Security Council authorised the secretary-general to increase the peacekeepers to 5500, but countries were reluctant to offer troops. The US, freshly out of Somalia, was unwilling to step into Rwanda. US Secretary of State Madeleine Albright admitted later, "Perhaps the only solution would have been a large and heavily armed coalition led by a major power, but because of Somalia, the US military wasn't going to undertake that. The French would have been strongly opposed by the Tutsis."[20]

The killing of the Tutsis soon led to a violent reaction from them. Kagame's troops entered Rwanda and started killing Hutus. On 27 May 1994, Boutros-Ghali told the media, "It is genocide. . . and more than 200,000 people have been killed, but the international community is still debating what to do." He wrote later in his memoir, "The US effort to prevent the effective deployment of a UN force for Rwanda succeeded with the strong support of Britain."[21]

The Security Council was paralysed on Rwanda. The US offered to use its air force and criticised Boutros-Ghali for blocking it. Senator Bob Dole, who was the Republican Party candidate for the presidency against President Bill Clinton, thundered that Boutros-Ghali and not Clinton was the commander-in-chief of the US army. But not just the UN, even Britain and France, who had forces on the ground were apprehensive of US air strikes.

Finally, France offered to send its troops for enforcement action. In June, it sponsored a resolution under Chapter VII which was adopted by the Security Council authorising member states, acting in cooperation with the secretary-general, to conduct an operation in Rwanda "using all necessary means" to achieve its humanitarian objectives.[22] France launched Operation Turquoise to set up a humanitarian safe zone, even though it was not considered to be neutral in the war since it had been arming the Hutu government forces. In July, a national unity government was formed and France withdrew its forces.

The Rwanda resolution had the same reporting requirement as the one on Somalia two years ago. It called upon the concerned member states and the secretary-general to report to the Security Council on a regular basis, with the first report within 15 days. No command structure was laid down for the forces. Its term was fixed at two months unless the secretary-general decided earlier that the UN peacekeeping force, UNAMIR, was in a position to deal with the situation. The resolution was able to muster the support of only 10 members. China, Brazil, New Zealand, Nigeria and Pakistan abstained. China expressed support for the proposal of the Organisation of African Unity that all international assistance should in the framework of the UN peacekeeping mission, which needed to be strengthened. Brazil also expressed apprehension that authorising enforcement action would undermine the UN peacekeepers.

The genocide in Rwanda was used later by the West to advocate the need for humanitarian intervention by the international community. Unfortunately, the key lesson, the need to equip the Security Council with a rapid reaction force to enable it to "take urgent military measures" as envisaged in Article 45 of the Charter for such situations, was ignored. The permanent members preferred to operate their forces themselves and intervene, with or without Security Council authorisation, where and when they chose.

Haiti

A military coup in September 1991 against President Jean Bertrand Aristide, in less than a year of his election, destabilised the country and led to an exodus of refugees. In June 1993, the Security Council determined that the situation was a threat to international peace and security and imposed an oil and arms embargo under Chapter VII.[23] The embargo was briefly suspended after an agreement among the parties but reinforced when it broke down very soon. The Security Council followed up with an authorisation to member states to take commensurate measures to enforce the embargo on arms and oil imposed by it.[24]

The Security Council expanded the scope of the embargo in May 1994 and, when this proved ineffective, authorised member states under Resolution 940 (1994) "to form a multinational force under unified command and control and, in this framework, to use all necessary means to facilitate the departure from Haiti of the military leadership......and the prompt return of the legitimately elected president...." China and Brazil abstained on the resolution, while Rwanda did not vote. China opposed the recourse to enforcement action by member states to deal with an internal matter of a country, while Brazil said the task could be adequately performed by the UN peacekeepers in Haiti (UNMIH). A multinational force of 28 countries, led by the US, landed in Haiti in September. The Haitian army did not resist and President Aristide was restored.

The Haiti resolution was sponsored by the US, France, Argentina and Canada. It was adopted under Chapter VII and was aimed at restoring the legitimately elected president of the country. Member states enforcing the resolution were requested to report to the Council "at regular intervals" and the multinational force was to terminate its mission when a secure and stable environment had been established and the UN peacekeepers had adequate force capability and structure to assume the full range of their functions.

Zaire (Democratic Republic of the Congo)

In 1996, Laurent Desiré Kabila led a revolt against the ailing Mobutu Sese Seko who it would be recalled from Chapter 8 had seized power in 1960 in the Democratic Republic of the Congo, which he had renamed Zaire. The country was also reeling under the burden of refugees from neighbouring Rwanda and Burundi and armed militias. In November 1996, the Security Council decided that the situation constituted a threat to international peace and security in the region and called for an urgent response by the international community. Acting under Chapter VII, it unanimously adopted Resolution 1080 (1996) sponsored by 30 countries, including the US, Britain and France, authorising member states to set up a "temporary multinational force" to "facilitate the immediate return of humanitarian organisations and the effective delivery by civilian relief organizations of humanitarian aid." The Council authorised member states to use "all necessary means" to achieve the humanitarian objectives of the resolution.

The resolution required member states participating in the multinational force to provide periodic reports, at least twice a month. It specified that the cost of the operation would be borne by the participating states, but a voluntary trust fund would also be set up for others to contribute. The resolution also anticipated UN peacekeepers taking over at a later date and requested the secretary-general to prepare a report on it.

However, there was little enthusiasm among countries to contribute troops to the operation. Both the US and France were reluctant and were also distrusted by African countries, who agreed to accept a Canada-led contingent. Canada sent an advance force, which stationed itself in Kampala and sent liaison teams to the Congo but it soon found the situation to be beyond its capacity and withdrew within a month. Meanwhile, Kabila seized Kinshasa in February 1997 and overthrew Mobutu. But the fighting continued. The Organisation of African Unity and the Southern African Development Community succeeded in mediating a ceasefire with the help of the UN representative in August 1999. The Security Council then deployed a peacekeeping force, MONUC, with powers under Chapter VII to "take the necessary action" to protect UN personnel. MONUC was renamed MONUSCO, when the situation stabilised by 2010, to reflect its changed role as a stabilisation force.

The Congo resolution once again exposed the Security Council's limitations. After the experience in Somalia and Rwanda, member states were wary of deploying ground troops in situations of civil strife in Africa. The only countries with the capacity to do so were the former colonial powers, which were unacceptable to African countries. Countries like Canada, which had greater acceptability, lacked combat experience.

Albania

In March 1997, the Security Council determined that there was a threat to peace and security in the region due to a financial crisis in Albania caused by ponzi schemes. Acting under Chapter VII, it adopted Resolution 1101

(1997) authorising member states "to establish a temporary and limited multinational protection force to facilitate the safe and prompt delivery of humanitarian assistance." The resolution, led by Italy and Greece, was sponsored by 21 countries, including the US, Britain, France and Albania. China was the only country that spoke in the debate. It said that it was opposed to the use of Chapter VII resolutions in the internal affairs of states, but in view of Albania's support, would not block it.

The operation was led by Italian forces, which had experience of invading Albania in the two world wars. Its duration was capped at three months but was extended later by another forty-five days. The participating member states were told to bear their own cost and were required to cooperate with the UN, the Organisation for Security and Cooperation in Europe (OSCE), the European Union and other international organisations engaged in rendering humanitarian assistance in the country. They were to submit periodic reports, at least every two weeks. The resolution received the support of all members of the Security Council, except China, which abstained, as it did on the subsequent resolution extending the period of the operation.

Libya

A civil war broke out in Libya in 2010 and the eastern city of Benghazi went under the control of forces fighting the country's military ruler, Colonel Muammar Gaddafi. Gaddafi's troops advanced towards Benghazi and reached its outskirts early next year. The Security Council adopted Resolution 1970 (2011), acting under Chapter VII, welcoming the appointment of a commission of enquiry by the Human Rights Council to investigate allegations of violations of human rights and imposed comprehensive sanctions including an arms embargo, travel ban on designated officials and an asset freeze. It also decided to refer the situation since 15 February 2011 to the Prosecutor of the International Criminal Court.

France and Britain, however, declared that they feared a genocide in Benghazi and appealed for Security Council authorisation to prevent it. France flew in its foreign minister, Alain Juppé, to pilot another resolution in less than a month, supported by three others, the US, Britain and Lebanon. Juppé said that while the rest of the Arab world was on the threshold of liberty and democracy, the forces of Gaddafi were hours away from committing a genocide in Benghazi. Germany cautioned against the optimism of quick military results. India advised the Council to wait till the reports of the UN special envoy for Libya and the African Union's high-level delegation on their visits to Libya were available. Russia feared destabilisation of the entire region, while China said that it was opposed to the use of force in international relations and supported the peace efforts of the UN special envoy, the African Union and the Arab League.

The Security Council adopted Resolution 1973 (2011) declaring that the situation in Libya constituted a threat to international peace and security and, acting under Chapter VII, demanded that Libyan authorities comply with international law, international humanitarian law, and international refugee law and provide protection to its civilians. It imposed a no-fly zone on the country and authorised member states that had notified the secretary-general to "take all necessary measures" to protect civilians and civilian populated areas under threat of attack in Libya, including Benghazi. The resolution ruled out "a foreign occupation force of any form on any part of Libyan territory". This disavowal was to make the resolution acceptable to the members who had reservation about the deployment of ground troops. The resolution could only garner ten votes in favour. Five countries, Brazil, China, Germany, India and Russia abstained. The refusal of Germany, a NATO ally, to support the resolution was a blow to the Western countries. It prompted an unusual provision in a subsequent resolution that the authorisation of military action would terminate at "23.59 Libyan local time on 31 October 2011".[25]

The Western countries deemed the text adequate to authorise them to bomb Libya while enforcing a no-fly zone. The bombing was carried out by Britain, France and NATO forces and lasted from March to October. However, once it started it, turned from saving civilians in Benghazi to removing Gaddafi from power. Gaddafi was killed by one of the armed militias operating with Western air support. With his death, the country passed into the hands of mutiple warring militias.

The resolution against Libya was not the last such to be adopted by the Security Council authorising member military action, although it was the last that led to a military invasion. Two more resolutions were adopted thereafter, both in Africa and both specifically authorising French forces to use force to support and protect UN peacekeeping missions. The first was Resolution 2085 in December 2012 authorising French forces "to use all necessary means" to provide protection to the UN peacekeeping mission (MINUSMA) in Mali. The second was Resolution 2127 of December 2013 authorising French forces "to take all necessary measures" to support the UN peacekeeping mission (MISCA) in the Central African Republic.

The Authorisation Resolutions

The Security Council's practice of authorising military action evolved erratically and never took definite shape. All such resolutions were drafted by Western countries and put through informal negotiations among the permanent five behind closed doors. They varied widely in content. The Security Council typically "authorised" or "called upon" them to use "all necessary means" to implement its provisions. Some resolutions used other phrases like "all necessary measures", "all means" and "all necessary action", all of which were interpreted by interested member states as authorisation to use military force on behalf of the Security Council. All military actions were taken by the Western countries, led by the US or NATO. Britain and France participated in most, while the Soviet Union and China stayed away from all.

The mandate was precisely defined in some instances and left vague in others. All resolutions were based on a determination by the Security Council that there existed a threat to peace and security, international or regional. But the restoration of peace and security was not the stated objective of all. On international threats, the interventions were mainly to vacate the aggression and restore the *status quo ante bellum* (situation prevailing before the war). On domestic issues, however, they were for a variety of reasons - preventing the proliferation of weapons of mass destruction, ensuring delivery of humanitarian aid, protecting human rights, restoring a democratically elected regime, enforcing economic sanctions, and enforcing peace settlements.

Most resolutions required reports to be submitted to the Security Council, either by the member states or the secretary-general, on the progress in implementation. When left to member states, the periodicity of the reports was not always specified. The secretary-general was usually asked to report periodically on the action taken by member states. However, in the later resolutions, on Albania and on the Congo, member states were required to report every two weeks.

The command and control structure of the forces was usually left undefined. In Korea, it was specifically assigned to the United States but in the First Gulf War, there was no reference to it. In Haiti, a 60-member advance team was set up for coordination with the multinational force and the secretary-general was asked to report on it. In Zaire and Rwanda, the resolutions authorised "member states cooperating with the Secretary-General". This was to confer the Council's blessings only on the military action of Belgium and France, not the interference by their African neighbours.

Regional organisations were sometimes given the authority along with member states to use military force, as in Bosnia and Herzegovina and in Kosovo. This was done to enable NATO and the European Union to join and even lead the operation.

The duration of the military action authorised was left open in most cases. This enabled the implementing powers to keep their operations going for as long as they wished since they could veto a resolution terminating the operation. In Albania, the force constituted was described as "temporary and limited".

Member states were expected to bear the cost of their military action themselves though this was not always mentioned in the resolution. In Albania, member states were told that they would have to bear the cost of their troops. No resolution provided for the cost to be borne by the UN.

The resolutions did not always provide for recourse to negotiations or mediation before military action, but many began by calling for a ceasefire. In the First Gulf War, Iraq and Kuwait were called upon to "begin immediately intense negotiations", but in most other cases it was presumed that there was no time for negotiations or that they would be fruitless.

Not all the resolutions authorising military action were adopted unanimously. The Western three and Russia supported all the resolutions in the 1990s. China abstained on the ones on Iraq in the First Gulf War, on one resolution on Bosnia-Herzegovina, and those on Rwanda, Haiti and Albania. The resolutions on Somalia and Zaire and all but one on Bosnia and Herzegovina were adopted unanimously. The resolutions on Rwanda and Libya had as many as five abstentions. India, which was a member of the Security Council in 1992 when Resolution 770 on Bosnia and

Herzegovina was adopted, abstained along with Zimbabwe and China. It also abstained on Resolution 1973 on Libya in 2011.

The effectiveness of military invasions has been mixed and continues to be debated. Only in Kuwait in the First Gulf War was the immediate objective attained – Iraq was compelled to withdraw and pay compensation. This was the only case which met the criterion of a threat to international peace and security. It was also the most specific in its reference to Article 39 and in its determination that there had been a "breach of international peace and security as regards the Iraqi invasion of Kuwait".[26] All the others were essentially internal affairs of countries. The goals of these international interventions were unclear and their success remains difficult to evaluate. In Bosnia and in Rwanda the action came late. Conflict continues in the Democratic Republic of the Congo and democracy in Haiti remains fragile. Libya has descended into civil war, with large parts becoming a failed state.

Equally serious are the questions about Charter-compatibility and legality of these military actions which impact the credibility of the Security Council and the reputation of the United Nations. This is discussed in Chapters 12 and 13.

Endnotes

1   Juergen Drifte. *The United Nations Security Council – Resurgence and Renewal.* (State University of New York, 2009), p. 4.

2   S/PV.3046 of 31 January 1992, pp.8-9.

3   UN Document, S/RES/665(1990), 25 August 1990.

4   UN Documents, S/RES/661 (1990), -662 (1990), -670 (1990) and -674 (1990).

5   UN Document, S/RES/678 (1990), 29 November 1990.

6   UN Document, S/RES/687 (1991), 3 April 1991.

7   UN Document, S/RES/833(1993).

8   Quoted in T. Eitel, *The Escape and Parole of the Imprisoned God of War: An Overview of the Second Gulf War from the Perspective of International law.* (35 GYIL, 1992), n. 292, p. 182.

9   George Bush and Brent Scowcroft. *A World Transformed* (New York: Alfred A. Knopf, 1998), p. 356.

10 UN Document, S/RES/1205 (1998), 5 November 1998.

11 Harry Kreisler. *Conversations with Sir Brian Urquhart, 19 March 1996, The UN in the Post-Cold War World* (Berkeley: UC Institute of International Studies), pp. 7-8. Quoted in Kaplan, p. 133.

12 UN Document, S/RES/713(1991).

13 The Serbs constituted 30 percent and the Croats 18 percent of the population.

14 UN Document S/RES/757 (1992).

15 UN Document, S/RES/770 (1992).

16 UNSC Resolutions 836(1993), 908(1994), 1031(1995) and 1088(1996).

17 New York Times, 1 September 1992.

18 Quoted in Annan. *Interventions,* p. 48.

19 UN Document, S/RES/794 (1992), 3 December 1992.

20 Albright, p. 152

21 Boutros Boutros-Ghali. *Unvanquished – A US-UN Saga* (New York: Random House, 1999), p. 138.

22 UN Document, S/RES/929(1994), 22 June 1994, para 3.

23 UN Document, S/RES/ 841 (1993), 16 June 1993.

24 UN Document, S/RES/875 (1993), 16 October 1993.

25 UN Document, S/RES/2016(2011), 27 October 2011, para 5.

26 UNSC Resolution 660 (1990) of 2 August 1990.

10 Sanctions

This is the most common coercive measure used by the Security Council. Unlike peacekeeping operations and authorised military actions, it has a specific provision for it in the UN Charter. Its effectiveness, however, remains open to question and its burden often falls on the innocent.

Article 41 empowers the Security Council to enforce sanctions as a non-military measure. Embargoes can cover trade, particularly in commodities and arms, and financial and travel sanctions on the entire country or specific entities and individuals in it. The permanent five have been willing to let sanctions of varying intensity be applied on their client states in order to ease pressure for visible action for defiance of the Security Council. There can be various explanations for this. Sanctions can be easily evaded through smuggling. They impose costs on the economy but it is the common people who bear the brunt of it. Sanctions make the client state even more dependent on its benefactor and help the government rally its citizens behind it.

In the Cold War days, economic sanctions were used only twice by the Security Council: an oil and arms embargo on Southern Rhodesia and an arms embargo on South Africa. Since 1990, 24 sanctions regimes have been imposed by the Security Council, of which 14 are still in force. These have been imposed for enforcing peace among parties in conflict, for nuclear non-proliferation and for counter-terrorism.

Arms embargo is the most commonly applied sanction. Angola, Somalia, Rwanda, Ethiopia and Eritrea have been among its targets of these. Iraq, Haiti and Yugoslavia have been targeted with comprehensive trade sanctions. Financial sanctions have been used on government assets and on private individuals and organisations after 1994. Angola, Sierra Leone, Afghanistan, Liberia, the Democratic Republic of the Congo, Sudan and Côte d'Ivoire were among countries affected. In Afghanistan, after the overthrow of the Taliban regime in 2001, sanctions were imposed on the Taliban and Al Qaeda which dispersed in the Afghan countryside and took shelter in Pakistan. Sanctions on the export of precious commodities, like diamonds and oil from Angola and logs from Liberia have been used to hit government revenues. In the case of Angola, sanctions were imposed on the territory under the control of the rebel organisation, the National Union for the Total Independence of Angola (UNITA).

Southern Rhodesia, 1965-1979

Europeans had been settling in Southern Rhodesia since 1923 when Britain invaded and conquered it. In 1965, a minority racist regime under Ian Smith declared itself independent. The UN had been trying to prevent such unilateral action and had sought Britain's help. Britain insisted that this was outside the competence of the UN as it was a domestic matter. The Security Council declared the action of Southern Rhodesia as illegal and under Resolution 217 (1965) called upon the United Kingdom to take action against it. It also asked all member states to break economic relations with the country and refrain from supplying arms to it. The Organization of African Unity imposed an economic blockade.

In April 1966, the Council called upon Britain to use force, if necessary, to prevent some ships carrying oil for Southern Rhodesia from reaching there. Resolution 221 (1966) stated that the Council had determined that the situation constituted a threat to the peace but did not mention any article of the Charter. The Council progressively tightened the sanctions by adding commodities such as iron and copper to the import ban. Southern Rhodesia was the first instance of economic sanctions being imposed by the Security Council, and also the first instance of it calling upon a member state to take action to implement it.

The sanctions were eventually lifted in 1979 when the United Kingdom brokered an agreement between the racist regime and the freedom fighters. Elections were held in 1980 and Southern Rhodesia, now called Zimbabwe, was admitted to the United Nations on 25 April 1980. It is generally accepted that while the sanctions imposed a financial burden on the country, it was the guerrilla attacks of the freedom fighters that forced the racist regime to capitulate.

South Africa, 1977-1994

One of the principles of the UN Charter is "promoting and encouraging respect for human rights and for fundamental freedoms for all without distinction as to race, sex, language or religion" [Article 1(3)]. However, the very next Article enjoins upon the UN not to "intervene in matters which are essentially within the domestic jurisdiction of any State." A group of 29 countries in Asia and Africa, including Japan, brought up the issue of apartheid in South Africa after a gruesome incident in Sharpville in 1960 in which nearly one hundred people were killed in police firing. Western countries, which were to later make human rights one of the primary goals of the UN, were either opposed to the issue being raised in the Security Council or extremely cautious about it. Britain and France opposed the adoption of the agenda and reminded the Council of the injunction contained in Article 2 on intervening in internal matters of a State. The French delegate, Armand Berard, said, "My delegation .... has serious doubts regarding the legal merits of the case which has been submitted to the Council and regarding the competence of the Council to deal with this question."[1]

Henry Cabot Lodge of the US was willing to go half way. He said that all members were required to respect their commitments made under the Charter and, therefore, the matter could be discussed in the Council. Italy's Ortona drew attention to the internal contradiction in the UN Charter "between the need to give practical expression to the provisions of the Charter concerning human rights and fundamental freedoms and those provisions in the protected States from interference in their internal affairs."[2]

India maintained that a matter as important as this had the potential to threaten international peace and security and, therefore, fell within the jurisdiction of the Security Council. India's ambassador, C.S. Jha, who participated in the discussion as an invitee, said, "Peace does not mean the mere avoidance of war; the threat to international peace does not merely connote a threatening war situation between two or more nations. Any issue which threatens to divide humanity as deeply as the present one is a threat to international peace."[3] He added, "Events which cause world-wide concern, which have potentialities for international friction and disharmony, and which are directly opposed to the spirit and letter of the Charter cannot be brought within the straitjacket of Article 2, paragraph 7."[4]

It was not the Security Council but the General Assembly that took the lead in the campaign against apartheid. In 1952, it declared that the UN had a commitment to protect human rights and was, therefore, competent to pronounce on apartheid. In 1962, it called for severance of diplomatic ties. Four years later it declared apartheid to be a crime against humanity. The General Assembly progressively adopted resolutions against South Africa recommending action against it. In 1968, it recommended to the Security Council to impose sanctions under Chapter VII. In 1973, it excluded South Africa from participating in its meetings and those of most specialised agencies, on the ground that it had no right to represent the people of South Africa.

The Security Council took its time responding to apartheid. In April 1960 it adopted a resolution moved by Ecuador calling on the UN secretary-general to take measures with the government of South Africa to enable it to fulfil its Charter obligations. France and the UK abstained in the vote. South Africa maintained that its apartheid policy was an internal matter and not subject to the jurisdiction of the UN. In 1963, the Council adopted Resolution 181 (1963) "solemnly" calling upon all states "to cease forthwith the sale and shipment of arms, ammunition of all types and military vehicles to South Africa." This resolution was an appeal and was not taken under Chapter VII. After the brutal killing of several hundred people in Soweto in 1976, it adopted Resolution 392 (1976) in which it agreed that apartheid was "a crime against the conscience and dignity of mankind" and a potential threat to international peace and security but refused to make a determination under Article 39 and impose sanctions.

The Security Council took action under Chapter VII only in 1977 when it imposed an arms embargo on South Africa under Resolution 418 (1977). It also set up a committee to monitor its implementation. However, despite a continuous demand from an overwhelming number of countries the Council refused to expand the scope of the sanctions. The sanctions were lifted in 1994 when apartheid was abolished.

Effectiveness of Sanctions

After the Cold War sanctions proliferated. They were imposed on countries, individuals and organisations. After the terrorist attacks in the US in 2001 restrictions were imposed on several terrorist organisations.

Sanctions are widely recognised to have limitations due to violations by countries and non-state entities. They are believed to have been relatively successful in Iraq, Yugoslavia (for its actions in Bosnia), Libya, Serbia, Cambodia and Sierra Leone but to have had little effect on Haiti, Angola, Somalia, Sudan, Liberia, Rwanda, Yugoslavia (for its actions in Kosovo) and Afghanistan. But it is also recognised that they are counter-productive because they oblige the people to rally behind their government in solidarity and the poor and vulnerable people suffer the most under their impact. Besides, they are very difficult to enforce and lead to profiteering by unscrupulous elements. Smuggling of the banned goods from neighbouring countries becomes hugely profitable. A far more insidious malpractice developed in Iraq in what is called the 'oil for food' program.

A comprehensive trade embargo was enforced on Iraq within four days of its invasion of Kuwait in 1990. In November 1994, when Iraq recognised the sovereignty of Kuwait, France, Russia and China sought to ease sanctions to alleviate the humanitarian suffering caused by it but the US and Britain blocked it. The only concession given on this count was the 'oil for food' program in April 1995 under which Iraq was allowed to use oil exports to finance humanitarian relief. Iraq initially refused to accept the plan as a violation of its sovereignty but agreed when it was given a greater say in it. The program started in January 1997. This, however, led to one of the biggest financial scandals in the UN. Oil sales under the scheme generated US$ 64.2 billion in revenue, but there were allegations that large sums were paid illegally by companies buying the oil to Iraqi, UN and other country officials. An Independent Inquiry Committee into the United Nations Oil-for-Food Programme (Volcker Committee) set up to investigate the allegations, estimated the illicit income paid to Iraqi officials to be US$ 1.8 billion.

The Security Council tries to mitigate the negative consequences of sanctions by seeking regular reports on their humanitarian impact. It has also sought to make sanctions smart. Arms embargos, financial sanctions, travel restrictions, commodity embargos and actions directed against specific individuals and organisations are believed to be smart sanctions that obviate the humanitarian impact and target the guilty more accurately. However, they are generally more difficult to enforce and are largely ineffective because they do little to deter those targeted by them. The most stringent sanctions currently imposed by the Security Council are against the Democratic People's Republic of Korea (North Korea) on account of its nuclear weapons program. They were first imposed in 2006 on the export to the country of military supplies and some luxury goods. They have since been progressively expanded to cover a wide range of goods and financial transactions. However, a UN Panel of Experts reported in August 2017 that North Korea has been able to evade the sanctions through a network of illicit banking channels.[5]

The United States and Britain regard sanctions as a useful tool to coerce countries. They support maintaining comprehensive sanctions for an indefinite period of time. On the other hand, France, Russia and China prefer incremental sanctions to be leveraged for limited periods of time. The US also imposes sanctions unilaterally, using its economic clout to punish countries. It is equally willing to inflict costs on third countries that seek to defy its sanctions. Under the Helms-Burton Act on Cuba and the Iran-Libya sanctions, it reserved the right to retaliate against any state or company that defied its sanctions on these countries.

Sanctions have been the most effective when the patron state is willing to put pressure for change. This enabled apartheid to come to an end peacefully in South Africa. China's willingness to allow tighter sanctions on North Korea can also be regarded as a factor in persuading its ruler to agree to talks. Sanctions against individuals, such as on travel abroad or on remittances to their bank accounts also pinch.

Legal Validity of Sanctions

The legal validity of sanctions has occasionally been challenged with some success. In Libya's case, the ICJ was cautious not to question the authority of the Security Council but its assertion of jurisdiction in case of treaty obligations of the target country enabled several developing countries to challenge Security Council sanctions. In July 1998, seven Arab countries wrote to the Security Council against its sanctions. In December, the Organisation of African Unity voted to ignore it.

A more direct confrontation to the Security Council came from the European Court of Justice in the *Kadi case*. While the ICJ has hinted at possessing powers to review decisions of the Security Council, such as in the *Lockerbie* and *Bosnia genocide cases*, it has held back from a direct challenge to it. However, the courts in the European Union examined and found the sanctions imposed by the Security Council against Yassin Abdullah Kadi and Al Barakaat International Foundation to be weak in law.[6] Kadi was a Saudi national whose assets in Europe were frozen by the European Union as part of sanctions imposed by the Security Council for links with Al Qaeda. He appealed in the Court of First Instance of the European Community in September 2005. The court ruled that it was bound to interpret and apply the European Community law in a manner compatible with the obligations of the member states under the Charter of the United Nations and, therefore, could not question the legality of the sanctions. However, it did go into the question of the lawfulness of the Security Council resolutions with regard to *jus cogens*, a body of higher rules of public international law binding on all its subjects and from which no derogation is possible, but it did not find the Security Council resolutions to be in violation of them. It declared that the freezing of funds was a temporary act and did not take away the plaintiff's right to them.

Kadi appealed to the European Court of Justice (ECJ) which gave its ruling in 2008. The ECJ disagreed with the lower court and ruled that "the obligations imposed by an international agreement cannot have the effect of prejudicing the constitutional principles of the EC Treaty." It held that the lower court had erred in concluding that the Council's decision could not be subject to judicial review. The Court examined in detail the procedure followed in the Security Council Sanctions Committee for freezing assets of individuals and the remedies available to them. It held that the Committee's procedure was, in essence, diplomatic and inter-governmental, since the accused could not appear before it personally or through his lawyer but only through his own State. Besides, the Committee could reject the request of the individual with no obligation to give reasons. The Court also held that since the permanent members of the Security Council had decisive powers in the Committee the process of scrutiny was political, not judicial, in character. The Court concluded, "The principle of effective judicial protection has been infringed."

However, the Court refused to lift the sanctions on Kadi since it felt that doing so would give him an opportunity to hide his assets. It instead asked the Council to remedy the infringement of his right within three months by establishing an independent and impartial appeals procedure. The Security Council took no action to comply with the ruling but it quietly removed Kadi from the sanctions list in 2012. The European Union followed suit.

Endnotes

1   French delegate Berard in 851st meeting of UNSC on 30 March 1960, SCOR, p. 2.

2   Italian delegate Ortona in 851st meeting of UNSC on 30 March 1960, SCOR, p. 3.

3   C. S. Jha on 852nd meeting of UNSC on 30 March 1950, SCOR, p. 16.

4   Jha. at the 852nd meeting of the Security Council, 30 March 1960, SCOR, 30 March 1960, para 97, p. 24.

5   Ramesh Jaura, Serious Doubts Whether Sanctions Against DPRK Are Effective(In-Depth News, International Press Syndicate, 24 August 2017).

6   European Court of Justice, *Kadi & Al Barakaat International Foundation v. Council and Commission, C-402/05P and C-415/05P, 3 September 2008.* Case summary on the website of the European Commission Legal Service: *http://ec.europa.eu/dgs/legal_service/arrets/05c402_en.pdf.*

11   New Mandates

The two decades of cooperation among the permanent five after the Cold War saw a steady escalation in the mandate of the Security Council, driven by the Western powers, not so much the United States as the two European members, supported by Canada. Humanitarian intervention, which had been frowned upon by them during the Cold War, was turned into a responsibility of the international community. The rise of terrorism became a serious global security concern and enabled the Security Council to expand its powers. It also added human rights, democracy, climate change, pandemics, human trafficking and empowerment of women to its agenda. It got involved in setting up international tribunals for trying individuals and took up the administration of Kosovo and East Timor (also called Timor Leste).

After the successful liberation of Kuwait in 1991, the Western countries pushed the Security Council into overdrive. In January 1992, Britain convened the first-ever summit meeting of the Security Council and got it to direct the new secretary-general, Boutros Boutros-Ghali, to prepare a report on strengthening the capacity of the United Nations in preventive diplomacy, peacemaking and peacekeeping. In his report, An Agenda for Peace, presented to the Security Council in June 1992, Boutros-Ghali stated that solving international problems required a commitment to human rights, fundamental freedom, self-determination of people and respect for democratic principles. He recommended accepting the general jurisdiction of the ICJ to settle disputes and providing armed forces to the Security Council under Article 43. In the interim, member states could keep troops available on call for peace-enforcement. He also advised the involvement of non-government organisations, academics, parliamentarians, business and the media in UN activities. There was no reference to Security Council reform – merely an advice to the permanent five not to lose their collegiality and carry other members of the Security Council and the United Nations with them.

The Western countries soon began defining the mandate of the Security Council according to their priorities by cherry-picking from the secretary-general's recommendations. They selected protection of human rights, empowerment of women, providing humanitarian relief and promoting democracy. Later, climate change, pandemics and human trafficking were added to the growing list. They declared that these were linked to international peace and security and should be brought within the Security Council's mandate. Humanitarian crises were designated as potential threats to peace and security. Democracy and human rights were projected as essential preconditions for it. There was no attempt to strengthen the Council's delivery capacity, broaden its representative base or streamline its decision-making procedures, factors that had been responsible for its earlier inaction. There was a great deal of talk of reform which to the US and Britain implied expanding the Security Council's mandate, not membership. Canada and the newly-formed European Union were in the forefront of this movement. The United States, believing in its own "exceptionalism", expounded the superiority of its economic and political principles and institutions, but did not share the enthusiasm of its allies on all new issues.

International cooperation for solving international problems of a humanitarian character is one of the stated purposes of the United Nations.[1] Human rights and economic and social development also find mention in the Charter. But Article 60 assigns the responsibility for the discharge of this function to the General Assembly and the Economic and Social Council, and states that they "shall have for this purpose the powers set forth in Chapter X". Chapter X authorises the Economic and Social Council to prepare studies and reports and make recommendations. It does not give powers of forcible enforcement to either organ. These provisions were not due to oversight. The powers of the Security Council and the Economic and Social Council are divergent and so are their functions. The coercive powers given to the Security Council were exclusively for maintaining international peace and security. Human rights and fundamental freedoms were not included in its mandate and the term 'democracy' does not figure in the Charter.

Non-interference in the domestic jurisdiction of a member state and respect for their territorial integrity and political independence are cardinal principles of the UN. Article 2(4), which provides for this is quite categorical. The *travaux préparatoires* also establish that the framers of the Charter did not wish to leave any loophole. Article 2(7) is even more emphatic. It declares that nothing in the Charter empowers the UN to intervene in a domestic matter, except in the case of an enforcement measure, which can only arise from a threat to or a breach of international peace and security.

In the 1990s, the Security Council declared terrorism and proliferation of nuclear weapons to be threats to international peace and security. In 2000, in a resolution on the need to protect UN peacekeepers from HIV/AIDS, it included a preambular paragraph stating that the HIV/AIDS pandemic, if unchecked, may pose a risk to stability and security.[2] In 2017, when there was an outbreak of ebola in Africa, the Security Council adopted a resolution expressing concern over its impact on security in the region.[3] It urged all countries and the World Health Organisation to take effective action. The Security Council also adopted a resolution on human trafficking.[4] In 2000, came a resolution on women and peace and security reaffirming the important role of women in the prevention and resolution of conflicts and calling for "increase in the participation of women at decision-making levels in conflict resolution and peace processes", both in the UN and at national levels.[5] While all these issues can potentially have security implications the Security Council gave little thought to its expertise in dealing with them, especially in view of the presence of other more specialised bodies within the UN system.

During this period, Security Council resolutions became more sweeping and open-ended in their application. Resolution 1373 (2001) on international terrorism was adopted under Chapter VII and obliged states to take a number of steps and undertake obligations against terrorism. This resolution was not with reference to any specific terrorist organisation and did not specify a time period for its implementation. In view of the fact that there is still no universally accepted definition of terrorism, such a resolution could be used for coercive action in any situation.

The Security Council also expanded its machinery for implementing its newly acquired powers. It created international criminal tribunals, peacekeeping operations with Chapter VII powers, and international transitional administrations. It set up committees to monitor sanctions regimes against states, organisations and individuals. However, even in these committees, the procedures were non-transparent and the permanent five retained their veto when performing quasi-judicial functions like indicting individuals. Despite talk of putting human beings at the centre of the UN system, individuals could not appeal directly to the Security Council or its committees if they had sanctions imposed on them. They had to go through their governments as seen in the Kadi case in Chapter 10.

Humanitarian Interventions

Hersch Lauterpacht, who edited the 8th edition of Oppenheim's International Law (Volume I) in 1955, wrote that humanitarian intervention is legally permissible "when a state renders itself guilty of cruelties against and persecution of its nationals in such a way as to deny their fundamental human rights and to shock the conscience of mankind."[6]

The Charter injunction against interference in the internal affairs of a country has been ignored by the Security Council in cases of a grave humanitarian threat to the people of that country. The Council's actions against Southern Rhodesia, South Africa, Somalia, Liberia, Iraq, Haiti and Rwanda were attributed to its concern for human rights. The principle that a purely domestic affair can trigger sanctions under Chapter VII has, however, never been expressly claimed or categorically established. In several cases, the Council has gone to great lengths to seek or cite an international dimension of the problem. Its inability to do so in situations like Somalia, where there was no threat to peace in any other country despite the violence inside, prompted some Western countries to seek a new principle to justify Council action. The genocide in Rwanda and the killings in former Yugoslavia triggered a campaign for a Security Council policy on humanitarian intervention.

Consistency is not a virtue in diplomacy and it is useful to keep memories short. In 1986, a policy document of the British Foreign Office had argued against humanitarian interventions, "The overwhelming majority of contemporary legal opinion comes down against the existence of a right to humanitarian intervention for three main reasons: First, the UN Charter and the corpus of modern international law do not seem specifically to incorporate such a right; secondly, state practice in the last two centuries and especially since 1945, at best provides only a handful of genuine cases of humanitarian intervention; and finally, on prudential grounds, that the scope for abusing such a right argues strongly against its creation."[7]

The position of Western countries on interventions in the internal affairs of a country on humanitarian grounds underwent a radical change once the moral burden of apartheid was off their shoulders. In 1966, the Security Council had determined that the unilateral declaration of independence by Southern Rhodesia constituted a threat to international peace and security and had imposed economic sanctions on it. Though the US did not veto the measure, its secretary of state, Dean Rusk, criticised the Council for interfering in an internal matter of a country. He said that the threat to international peace and security came from the neighbouring African countries that were supporting the opposition to the Ian Smith's regime in Southern Rhodesia.

In 1978, the US permanent representative to the UN, Daniel Patrick Moynihan, wrote a book on the UN and gave it the title, "A Dangerous Place". This followed numerous successful attempts by the newly independent countries of the South to get resolutions condemning countries like South Africa, Rhodesia and Israel for their policies on issues that the West regarded as their internal affairs. In 1970, Franck lamented the "death of Article 2(4)", which bars member states from using or threatening the use of force against the territorial integrity or political independence of another. He wrote that the prohibition against the use of force in relations between states had been eroded by wars of national liberation, the threat of a nuclear war and by regional organisations dominated by the superpowers. Both superpowers expected countries in their backyard to conform and were quite prepared to use force for this purpose. He accused India of using force against the Portuguese in Goa on the pretext of self-defence.[8] The support extended by the countries of the South, with Soviet backing, to wars of liberation and their claim that these were exceptions to Article 2(4) was characterised as anarchy by Western countries, who lamented that the safeguards incorporated in the UN Charter had been severely weakened and regional organisations supported by the Soviet Union were behaving in an authoritarian and irresponsible manner.

Moynihan also chided the United Nations for getting involved in "social, humanitarian and cultural affairs" instead of focusing on its primary task of international security. He wrote, "The League of Nations was by now vaguely remembered as having sought to distract attention from the collapse of its collective security efforts – high politics – by busying itself with the standardisation of road signs and the suppression of white slavery. The United Nations seemed to be following much the same pattern." He said that social, humanitarian and cultural matters were of importance only to the 'third world' and successive American presidents followed their lead by sending liberal ambassadors to the United Nations, which he considered the same as sending symphony orchestras abroad, where they would "testify to American concerns for social problems and do no great harm." He said that this was being done at the expense of the "legitimacy of Western political systems and democratic beliefs that the UN Charter embodied."[9]

Three major humanitarian crises during the 1970s failed to elicit action by the Security Council and Western countries regarded the intervention of their neighbours as contrary to the UN Charter. India in East Pakistan/Bangladesh in 1971, Vietnam in Cambodia in 1978 and Tanzania in Uganda in 1979 were left to their own devices to deal with the fallout of genocide in these countries. All three intervened militarily but declared their actions to be in self-defence. This was because self-defence was the only provision in the UN Charter they could cite to justify the use of force, there being no right to humanitarian intervention.

India faced three resolutions in two weeks on its intervention to stop Pakistan's atrocities in its eastern wing. The first resolution, moved by the United States, received eleven votes in favour. France and Britain abstained while Poland and the Soviet Union voted against. This resolution called upon India and Pakistan to cease hostilities and create a climate conducive to the voluntary return of the refugees to East Pakistan. Another resolution moved the next day by 8 countries, none from the permanent five, met with the same fate as did the third resolution, moved by the United States.

In the course of the debate on the first resolution the US ambassador, George H.W. Bush, commenting on India's action, declared, "The time is past when any of us could justifiably resort to war to bring about change in a neighbouring country that might better suit our national interests as we see them. All of us know – certainly the leaders of India and Pakistan know – that the human needs of our people are not met through the terrible cost of war."[10] This criticism was despite his government's awareness of the extent of the tragedy. The US consul-general to Bangladesh, Archer Blood, and 19 of his colleagues had sent a telegram lamenting their government's decision not to intervene in East Pakistan on the plea that it was an internal matter of a sovereign state, "Our government has failed to denounce the suppression of democracy. Our government has failed to denounce atrocities... [W]e have chosen not to intervene, even morally, on the grounds that the Awami conflict in which unfortunately the overworked term genocide is applicable, is purely [an] internal matter of a sovereign state."[11]

Before the outbreak of the war, India had pleaded for Security Council action to stop the genocide and violation of the human rights of the people of East Pakistan. However, it justified its use of military force as an act of self-defence against Pakistan's invasion.

Vietnam faced a similar situation when it invaded Cambodia in 1978 to put an end to the atrocities of the Pol Pot regime. Bangladesh, Bolivia, Gabon, Jamaica, Kuwait, Nigeria and Zambia introduced a resolution calling for all foreign forces to withdraw from Cambodia. The resolution stated that the preservation of sovereignty, territorial integrity and political independence of every state is a fundamental principle of the UN Charter and all countries should strictly adhere to the principle of non-interference in the internal affairs of states. The resolution was supported by 13 members of the Security Council and opposed by Czechoslovakia and the Soviet Union.[12] Akehurst summarised the international reaction, "Several of these states mentioned the Pol Pot regime's appalling violations of human rights, but nevertheless said that those violations did not entitle Vietnam to overthrow that regime. Not a single state spoke in favour of the existence of a right of humanitarian intervention."[13] Vietnam too based its military action on border incursions by Cambodia which, it claimed, had threatened its security.

During the debate, the French delegate, Jacques Leprette, acknowledged that excesses had been committed by the Pol Pot regime but asserted, "The notion that because a regime is detestable foreign intervention is justified and forcible overthrow is legitimate is extremely dangerous. That could ultimately jeopardize the very maintenance of international law and order and make the continued existence of various regimes dependent on the judgment of their neighbours."[14] The British delegate, Lord Richard, agreed, "Whatever is said about human rights in Kampuchea, it cannot excuse Vietnam, whose own human rights record is deplorable, for violating the territorial integrity of Democratic Kampuchea, an independent State Member of the United Nations . . . Respect for the sovereignty, territorial integrity and political independence of Member States is one of the corner-stones of the Charter and of the United Nations system."[15] The US ambassador, Andrew Young, was equally categorical, "[T]he fundamental principles of human rights must be respected by all Governments, one State must not use force against the territory of another State, a State must not interfere in the affairs of another State and if there is a dispute between States it must be settled peaceably."[16]

Tanzania too did not call its invasion of Uganda in 1979 to overthrow the brutal regime of Idi Amin a humanitarian intervention. It instead accused Uganda of invading its territory and justified its use of force as self-defence. Two other interventions for regime change in Africa in the same year, by France in the Central African Republic and Spain in Equatorial Guinea also did not call their actions humanitarian interventions.

When Ireland sought UN action against Britain in 1969 for its repression in Northern Ireland, the British ambassador, Lord Caradon, put up a sterling defence of national sovereignty and non-interference in internal affairs, "The principle of domestic jurisdiction is fundamental for us all. If it were breached, if it were eroded, the consequences for the United Nations and for all of us would be most serious. It needs no effort of the imagination to realize that if this necessary safeguard were no longer accepted and respected and effective, the way would be wide open to the encouragement of disunity and division and disorder. . ... There is no representative in this Council, nor indeed in the United Nations, who would be prepared to accept unwelcome interference in the domestic national affairs of his country." Lord Caradon then expounded the supremacy of Article 2 (7) in the Charter, "Neither Article 35 nor any other article can possibly be regarded as prevailing over the specific provisions of Article 2 (7)."[17]

The success of the West in the First Gulf War and its control over the Security Council, however, led to a spurt in interventions. Non-government organisations championed human rights and satellite television brought the brutalities of war directly to people's homes creating a groundswell of public demand for international action. The genocide in Rwanda and the atrocities in the civil war in Yugoslavia led to public outrage and calls for international intervention.

State sovereignty now came to be identified by Western writers as the chief impediment to effective global governance. Kate Seaman wrote, "The continuing importance which many states place on their perceived sovereign rights, and the reality that international organisations are severely limited in their abilities to challenge this also challenges that assumption, and serves to highlight the potential unsustainability of international norms."[18]

Responsibility to Protect (R2P)

Secretary-General Kofi Annan started as an ardent protagonist of humanitarian intervention. Addressing the UN Commission on Human Rights in Geneva on 7 April 1999 he recalled the killings by the Pol Pot regime in Cambodia and then the more recent ones in Rwanda, Bosnia and Kosovo and hinted at the need for redefining national sovereignty, "No government has the right to hide behind national sovereignty in order to violate the human rights or fundamental freedoms of its peoples."[19] He developed this idea further in his address to the General Assembly on 20 September 1999, in which he advocated forcefully, "To avoid repeating such tragedies in the next century, I believe, it is essential that the international community reach consensus - not only on the principle that massive and systematic violations of human rights must be checked, wherever they take place, but also on ways of deciding what action is necessary, and when, and by whom."[20]

The idea was pursued by Canada, which appointed its own commission, calling it the International Commission on Intervention and State Sovereignty (ICISS). In 2001, the Commission produced a report expounding the principle of "Responsibility to Protect". It demanded curbs on national sovereignty, "Based on our reading of state practice, Security Council precedent, established norms, guiding principles, and evolving customary international law, the Commission believes that the Charter's strong bias against military intervention is not to be regarded as absolute when decisive action is required on human protection grounds."[21] The Commission prefaced its proposal with a "responsibility to prevent." It recommended prevention of humanitarian catastrophes through aid and development assistance and added that non-forcible manoeuvres, such as diplomatic negotiations and economic sanctions should be preferred to armed intervention. It also advocated a 'responsibility to rebuild' after armed intervention, including both peacekeeping and reconstruction.

In his address to the General Assembly on 23 September 2003, Kofi Annan said that the original vision of the founding fathers of the UN was to create a world governed by rules of international behaviour and a network of institutions with the United Nations at its centre, "in which the peoples of the world could work together for the common good."[22] Annan then asked rhetorically whether it was possible to continue on the basis agreed then or whether radical changes were needed. He asserted boldly that the adequacy of both the rules and the instruments should be examined. He also noted, "Among these instruments, none is more important than the Security Council itself."

Annan appointed a high-level panel of eminent persons to examine and advise on four principal issues: (i) current challenges to international peace and security; (ii) the contribution which collective action could make to addressing these challenges; (iii) review of the functioning of the major organs of the UN; and (iv) strengthening the UN through the comprehensive reform of its institutions and processes. He also set up an inquiry under an American economist, Jeffrey Sachs, on how to promote international cooperation in solving global economic and social problems.

The high-level panel gave its report late in 2004. It was called, "A More Secure World: Our Shared Responsibility: Report of the High-level Panel on Threats, Challenges and Change."[23] It accepted the concept of R2P and maintained that the Security Council has a responsibility to protect people facing insecurity even if there is no threat to international peace and security. It concluded, "We endorse the emerging norm that there is a collective international responsibility to protect, exercisable by the Security Council authorising military intervention as a last resort, in the event of genocide and other large scale killings, ethnic cleansing or serious violations of international humanitarian law which sovereign governments have proved powerless or unwilling to prevent."[24] Jeffrey Sachs gave his report early in the following year.

Based on the reports of his two panels, Annan introduced his proposals in the General Assembly for reform on 21 March 2005, "In Larger Freedom: Towards Development, Security and Human Rights for All." Annan's proposals sought to expand the concept of security to include human security, in which development and human rights issues were intertwined with peace and security. Freedom from want and from fear was posited as a pre-requisite for peace and security and the need was asserted for the international community to be bestowed the responsibility to protect people in other countries from threats to it.

World Summit, 2005

Annan included R2P in his report and recommended it for acceptance to world leaders at the World Summit in New York in September 2005 to mark the sixtieth anniversary of the United Nations. Western countries supported the idea as did several African nations. President Benjamin Mkapa of Tanzania was among the early African leaders to call for R2P. Latin America was less enthusiastic and many developing countries in Asia opposed it. There was strong opposition from countries like India, Egypt, Syria, Iran and Pakistan. Russia and China were cautious. Significantly, the United States too had certain technical reservations. It objected on the ground that responsibility implied a legal liability, which would expose it to law suits for non-fulfilment.

Kofi Annan's task was made particularly difficult by the US ambassador to the UN, John Bolton, an unrepentant UN-baiter and ardent unilateralist, who could antagonise even the strongest US allies. Bolton was opposed to any outcome at the world summit but had to accept it due to pressure from Washington, which realised that its Western allies were keen. Nevertheless, Bolton was able to exorcise many concepts and ideas abhorrent to him. These included references to nuclear disarmament, extending cooperation to the International Criminal Court and mention of the Kyoto Protocol on climate change. A reference to the international community's "shared responsibility" to act against crimes against humanity was deleted and replaced by a more general phrase stating that the international community could "decide" to act in such circumstances. R2P was to be a right, not a legal obligation.

The text went through several changes and it appeared that no agreement would be reached. However, a late compromise text that severely qualified the concept eventually found acceptance among the tired delegates. The final text read as follows, "In this context, we are prepared to take collective action in a timely and decisive manner, through the Security Council in accordance with the Charter, including Chapter VII, on a case-by-case basis and in cooperation with relevant regional organizations as appropriate, should peaceful means be inadequate and national authorities are manifestly failing to protect their populations from genocide, war crimes, ethnic cleansing and crimes against humanity."[25] Canada championed the idea along with its proposal for a Peace Building Commission.

The Security Council then adopted Resolution 1674 which reaffirmed the "provisions of paragraphs 138 and 139 of the 2005 World Summit Outcome Document regarding the responsibility to protect populations from genocide, war crimes, ethnic cleansing and crimes against humanity."[26] However, the issue of responsibility was left vague and it was unclear if the Security Council was to be the source of authorisation or the agency for execution. The resolution did go on to demand that "all States fully implement all relevant decisions of the Security Council..."[27]

The resolution also listed the responsibilities of governments. These included the promotion of economic growth, poverty eradication, national reconciliation, good governance, democracy, the rule of law and the protection of fundamental human rights. However, the responsibilities of the international community recommended by the ICISS on conflict prevention and to nation-building were lost in the fine print as were all references to Security Council reform. The ICISS, for example, had recommended that the Security Council should keep four criteria in mind while authorising R2P: (i) The principle of right intention: the primary objective should be the alleviation of human suffering; (ii) The principle of last resort: all less invasive means should have been exhausted; (iii) The principle of proportional means: these should be the minimum required; and (iv) The principle of reasonable prospects: there should be a reasonable likelihood of success. Above all, the ICISS had recommended that the permanent five should voluntarily relinquish their exercise of veto when an action was being considered in response to a situation of genocide.

The R2P doctrine identifies four international crimes - genocide, war crimes, crimes against humanity and ethnic cleansing - as serious enough to warrant international intervention. It rejects the notion that national sovereignty can be a defence against non-interference in internal affairs in the face of these crimes. These crimes have never been defined, though in the Rome Statute of 1998, which led to the setting up of the International Criminal Court, a number of crimes drawn from various international treaties applicable to armed conflicts have been listed. However, several major countries, including three of the permanent five – the United States, Russia and China - are not parties to the Rome Statute.[28] Besides, the 2005 summit declaration was only a declaration, not a treaty ratified by member states. Declarations are statements of political intent and must be converted into treaties before they can be treated as international law. The Security Council's endorsement of the interventionist provisions of the declaration adds weight to it but it still falls short of becoming international law. This is discussed in Chapter 13.

R2P circumscribes and redefines state sovereignty by turning it from a right to a responsibility and, inducting shades of the social contract theory, maintains that a state unable to provide security to its citizens forfeits it. When this happens, the international community must step in to assume this responsibility. In principle, the concept built into the world summit declaration is that R2P is to be exercised by the international community against a state committing any of the four identified international crimes. However, R2P enthusiasts also include protecting human rights in this list.

The collection of 150 heads of state and government at New York at the World Summit was intended to herald a new era of activism in its work. R2P was intended to make the United Nations the protector of the people of countries ruled by repressive regimes. However, after the grand declaration, the details were left vague. No legal accountability was imposed on the Security Council and the responsibility to protect was vested safely in the amorphous 'international community'. This was because few governments had the will or economic stamina for nation-building. The misadventures of the United States in Afghanistan and Iraq had reduced its enthusiasm. In a frank admission of this, Julianne Smith, a former deputy national security adviser to the US Vice President, Joseph R. Biden, said about the US invasion of Iraq: "We have to be clear-eyed about the limits of US engagement . . . At the end of the day, the United States does not control what happens in Iraq." Smith, who is now at the Centre for a New American Security, was outlining the limits of responsibility the US is prepared to undertake when it exercises R2P.[29]

Security Council Resolution 1706 (2006) invoked the concept of R2P for the first time while deploying a peacekeeping force in Darfur in Sudan. In its preambular section, it recalled UNSC Resolution 1674 (2006) on the protection of civilians in armed conflict and which reaffirmed paragraphs 138 and 139 of the 2005 UN World Summit outcome document.[30] It was once again cited in Resolution 1973 (2011) on Libya. While Kofi Annan billed R2P as a revolution in international affairs, others downplayed it by saying that it was not a new concept. They also pointed out that there was limited agreement at the summit. The primary responsibility for protecting its people still vested with the state and R2P could be exercised only with specific approval of the Security Council.

Human Rights

One of the principles of the UN Charter is "promoting and encouraging respect for human rights and for fundamental freedoms for all without distinction as to race, sex, language or religion" [Article 1(3)]. However, the very next Article enjoins upon the UN not to "intervene in matters which are essentially within the domestic jurisdiction of any State." During the Cold War, the Security Council rarely imposed sanctions or took any other measures against a state for human rights violations. The only exceptions were Southern Rhodesia and South Africa on which limited sanctions were imposed. The Security Council made occasional references to human rights in its resolutions, such as in Resolution 120 on Hungary in 1956, Resolution 161 on the Congo in 1961 and Resolution 203 on the Dominican Republic in 1965, but it was treated as an internal matter.

After the Cold War, the Security Council started taking interest in human rights but it remained ambivalent about its link with international peace and security. Resolution 688 (1991) on Iraq is considered to have drawn such a link in its preambular paragraph which reads as follows, "Gravely concerned by the repression of the Iraqi civilian population in many parts of Iraq which led to massive flow of refugees towards and across international frontiers to cross-border incursions which threaten international peace and security in the region." A close reading of this text reveals that the threat to international peace and security is attributed to the cross-border flow of refugees, not to the repression of civilians. A Security Council Research Report in 2016 noted that the Council had never held a formal meeting with a stated focus on human rights.[31] It had only been discussed in informal meetings and retreats. The Security Council has tried to show its commitment to human rights by making its protection part of the objectives of some peacekeeping missions. The Council also holds regular briefings by human rights investigators, a practice that started in 2002. The High Commissioner for Human Rights also briefs the Council periodically.

Although human rights are now projected as one of the pillars of the UN all permanent five members have vetoed resolutions against their allies and friendly states. The US, Britain and France did so on numerous occasions in the past in the case of Southern Rhodesia, South Africa and Namibia and continue to do so in the Middle East. Russia and China have worked together to defeat resolutions on Myanmar, Syria and Zimbabwe.[32]

The Office of the High Commissioner for Human Rights in Geneva lists nine treaties as core international human rights instruments.[33] None of the permanent five has ratified all nine. France with eight and Britain with seven display a high degree of commitment. Russia and China with six each can be said to pass muster. But the United States, which has ratified only three, can hardly boast of setting an example of good international behaviour. China's record may look good in numbers, but the fact that it has not ratified the International Covenant on Civil and Political Rights, which has been by 170 countries also sets a poor example.

Terrorism

After the terrorist attacks on its territory on 11 September 2001, commonly called 9/11, the US invaded Afghanistan, where the Al Qaeda, which had carried out the attack, was based. It did not seek authorisation from the Security Council and decided, instead, to act under its right of self-defence. As Marquand put it, "The Bush administration's answer was a new strategic doctrine, based on an explicit principle of 'pre-emption', or preventive war. It was not enough to wait to be attacked and then fight back. It was necessary to take 'anticipatory action' – if need be, 'pre-emptively' and unilaterally."[34] The legality of this action has not been sufficiently examined. The view that a terrorist act by a non-state organisation constitutes an armed attack warranting retaliation against another country in self-defence also has many adherents but is by no means universally accepted.

There is no comprehensive international convention on terrorism, nor is there a universally accepted definition of it. Global rules on terrorism flow from about a dozen treaties and protocols prohibiting specific acts. These treaties deal with acts and sectors like aviation, the safety of nuclear materials, marking of plastic explosives, financing of terrorism, attacks on government officials and diplomats, hostage-taking, terrorist attacks on airports, off-shore oil platforms, ships, and such others. Security Council resolutions lay down the obligations of member states in combating terrorism, without attempting to define it. It first condemned terrorism in 1985 when addressing the problem of hostage-taking and abduction (Resolution 579). Four years later it condemned terrorism twice, against attacks on civil aviation (Resolution 635) and against hostage-taking (Resolution 638). It did so again in 1991 while demanding that Iraq renounce terrorism as a condition for a ceasefire (Resolution 687). A year later it demanded that Libya surrender the two accused in the Lockerbie case. When Libya refused it imposed sanctions (Resolutions 731, 748 and 883).

In 1995, the Council imposed sanctions on Sudan when it refused to extradite three suspects to Ethiopia (Resolutions 1044 and 1070). In 1998 it asked all states to punish those who had attacked the US embassies in Kenya and Tanzania (Resolution 1189). The next year it asked Afghanistan not to harbour terrorists and to surrender Osama bin Laden (Resolutions 1214 and 1267) and when the Taliban regime in Afghanistan refused, sanctions were imposed by Council (Resolutions 1333 and 1390).

In 2001, the Council asked all States to punish the perpetrators of 9/11. A Counter-Terrorism Committee was set up to monitor the implementation of Resolution 1373. Later, in 2005 the Security Council authorised multinational forces in Iraq to use force to prevent and control terrorism (Resolution 1546). The US itself has used force frequently in response to terrorism without seeking UN authorisation. It treats the resolutions adopted by the Security Council after 9/11 as an open-ended authorisation and also considers its anti-terror strikes as self-defence in the ongoing war on terror.

Democracy

Democracy and decolonisation were not on the agenda of the permanent five when they drafted the UN Charter nor was it a foreign policy objective of any of them. Few of the countries participating in the San Francisco conference were democracies, and some, like India, were not even independent. During the Cold War, the Western countries did not make democracy a goal of their foreign policy, even though they styled themselves as the 'free world'. It was the Soviet Union, a communist country that espoused the dictatorship of the proletariat, that played a key role in the first declaration on decolonisation adopted by the General Assembly in 1960, the 'Declaration on the Granting of Independence to Colonial Countries and Peoples'.[35] This resolution reaffirmed the right of self-determination and the right of all peoples to determine their political status. It declared that subjecting people to alien subjugation constitutes the denial of human rights and is an impediment to attaining world peace. The resolution was made possible by 19 newly-independent states joining the UN that year. It was adopted by 89 votes to none, but there were 9 abstentions, three of them permanent members of the Security Council – the US, Britain and France. Other colonial powers – Belgium, Portugal, and Spain also abstained, as did Australia, South Africa and the Dominican Republic. The US declared that the resolution was unnecessary since the application of Article 73 of the Charter had successfully enabled 34 countries to become independent since 1946. This view ignored the fact that this article dealt only with the trust territories, not the colonies of its European allies. Britain argued that going through colonial rule was a necessary phase of development for the colonies before attaining independence.

However, while the General Assembly tried to guide the United Nations towards decolonisation, the Security Council remained mired in its post-war colonial mindset even a decade later. As early as in 1961, Security Council Resolution 163 had declared that the conflict in Angola could endanger international peace and security but Portugal took no action to withdraw. Angola and Mozambique continued to be under Portuguese occupation as also Guinea Bissau and Cape Verde. Speaking in the Security Council on 22 November 1972 India's ambassador, Samar Sen, demanded that the UN declare the territories independent as Portugal had no legal authority on them and that its presence in these territories was a form of aggression. The British ambassador, Colin Crowe, expressed support for self-determination in the territory but insisted that the freedom struggle "should be pursued only by peaceful means and in accordance with the provisions of the Charter." The US ambassador, George Bush, said, "We recognize Portuguese sovereignty, even while we continually urge Portugal, as we do, to permit the exercise of self-determination in these territories." The United States maintained that full freedom was only one of the alternatives available to people in their exercise of the right of self-determination. They could decide to have other forms of political status as mentioned in the 1960 resolution of the General Assembly.

After the Cold War, the Western countries turned the tables on the South by declaring that democracy was an essential pre-requisite for international peace, for human rights and for sustainable development. The goal of democracy was placed on the agenda of the UN by Boutros-Ghali in his 'Agenda for Democratisation', presented to the General Assembly in December 1996. He declared that democracy leads to a more open, more participatory and less authoritarian society and that the idea was gaining adherence all over the world and countries were turning to the UN for assistance in attaining it, "......just as newly-independent states turned to the United Nations for support during the era of decolonization, so today, following another wave of accessions to statehood and political independence, member states are turning to the United Nations for support in democratization."[36] He noted that peacekeeping mandates of the UN now included both the restoration of democracy and the protection of human rights. The report declared that the UN Charter, the Universal Declaration of Human Rights and the Declaration on the Granting of

Independence to Colonial Countries and Peoples are the three primary documents which provide a clear and solid foundation for the UN's role and responsibility in democratisation. He also conceded, in passing, that there was growing interest among member states in the democratisation of the United Nations itself.

If the Security Council is to promote democracy in member states, it is legitimate to look at the permanent five and examine their commitment to it. Four of the permanent five declare themselves to be democracies. The constitution of China, however, declares it to be a socialist state "under the people's democratic dictatorship".[37] Whatever be the legal interpretation of this phrase it puts in doubt the country's commitment to democracy at home even if it seeks to promote it abroad through its permanent membership of the Security Council.

Climate Change

The idea that a change in the earth's atmosphere could be a threat to international security was recognised in one of the first international conferences on this issue, the Toronto Conference in 1988. Climate change negotiations have been taking place in the UN in the UN Framework Convention on Climate Change, formed in 1992. However, some Western countries have been pressing for the matter to be taken up by the Security Council as well. Britain convened a meeting of the Council to discuss the issue in 2007. India, China and Russia opposed the discussion on the plea that the Security Council lacked expertise in the matter. No resolution was adopted at the meeting, but in 2012 the Council issued a Presidential Statement on the security implications of climate change.[38] The Security Council has not been able to adopt a resolution on climate change due to the opposition of several countries, including the US, but in 2017 it adopted a resolution on the conflict-affected population of Lake Chad Basin. The lengthy resolution was on the threat of the terrorist group, Boko Haram, to the countries in the region, Cameroon, Chad, Niger and Nigeria, but included a paragraph acknowledging the impact of climate change on their stability.[39] Such resolutions on issues that capture the imagination of people may give the impression that the Security Council is doing its job but they divert its attention from its primary responsibility.

International Tribunals

After the collapse of the Soviet Union, Western countries set up a new genre of courts to try people in high places for crimes committed by them, including actions in the exercise of the sovereign authority of states. The International Criminal Tribunal for Yugoslavia (ICTY) in 1993 and the International Tribunal for Rwanda (ICTR) in the following year were *ad hoc* judicial bodies appointed by the Security Council to try specific individuals for "serious violations" of insufficiently defined in "international humanitarian law".

Under international law, it is for states to prosecute violations of it in their national courts. Jurisdictional disputes are frequent in international law, especially in extra-territorial crime, since states claim both territorial jurisdiction and jurisdiction over their nationals and means of transport, such as ships and aircraft. However, until the Second World War, national courts were the only judicial system for trying violators. After the war, the victors set up war crimes tribunals for Germany and Japan. The United Nations was not involved in these tribunals. The UN Charter did not provide for any international judicial system for trying individuals for violations of international law.

In 1993, the Security Council constituted the first international tribunal, the International Criminal Tribunal for Yugoslavia, after making a determination that the situation constituted a threat to international peace and security.[40] It recalled Resolution 764 (1992) which had provided that all parties must abide by their obligations under the Geneva Conventions of 1949 and "persons who commit or order the commission of grave breaches of the conventions are individually responsible in respect of such breaches."[41] The tribunal was charged with prosecuting those who had violated international law in the wars conducted by former Yugoslavia.[42] It indicted a head of state, Slobodan Milosevic. It was the first to convict anyone for genocide and the first to treat rape as a crime against humanity. The tribunal indicted 161 individuals of whom 90 were convicted. It was wound up at the end of 2017.

In 1994, the Security Council set up the International Criminal Tribunal for Rwanda. Resolution 955 (1994) stated that the Security Council was acting under Chapter VII and in response to a request from the Government of Rwanda for prosecuting persons responsible for genocide and other serious violations of international humanitarian law. The secretary-general was asked to make arrangements for the effective functioning of the tribunal and a detailed statute was appended to the resolution. The statute identified crimes like genocide, crimes against humanity, violations of Article 3 common to the Geneva Conventions, and of Additional Protocol II of 1977 to the Geneva Conventions. The tribunal was given primacy over national courts. Its statute also provided for the procedure for the election of judges by the General Assembly and stated that the other rules of procedure would be adapted from the ICTY. The resolution stated that the penalty would be limited to imprisonment and return of any property acquired by criminal conduct. It provided for an Appeals Chamber and all states were asked to cooperate with the tribunal in the arrest and other trial procedures of the accused.[43] ICTR was the first international tribunal to convict a former head of state, Prime Minister Jean Kambanda of Rwanda, for genocide. The ICTR indicted 93 individuals of whom 62 were convicted. The tribunal was closed at the end of 2015, but its Appeals Chamber is still working.

While the details of the ICTY had been left to be determined by the secretary-general, the statute of the ICTR was adopted by the Security Council. The prosecutors of both tribunals were approved by the Security Council on nomination by the secretary-general. The Security Council in association with the General Assembly appointed not only the prosecutor but also the judges of the tribunal, laid down the procedures, defined the crimes and the penalty on a case-by-case basis. The tribunals enumerated the crimes very broadly. In both, personal responsibility was to be fixed for violations of the Geneva Conventions even though the conventions themselves do not provide for such liability. Besides, the United States is not even a party to the Additional Protocol II. The Security Council summarily decided that violations of the Geneva Conventions constituted a threat to international peace and security and, therefore, came within the purview of its powers. No reference was made to the ICJ to ascertain if the actions of the Security Council or the procedures of the tribunals were in conformity with the Charter. The tribunals were given primacy over national courts in supersession of the sovereignty of these countries.

Both Yugoslavia and Rwanda tribunals had similar structures. They had a chamber of judges and a prosecutor. Until 2003 they had the same prosecutor. The judges were elected by the General Assembly for a term of 4 years. The chamber was divided into multiple trial chambers and an appeals chamber. The internationally recognised principles of due process were applied: presumption of innocence, trial in the presence of the accused, right to a speedy trial, right to examine witnesses, right to appeal, provision of legal aid, witness protection program, and life term as the maximum sentence. The sentence was to be served in a country willing to accept the prisoner. The Yugoslavia tribunal was based in The Hague and the Rwanda tribunal in Arusha. The Rwanda tribunal was the first to develop the concept of genocide under the Geneva Conventions of 1948 and make indictments for it.

The tribunals proved to be extremely slow, expensive and riddled with serious logistical problems. They spent $ 1 billion to prosecute about 250 persons. In 2003, the Security Council had called upon them to finish their work by 2008. They had no enforcement powers, so they depended upon states to arrest and bring the accused to them. NATO accounted for one-third of all arrests for the Yugoslavia tribunal. Serbia itself surrendered Milosevic in June 2001 under threat of sanctions.

The US generously funded ICTY and ICTR. This ensured that the ICTY Prosecutor decided not to investigate the bombing of Serbia by NATO in 1999. Western countries had also provided personnel free of cost from their own bureaucracies for these tribunals. However, in 2000, when Sierra Leone asked the Security Council to constitute a tribunal to try those responsible for crimes during its civil war, which included killing some UN peacekeepers, the Council balked at the suggestion. It instead authorised the UN secretary-general to help Sierra Leone set up a tribunal, a hybrid, called the Special Court for Sierra Leone.[44]

The absence of Security Council authority made it difficult for the Sierra Leone court to get one of its accused, Liberian President Charles Taylor, extradited first from Ghana where he was when indicted in 2003 and later from Nigeria where he fled. He was finally arrested by Nigeria, under African pressure, while trying to flee to Cameroon. The Sierra Leone court also had difficulty prosecuting minors, though nearly half of the Revolutionary United Front soldiers were minors.

Another hybrid court was the Extraordinary Chamber for Cambodia in June 1997. Cambodia sought UN assistance to prosecute those in Khmer Rouge regime from 1975 to 1979. The Security Council did not act because of the fear of a Chinese veto. The matter was taken up in the General Assembly which authorised the secretary-general to assist Cambodia. Indecision in Cambodia and issues of sovereignty led to delays but the chamber was finally set up in March 2003 and remains in operation.

What was the source of authority of the Security Council to set up the tribunals? Kirgis finds none, "No legislative authority for statutes such as these is to be found in the Dumbarton Oaks or San Francisco plans." Dusco Tadic, an accused, questioned the jurisdiction of the ICTY. The Appeals

Court of the ICTY, which was part of the trial framework set up by the Council, examined the issue and declared that the tribunal was competent to examine the validity of its establishment. It said that there should be limits to the powers of the Council and tried to put a juridical construct on the Charter, "The Security Council is an organ of an international organization, established by a treaty which serves as a constitutional framework for that organization. The Security Council is thus subjected to certain constitutional limitations, however broad its powers under the constitution may be. Those powers cannot, in any case, go beyond the limits of the jurisdiction of the organization at large, not to mention other specific limitations or those which may derive from the internal division of power within the organization. In any case, neither the text nor the spirit of the Charter conceives of the Security Council as *legibus solutus* [unbound by law]."[45]

However, the Appeals Chamber then declared that under Article 39 the Security Council "exercises a very wide discretion." It held that the only limit to this power was that its decisions must remain "within the limits of the Purposes and Principles of the Charter."[46] As regards the powers of the Council under Articles 41 and 42, it observed, "Articles 41 and 42 leave to the Security Council such a wide choice as to not warrant searching, on functional or other grounds, for even wider and more general powers than those already expressly provided for in the Charter."[47] It declared that the measures set out in Article 41 are merely illustrative examples and do not exclude other measures. The only limit the Chamber could find was that under Article 41 the Council could not use force. This was reserved under Article 42. After examining various provisions of Chapter VII, the Chamber concluded, "The establishment of the international tribunal falls squarely within the powers of the Security Council under Article 41." The Chamber argued that the list of sanctions in Article 41 was not exhaustive and the Security Council with its wide powers under Chapter VII could establish an international tribunal under it. This was notwithstanding the fact that the Security Council resolution itself did not mention any article.

Equally unclear is the understanding of what constitutes a violation of international humanitarian law. Kirgis cites the US permanent representative, Madeleine Albright, to show her extreme interpretation of international humanitarian law. She considered any interference by the Bosnian factions in the delivery of emergency food supplies to be a violation. Nevertheless, Kirgis concludes that the tribunals were independent of political control and their adjudicative procedure "appears" to be "essentially fair".[48]

International Criminal Court

The success in setting up the *ad hoc* tribunals for Yugoslavia and Rwanda set in motion the creation of a permanent international criminal court. Delegates from 140 countries met in Rome in 1998 to negotiate the Rome Statute which set up the International Criminal Court (ICC). The statute was adopted on 17 July 1998 by 120 to 7 with 21 abstentions. The seven countries voting against were: the US, China, Iraq, Libya, Yemen, Qatar and Israel. The ICC came into existence on 1 July 2002.

The US favoured adhoc tribunals set up by the Security Council rather than a permanent body with universal jurisdiction to try cases of genocide, crimes against humanity and war crimes. In the Rome talks, it argued that the ICC should only have jurisdiction in cases where the state consents to the trial of its national or citizens of non-party states through Security Council authorisation. Due to this opposition, the ICC was given "complementary", not "universal" jurisdiction. The ICC has jurisdiction only if the accused is a national of a state party or the crime has been committed on the territory of a state party. Otherwise, the case can only be taken up by the ICC when referred to it by the Security Council. Article 98 of its statute also does not permit the ICC to proceed with a request for surrender which would require the requested state to act inconsistently with its obligations under international agreements. The US then went to great lengths to safeguard its nationals from being taken to the ICC. It signed bilateral treaties with over 100 countries obliging them not to refer US nationals to the ICC if a crime was committed on their territory. The US Congress passed the American Service-Members Protection Act, 2002, cutting off military aid to countries that did not sign the treaty. The Act, nicknamed 'The Hague Invasion Act', authorises the US president to use "all means necessary" for the release of an American or allied personnel detained in a country on behalf of the ICC. India also signed such a treaty, which provides mutual protection against a reference to the ICC. This, however, has not prevented the US from supporting a Security Council resolution in 2011 on Libya, referring it to the ICC though it had abstained on a similar resolution on Sudan six years earlier.[49]

Administration of Territories

After the First World War, the administration of the colonial territories of Japan and Germany, including those under the mandate of the League of Nations since World War I, was assigned to the Allied powers, the US, the Britain, Italy, Australia, New Zealand, France and Belgium, under the supervision of the Trusteeship Council of the UN. Over the next five decades, eleven countries were formed out of these colonies and given independence.

In the late 1990s, the Security Council found itself holding two territories that had broken away from their parent country but were unable to function immediately as sovereign countries. Kosovo's secession from Serbia and Timor Leste's from Indonesia came in divergent circumstances but in both cases, the Security Council chose to place them under its own administration. In Kosovo, it set up the 'UN Interim Administration Mission in Kosovo' (UNMIK) under Resolution 1244 (1999), with the mandate to promote democracy, human rights, self-governance and development, run the civil administration, support coordination with international humanitarian organisations and ensure the safe return of refugees. Kosovo unilaterally declared itself independent in 2008 and UNMIK reduced its operations, handing most of it to European Union mission there. Kosovo's recognition as a sovereign country remains controversial and its entry to the UN has been blocked by Russia, which wants it to settle its differences with Serbia first.

Timor Leste's separation was less violent since Indonesia agreed, albeit reluctantly, to a UN-supervised referendum in 1999 which was overwhelmingly in favour of independence. This former Portuguese colony had been annexed by Indonesia, soon after it broke away from Portugal in 1975. The Security Council set up a UN interim administration, the UN Transitional Administration in East Timor (UNTAET), which eventually arranged for its independence. Timor Leste became independent and a member of the UN in 2002.

Both these interim administrations were set up by the Security Council under its own jurisdiction, instead of being handed over to the Trusteeship Council. The Security Council saw nothing unusual in turning itself from a policeman to an administrator. In both Kosovo and Timor Leste, the Security Council authorised member states to set up an occupation force and it ran the civil administration itself. While this worked reasonably smoothly in Timor Leste it ran into serious problems in Kosovo.

The Authority for the New Mandates

The Security Council has been adding these powers to its armoury without any amendment to the Charter. In a constitutional democracy, the executive wing of the government requires a constitutional amendment or legislative mandate for such accretion of power. If the Security Council deserves the power to intervene in the domestic matters of a state to perform such functions as enforcing human rights or delivering humanitarian assistance, the UN Charter should be suitably amended. The Security Council cannot expand its powers on its own, especially since its actions are neither subject to the General Assembly's control nor to review by the ICJ. Member states had ratified the UN Charter and agreed to accept and carry out the decisions of the Security Council under Article 25, despite its undemocratic structure and procedures, on the explicit understanding that it would not interfere in their internal affairs. The mandated review of the Charter has not taken place for half a century and Security Council reform remains stuck. The permanent members are vehemently opposed to any reform, especially of their veto. More than seventy years have passed without any substantive change in the composition and working methods of the Security Council. This state of affairs has seriously affected the authority and functioning of the Security Council and will continue to undermine its legitimacy.

Another problem with this increase in the Security Council's powers is that the countries championing it are unable to back their promises with action. Public support for such interventions has been distinctly lacking, especially in Europe. Writing about R2P in his autobiography, the British prime minister, Tony Blair was candid enough to admit, "But however much it fascinated me (and some others), it didn't cut much ice with the British public. Throughout 1999 and particularly around Kosovo, we were aware the government was losing support."[50] Despite his forceful espousal of ground intervention in Kosovo, Blair could not persuade his allies in NATO and had to settle for bombardment from the air, with its concomitant collateral damage. A look at the military interventions establishes that only the United States, and to some extent, Russia, have the capacity to intervene in lands beyond their borders. All other countries can at best intervene in neighbouring countries. This places the Security Council at the mercy of the superpowers for the implementation of its resolutions.

Endnotes

1   Article 1.3 of the UN Charter.

2   UN Document, S/RES/1308 (2000) of 17 July 2000.

3   UN Document, S/RES/2177(2014) of 18 September 2014.

4   UN Document, S/RES/2331(2016) of 20 December 2016.

5   UN Document, S/RES/1325 (2000).

6   Quoted in Brownlie, p. 341.

7   Policy Document No. 148, British Year Book of International Law, Vol. 57, 1986, p. 614.

8   T. M. Franck. *Who Killed Article 2(4)? Or: Changing Norms Governing the Use of Force by States*. (64, American Journal of International Law 809, 1970), p. 811 and 835. Goa was a Portuguese colony in India since 1510. Unlike the French who left their colonies in India soon after the British, the Portuguese held on until they were ousted in 1961.

9   Daniel P. Moynihan. *A Dangerous Place* (Bombay: Allied Publishers, 1979), pp. 10-11.

10 George Bush, Statement at the 1606th meeting of the UNSC on 4 December 1971. UN Document S/PV/1606 on draft resolution S/10416, p. 19.

11 Gary Jonathan Bass. *The Blood Telegram* (New York: Random House, 2013), pp. 77-78.

12 UNSC draft resolution S/13027, 15 January 1979.

13 Michael Akehurst. *Humanitarian Intervention*. Chapter in Hedley Bull [Ed.], *Intervention in World Politics*. (Oxford: Clarendon Press, 1984), p. 97.

14 SCOR, Meeting No. 2108, 11 January 1979, p. 4.

15 SCOR, Meeting No. 2108, 11 January 1979, pp 6-7.

16 SCOR, Meeting No. 2108, 11 January 1979, p. 7.

17 SCOR, Meeting No. 1503, 20 August 1969, p. 1.

18 Kate Seaman. *UN-Tied Nations: The United Nations, peacekeeping and Global Governance* (Farnham, Surrey: Ashgate, 2014), p. 16.

19 Kofi Annan. *We the Peoples – A UN for the 21st Century* (London: Paradigm Publishers, 2014), p. 205.

20 Annan. *We the Peoples*, p. 208.

21 ICISS, 2001, p. 16.

22   Annan. *We the Peoples*, p. 98.

23 UN Document A/59/565.

24 UN Document A/59/565, p. 35

25 UN Document A/59/565, para 139.

26 UN Document S/Res/1674(2006), para 4.

27 UN Document S/Res/1674(2006), para 10.

28 The United States, Russia and China.

29 International New York Times, 10 January 2014.

30 UN Document S/Res/1706 (2006), preambular para 2.

31 UNSC Research Report, 25 January 2016. (www.securitycouncilreport .org).

32 For more details see Bruno Stagno Ugarte and Jared Genser. *The United Nations Security Council in the Age of Human Rights*. (Cambridge University Press, 2014), pp. 25-26.

33 International Convention on Elimination of Discrimination against Women, International Convention on Elimination of Racial Discrimination, International Covenant on Economic, Social and Cultural Rights, International Covenant on Civil and Political Rights, Convention on the Rights of the Child, Convention on the Rights of Persons with Disabilities, Convention against Torture, Convention for the Protection of All Persons from Enforced Disappearance, and Convention on the Rights of Migrant Workers.

34 David Marquand. *The End of the West* (Princeton University Press, 2009), p. 25.

35 UN Document A/Res/1514(1960) of 14 December 1960.

36 UN document A/51/761, para 5.

37 Article 1 of the Constitution of the People's Republic of China. [www.npc.gov.cn/englishnpc/Constitution/2007-11/15/content_1372963.htm].

38 UN Document, S/PRST/2011/15.

39 UN Document, S/RES/2349(2017).

40 UN Document, S/RES/808(1993).

41 UN Document, S/RES/764 (1992), para 10.

42 UNSC Resolution 827 (1993).

43 UNSC Resolution 955 (1994).

44 UNSC Resolution 1315 (2000).

45 Appeals Chamber of the International Tribunal for Yugoslavia, Decision on the Defence Motion for Interlocutory Appeal on Jurisdiction in *Prosecutor v. Dusko Tadic*, 2 October 1995, para 28.

46 ICTY, Appeals Chamber Decision in Prosecutor v. Dusko Tadic, 2 October 1995.

47 Appeals Chamber of the International Tribunal for Yugoslavia, Decision on the Defence Motion for Interlocutory Appeal on Jurisdiction in *Prosecutor v. Dusko Tadic*, 2 October 1995. Para 31.

48 Frederic L. Kirgis. *The Security Council's First Fifty Years.* (American Journal of International Law, Vol. 59, 1995, pp. 506-539), p. 523.

49 UNSC Resolutions 1593 (2005) on Sudan and 1970 (2011) on Libya.

50 Tony Blair. *A Journey* (London: Hutchinson, 2010), p. 250.

12 Charter-Compatibility of Military Actions

The compatibility with the UN Charter of the Security Council's practice of authorising member states to undertake military action on its behalf is taken for granted. Certain provisions of the Charter are cited in support and various other arguments put forward. In the absence of review by the International Court of Justice or accountability to the General Assembly, the validity of these arguments has never been independently and authoritatively examined.

Is the Security Council's practice of authorising member states to take military action on its behalf compatible with the Charter? Does the Charter provide for the Council to delegate its authority of military action under Article 42 and is the Council fulfilling its mandate under the Charter by doing so?

In its advisory opinion on the *Continued Presence of South Africa in Namibia case, 1971,* the ICJ had noted that the Charter gives extraordinarily wide powers to the Security Council for maintaining international peace and security. The only condition it imposes is that it should act within "the fundamental principles and purposes found in Chapter I of the Charter". The Security Council should ordinarily have no need to transgress such generously endowed powers in order to fulfil its mandate, but it has made heavy weather of it. The divide within the permanent five and their refusal to meet their Charter commitments has compelled it to resort two innovative practices – peacekeeping operations and authorised military action. Both had innocuous origins in the impromptu measures taken in the late 1940s. Peacekeeping operations are non-coercive and consensual and have been relatively easily accepted by member states. Authorised military actions, on the other hand, have been questioned and remain controversial.

Enforcement action using military force has always been delegated by the Council to member states. A report by Lakhdar Brahimi in 2002 had noted, "Where enforcement action is required, it has consistently been entrusted to coalitions of willing States, with the authorization of the Security Council, acting under Chapter VII of the Charter."[1] This practice has been given different names by critics - privatisation, franchise, contracting, self-help and half-way house. It has also been described as taking recourse to Article 42 ½. The World Summit meeting in 2005 used the term 'mandated' action. The Security Council itself has used 'authorised' when addressing member states in some resolutions but also 'recommend' or 'call upon' in others.

Chapter VII of the UN Charter, while conferring the power of military action on the Security Council, is silent on whether it can delegate it to member states. Bjola points out, "The legal provisions of the United Nations' Charter offer imprecise and insufficient criteria for discriminating properly between legitimate versus illegitimate uses." He adds, "[T]he adoption of a resolution by the UN Security Council is usually deemed sufficient for granting full legitimacy to certain military intervention, although the manner in which this consensus is reached is rarely questioned."[2] The issue of its compatibility with the Charter has engaged international law experts since the Korea operation.

The Charter's prohibition of the use of force by member states is quite categorical. Member states have pledged to abjure the use of force, even the threat of it, under Article 2(4). It permits them to use force only in self-defence, a provision that was not present in the Dumbarton Oaks text. It was inserted at San Francisco on the insistence of some member states but was made distinctly subordinate to the authority of the Security Council. Member states were required to report the measures taken by them immediately to the Security Council and cease operations as soon as it took appropriate measures. In addition, the Charter provided an interim provision in Article 106 for the permanent five to take 'joint action' pending the formation of the UN Force.

What provisions of the Charter can be said to permit such authorisation being given to member states to take military action on behalf of the Security Council?

Interpretation of Article 48

Article 48 is often cited as the authority for authorising military action. Votaries of this view maintain that since differences with the Soviet Union were never far from the surface, the framers of the Charter kept open the possibility of member states taking military action on behalf of the Security Council to implement its decisions. The article states, "The action required to carry out the decisions of the Security Council for the maintenance of international peace and security shall be taken by all the members of the United Nations or by some of them, as the Security Council may determine." The article empowers the Security Council to determine which states shall take action to carry out its decisions, either directly or through international agencies of which they are members.

However, Article 48 does not specify if the 'action' it refers to are sanctions under Article 41 or military action under Article 42. Various terms have been used interchangeably in the Charter for the two actions. Article 50 uses the terms "preventive or enforcement measures" without clarifying whether it is referring to sanctions or military action. Later, in the chapter on regional arrangements, the Charter, while authorising the Security Council to utilise regional arrangements, uses the term "enforcement action" and provides that the Security Council may utilise regional arrangements for enforcement action "under its authority." This is a much more explicit reference to authorisation of military action than Article 48. It is an authority conferred on the Security Council, not on regional arrangements, and specifies that the action will be taken under its authority. Article 53 further reinforces this point by stating, "[N]o enforcement action shall be taken under regional arrangements or by regional agencies, without the authorization of the Security Council." There is only one exception permitted to this and that is action against an enemy state of World War II. These provisions confirm that the framers of the Charter wanted military action to be taken only by the Security Council or by regional organisations acting under its authority. Article 48 does not contain the safeguards provided in Article 53 and the 'action' mentioned in it can only be construed to refer to sanctions under Article 41, not military action.

It would also be useful to look at the interpretation of the article by Stettinius in his report to the US President after the San Francisco Conference. Stettinius had reported, "While security and world peace are of universal concern, the reality of geography must also be considered. This applies especially, though not solely to the lesser powers, whose military effectiveness in areas remote from their home territories is likely to be slight. One must recognize also a distinction between world-wide responsibilities of the Great Powers and the more restricted scope of activities of the lesser states. These considerations are accounted for in Article 48, Paragraph 1, which provides in substance that the Security Council may determine each instance which states or groups of states are to carry out its decisions. In addition, this Article provides that the member states shall fulfil their undertakings not only directly but also through their action in other international agencies of which they are members. Under this provision, for example, in the event of economic sanctions against a particular aggressor, the Members would use their influence to prevent the International Monetary Fund from giving financial or other assistance to the aggressor."[3] It is evident from this that the framers of the Charter drafted Article 48 to enable "lesser" states to be given commensurate responsibilities in the enforcement of sanctions. It was not intended to authorise the big powers to take military action.

Simma has a similar take on the article, "Basically, Art. 48 constitutes an affirmation of members' obligation under Art. 25 to accept binding decisions by the Security Council. Article 48(1) allows the Council to limit such duties to selected members while Article 48(2) makes an attempt to co-opt other international organizations into the UN peace-keeping system."[4] This point is further clarified by Simma from the debate in the Security Council on Iraq before the First Gulf War, "In the Kuwait crisis, Art. 48 was discussed as a possible basis for SC Resolution 678 (1990), authorizing the use of force by those states co-operating with the government of Kuwait. According to the clear wording of Article 48, however, this provision refers only to the execution of decisions of the SC which find their basis in other provisions of the Charter, notably Articles 41 and 42, and cannot, therefore, be used as an independent authority for enforcement measures."[5]

Schachter also takes the same view in the context of Resolution 678 on Iraq, "Article 48 was not applicable, however, to the use of armed force authorized by the Council in Resolution 678....by its terms Article 48 did not apply to such permissive action, whereas it did apply to the mandatory economic and transportation embargoes required by all members."[6]

Interpreting the action referred to in Article 48 as enforcement action under Article 42, therefore, does not sit well with the security arrangement envisaged in the Charter. This provision, if so interpreted, would decentralise military action by the UN and take it back to the days of the League.

ICJ's Advisory Opinion

The advisory opinion of the International Court of Justice in the *Certain Expenses of the United Nations case, 1962,* is also cited as judicial endorsement of this practice. The question on which the Court was asked to give its advisory opinion was whether the expenses on the UN peacekeepers in the Congo and the UN Emergency Force in the Middle East, authorised by the General Assembly, constituted "expenses of the Organization" within the meaning of Article 17(2) of the UN Charter. France had questioned the authority of the General Assembly to set up these peacekeeping operations and the Soviet Union was opposed to peacekeeping *per se*. Both argued that the troops in these operations had not been provided under Article 43. The Court held that the Security Council could not be left impotent in an emergency situation in the absence of agreements under Article 43 and took the view that it was possible for it to take action under other provisions of the Charter. It said that the Security Council could, for instance, decide to police a situation without resorting to military action under Article 42. Such actions of the Security Council would constitute expenses of the organisation within the meaning of Article 17(2).

The ICJ contended, "......an argument which insists that all measures taken for the maintenance of international peace and security must be financed through agreements concluded under Article 43, would seem to exclude the possibility that the Security Council might act under some other Article of the Charter. The Court cannot accept so limited a view of the powers of the Security Council under the Charter. It cannot be said that the Charter has left the Security Council impotent in the face of an emergency situation when agreements under Article 43 have not been concluded."[7] The Court's advisory opinion was, ".....the Charter does not forbid the Security Council to act through instruments of its own choice: under Article 29 it 'may establish such subsidiary organs as it deems necessary for the performance of its functions'; under Article 98 it may entrust 'other functions' to the Secretary-General."[8] It is clear from this that the Court while referring to other means of action available to the Security Council was not referring to the delegation of military action to member states but other responsibilities to its own subsidiary organs or to the Secretary-General. This was a case of validation by the ICJ of peacekeeping operations. Authorising member states to take military action was not the issue under consideration and the advisory opinion cannot be extrapolated to it.

Better than Inaction

Another argument, which is more of a plea, is that authorised military action is a necessity since it is better than inaction. Authorising member states to take action on its behalf is better than doing nothing in the face of a threat to international peace and security. It should be treated as an implied power in the Charter because in the absence of appropriate means the Security Council would be seriously handicapped. Instead of a narrow legalistic view, a wider interpretation of the Charter is required to enable it to fulfil its Charter responsibility.

De Wet supports this line of argument, "The prevailing opinion is that the existence of Article 43 agreements is not a pre-requisite for the Security Council to resort to Article 42 of the Charter, as this would severely limit the discretion of the Security Council under this Article. Consequently, Article 42 implies that the Security Council can authorise member states to undertake military measures for the restoration or maintenance of international peace and security, where they are willing to do so."[9]

This is also the line of reasoning of Blokker, who begins by accepting that the Security Council "does not seem to take this responsibility very seriously if it leaves member states largely free to carry out these operations and if it gives away the possibility of stepping in if this went out of hand."[10] He then applies the *reductio ad absurdum* argument, "Without such powers the Council is left impotent if it is necessary to take military enforcement measures and thus the UN cannot perform the functions assigned to it by the member states."[11] He concludes, "This development of Security Council practice is clearly in line with the thrust of the relevant Charter provisions and with general principles of delegation under international law."[12]

Higgins argues that just as in the absence of Article 43 agreements the UN developed the concept of peacekeeping forces it should be within its authority under Article 42 to authorise military enforcement action to willing member states. She writes, "I could see no reason of legal analysis which proscribed any member or members from volunteering forces and the Security Council being able to use them under Article 42."[13]

Moir also uses the 'delegation better than inaction' line after offering others, "Consistent practice....... pointed to the acceptance of this, especially since the Security Council, in the continuing absence of any standing military capacity under Article 43 has had no practical option but to rely on member states."[14]

Franck says that the "franchise" approach is preferable to global inaction as it gives the UN "a modicum of influence over, and slightly multilateralizes, what would otherwise be no more than a return to a world of regional dominance by the most powerful nations of the regions."[15] He quotes from the Clinton Administration's Policy on Reforming Multilateral Peace Operations of 1994 to point out that the US will never agree to place its troops under UN command, "The greater the U.S. military role, the less likely it will be that the U.S. will agree to have a UN commander exercise overall operational control over U.S. forces. Any large-scale participation of U.S. forces in a major peace enforcement mission that is likely to involve combat should ordinarily be conducted under U.S. command and operational control or through competent regional organizations such as NATO or *ad hoc* coalitions."[16] Thus, for the UN the choice is between franchising its operation to the US and forgoing its contribution.

This argument may appear attractive but it does not stand legal scrutiny. The incapacity of the Security Council emanates directly from the refusal of the permanent five to provide troops to the Security Council. Their unwillingness to place their troops under the command of the Council should not give them to the right to use their military on its behalf. It has been seen from the *travaux préparatoires* that the permanent five were quite prepared to let the Security Council be frozen into inaction in the absence of consensus among them. The same should apply to military action in the absence of agreements under Article 43.

Authorising Regional Organisations

It is also argued by the supporters of this practice that the principle of delegated military action is recognised in the Charter in Article 53 under which the Security Council can utilise regional organisations for enforcement action. Moir contends that the Security Council has been using regional organisations and peacekeeping missions for enforcement action so it should be allowed to delegate such action to member states as well. Blokker also holds that the principle of the Security Council utilising member states is not alien to the Charter, although he adds, "The widely used practice of authorization resolution fits in badly with the Charter system."[17] It should be kept in mind, however, that this provision was incorporated on the understanding that regional organisations could be entrusted with security responsibilities at the regional level just as the Security Council had been at the global. Regional organisations are based on the principle of collective security and the Security Council can fruitfully utilise them to provide security to their members. Individual member states, however, cannot claim the right to provide collective security on the analogy of regional organisations.

No Challenge from Member States

Another argument used to claim the legitimacy of delegated military action is that member states have not challenged it. A general principle of international law is that a violation of the law if not effectively challenged becomes the law. The repeated delegation of military action has made it so commonplace that it is now no longer questioned. World leaders endorsed it in 2005, "We further reaffirm the authority of the Security Council to *mandate* coercive action to maintain and restore international peace and security. We stress the importance of acting in accordance with the purposes and principles of the Charter."[18] [Emphasis added]. This declaration was not a binding resolution or treaty, but it gave greater sanctity to the protagonists of authorised military action. McCoubrey and White argue that authorisation "does appear to be legitimate exercise of power by the United Nations under Article 39, particularly as most members accept such actions as legitimate."[19]

This, however, ignores the fact that there is no forum in the UN or outside for challenging Security Council's decisions. The General Assembly is debarred from pronouncing on an issue on the agenda of the Security Council and the ICJ has no authority of judicial review. A state against which the Security Council decides to take action cannot appeal to any other organ of the United Nations. Some members, like Libya, have challenged the actions of the Security Council but to no avail. This is in contrast to the League where the affected member could request the matter to be referred to the Assembly. Though this happened in only three cases, of the 66 disputes that were brought before the League's Council, providing the alternative made the system a lot fairer.

It would not also be correct to say that authorisation resolutions have not been questioned by member states and experts. Secretary-General Pérez de Cuéllar expressed his reservations in his memoirs on the Kuwait operation against Iraq, "The Council's action in getting *carte blanche* for the conduct of military action without retaining control or influence on the command of operations on overall strategy or on conditions for terminating military action raises serious questions." He recalled that just before Resolution 678 (1990) was adopted the US Secretary of State James Baker had called on him in his office and given him a cheque of $ 185 million covering the outstanding dues of the US to the UN and said that it was exciting to be involved in making the dream of the UN founders come true.[20]

The support for authorised military action is based more on assertions than arguments well summarised by Wilson, "It must surely be the case that if the Security Council can undertake enforcement action, it should also be entitled to authorise willing actors to undertake this function on its behalf." He maintains that this view has "overwhelming support" among international lawyers.[21]

Incompatibility with the Charter

There is nothing in the proceedings of the San Francisco Conference to indicate that the framers ever considered the possibility of member states taking military action on behalf of the Security Council. They had one paramount objective – avoiding the mistakes of the League. They were determined to create an organisation with real power to act, not a debating society. The Security Council was the core of the new organisation and Chapter VII was drafted to give it absolute power to maintain international peace and security and the means to enforce it. The framers took pride in providing a military force to the Security Council and giving it the exclusive power of military action. This was one of the two main improvements in the security system of the United Nations over that of the League. The League was dependent upon the goodwill of its member states to take action against a state that threatened international peace and security. The other improvement was in the voting procedure. While the League Council required unanimity among all members for a decision, the UN Security Council could take decisions with a simple majority and unanimity was required only among the permanent members. The League's inability to take action against Japan's invasion of Manchuria and Italy's invasion of Ethiopia went unpunished, setting precedents of inaction for Hitler to take advantage of in Czechoslovakia. This was widely believed to be an important reason for the League's failure.

As seen in the previous chapter, the practice of authorising military action had a tentative and controversial beginning in the Security Council in the Korean War and, but for the Southern Rhodesia authorisation, was not resorted to again during the Cold War. Its utilisation in the subsequent two decades has always raised questions about its compatibility with the Charter.

Violation of Principle of Unanimity

The principle of unanimity among the permanent five is cardinal to the UN security system. It is the basis of their right to veto a resolution. Even the interim arrangement under Article 106 for action pending the formation of a UN Force provides for "joint action" by them.

The US violated this principle in its Korea action on a questionable technical ruling. This critically damaged the unity of the permanent five and condemned the Security Council to inaction for four decades. In the debate in the General Assembly on the Uniting for Peace resolution, the US delegate, John Foster Dulles, admitted that it was doubtful that the Security Council would have acted in the Korean War if "one of the permanent members" had not been absent. He conceded that the Korean invasion was launched on the basis of a "recommendation" of the Security Council but he argued that the Korea operation had shown that the voluntary response to a Council recommendation could be more effective than obedience to an order. He said that although the Security Council had not itself carried out the action, 53 members had done so on its recommendation. Dulles also justified taking the issue to the General Assembly under the Uniting for Peace procedure. He declared that the General Assembly, better than any other organ, reflected world opinion on the question of what was right.[22]

Kelsen examined the constitutionality of the Acheson Plan, under which the Uniting for Peace resolution had been adopted by the General Assembly, and concluded that it could be considered "as being in conformity with the Charter; but only in conformity with its wording, not in conformity with the original intention of those who framed the Charter."[23] He said that the General Assembly could hardly be considered to be competent to "recommend" the use of armed force by member states. He concluded, "Only armed forces which are placed at the disposal of an organ of the United Nations competent to dispose of these forces by decisions binding upon the members may be considered as a 'unit of the United Nations'."[24]

Interference in Domestic Affairs

Several military actions authorised by the Security Council have been to resolve internal disputes in member states. This flies in the face of a specific Charter injunction. The inviolability of national sovereignty is enshrined in Article 2(7), "Nothing contained in the present Charter shall authorize the United Nations to intervene in matters which are essentially within the jurisdiction of any State or should require the members to submit such matters under the present Charter." The article goes on to state that the principle "should not prejudice the application of enforcement measures under Chapter VII." This stipulation is interpreted by some Western experts to claim that Chapter VII powers can be invoked by the Council in the internal matters of a State, even if they do not present a threat to international peace and security. They insist that this caveat was deliberately inserted by the framers as a farsighted measure, anticipating humanitarian interventions.

In the *Tadic case*, the Appeals Chamber of the International Tribunal for Yugoslavia examined the inviolability of state sovereignty invoked by the defendant and dismissed it by claiming that certain crimes transcend it, "It should be noted that the crimes which the international tribunal has been called upon to try are not crimes of a purely domestic nature. They are really crimes which are universal in nature, well recognized in international law as serious breaches of international humanitarian law and transcending the interest of any one state. The trial chamber agrees that in such circumstances the sovereign rights of States cannot and should not take precedence over the right of the international community, to act appropriately as they affect the whole of mankind and shock the conscience of all nations of the world."[25]

This interpretation, however, needs to be examined in the context of the *travaux préparatoires* of the Charter, rather than principles of international law conjured subsequently. The principle of national sovereignty was paramount for the founders, essentially the big three. They were determined to keep the UN out of their internal matters. Their primary concern was to prevent another war that could threaten them and other members. The provision of non-intervention in the internal affairs of a state was strengthened at the San Francisco Conference on the behest of the United States, the Soviet Union, Britain and China. In the Dumbarton Oaks draft, the provision was positioned in the section dealing with the peaceful settlement of disputes by the Security Council.

At the San Francisco Conference, it was moved to the first chapter so that it could cover the actions of the entire UN, not just of the Security Council. Even the text of the article was strengthened by the US representative who opposed the replacement of "essentially" by "solely" on the ground that the former was wider in its coverage and, therefore, allowed greater protection to member states in their internal affairs.[26]

The caveat in Article 2(7) has to be read in this overriding context since the member states have pledged their obedience to the Council with this safeguard. The first part of the article affirms that the Council cannot intervene in the domestic matters of a State and the second clarifies that when the Council acts under Chapter VII the stipulated condition should not prejudice it. The caveat applies to the enforcement measure not the cause that triggers it. Thus, the Security Council can use Chapter VII to intervene in a State but only when there is a threat to international peace and security. Matters which are in the domestic jurisdiction of the State and do not constitute a threat to international peace and security cannot attract the provisions of Chapter VII.

Falk identifies intervention in the internal affairs of a country as a key problem of international law, "No contemporary problem of world order is more troublesome for an international lawyer than the analysis of the international law of 'internal war'."[27] He cited Dulles to illustrate the contradictions on this issue in the thinking of such an advocate of interventionism. Dulles stood for interventionism to combat communism but in a Congressional hearing in 1957 he warned of the risk of a third world war breaking out "......if you open the door to saying that any country which feels it is being threatened by subversive activities in another country is free to use armed force against that country...."[28]

The Security Council resolutions on apartheid policies of South Africa and Southern Rhodesia, which had been supported by the countries of Africa and Asia, are cited as an affirmation that a country cannot claim sovereign immunity in the face of human rights violations. Reisman states, "Since the white minority government of Rhodesia declared its independence and 'sovereign' right to suppress the black majority, it has been settled by UN law that gross violations of human rights which the Rhodesian Government insisted were entirely 'domestic' – can constitute threats to the peace and can justify action under Chapter VII."[29] While this line of reasoning has a certain degree of validity, it is undeniable that the Security Council's actions against both Southern Rhodesia and South

Africa, limited to arms embargos, were soft. The Council never went beyond them despite their ineffectiveness.

It can be argued that the Charter's provisions on state sovereignty are antiquated and should be brought in line with contemporary norms but this can only be done by suitably amending the Charter.

Imprecise Drafting of Resolutions

The authorisation resolutions are the result of political negotiations, usually behind closed doors, and suffer from ambivalent drafting that leads to divergent interpretations. Freudenschuss calls them "careless if not haphazard".

The action to expel Iraq from Kuwait in 1991 is considered the most successful instance of authorised military action by the Security Council but the loose text of Resolution 678 (1990) raised serious questions of interpretation. Schachter notes, "By avoiding reference in Resolution 678 to any particular article of Chapter VII, the Council left the matter in doubt, giving rise to questions of authority that may require specific legal grounds."[30] The resolution was justified both as self-defence under Article 51 and collective authorised military action under Article 42. But self-defence is not mentioned in the resolution and one of its stated objectives, to "restore international peace and security in the area", went well beyond it. Besides, self-defence is a right of a member state under the Charter and does not require Security Council authorisation.

Wilson maintains that the imprecise text of the Iraq resolution was used to prolong the enforcement action and for objectives not intended in the resolution, "While this author shares the view of most international lawyers that there was no legal basis in UN Security Council authorisation for the action, the key point for our purposes is that if resolution 678 had been more specific, providing in clear terms that military action was authorised solely for the purpose of liberating Kuwait, it would have been difficult for it to be invoked as a basis for any of these later actions which it could not possibly have contemplated."[31]

Lobel and Ratner agree that imprecisely worded resolutions have been convenient for powerful member states to justify their military actions. They cite Britain, the US and France using their air force to enforce no-fly zones in northern Iraq and provide assistance to Kurds under Resolution 688 which made no mention of the use of force.[32] They note that "ambiguous, open-textured resolutions to exercise control over the initiation, conduct and termination of hostilities" leave very wide discretion with member states which they can misuse for their national interest. They hold that such 'contracting' resolutions should be explicit and time-bound and should provide for the termination of hostility as soon as there is a ceasefire. However, they note that this 'legal realist' theory of willingly tolerating forceful action by individual states and treating it as being lawful even if it conflicts with the UN Charter can cause harm to the security system set up by the UN, "A world order that would allow nations to use force unilaterally under the guise of creative or disputed interpretations of vague language in Security Council resolutions or by the Council's failure to act would undermine Article 2 (4)."[33]

Selectivity and Lack of Accountability

By delegating military action to member states the Security Council dilutes its accountability and leaves all decisions on military action to the big powers. Weston maintains that Resolution 678 (1990) on the use of force against Iraq violated the UN Charter because it "eschewed direct UN responsibility and accountability for the military force that ultimately was deployed, favouring, instead, a denigrated, essentially unilateralist determination and orchestration of world policy, coordinated and controlled almost exclusively by the United States. And, in doing so, it encouraged a too-hasty retreat from the pre-eminently peaceful and humanitarian purpose and principles of the United Nations. As a consequence, it set a dubious precedent, both for the United Nations as it stands today and for the "new world order" that is claimed for tomorrow."[34]

On selectivity, Freudenschuss questions whether the permanent five are interested in taking on all global threats on behalf of the Security Council, "Disregarding Russia and particularly China, it would appear that even the Western Permanent Members have no real interest taking on all burdens."[35] By delegating military action the Security Council makes the security system selective and dependent on the whims of the big powers.

Although there is no UN forum to adjudicate the legality of authorised actions they have sometimes been questioned within the governments of the countries taking them. Manusama recounts the controversy in the Netherlands on its government joining the military action against Iraq in 2003. Dutch legal experts differed on whether the Security Council needed to adopt a second resolution to authorise military action. The government's legal adviser believed that it did and that in its absence an invasion could be challenged in the ICJ. But this view was not expressed in the letter sent to the government by the law department. The letter merely stated, "A second resolution is desirable but not necessary."[36]

Britain faced a similar controversy on this operation and, in 2009, the Chilcot Inquiry took place into the government's participation in it. The fallout was that when the invasion of Libya was being discussed in 2011 the British government made sure that the resolution was to the satisfaction of its own legal experts. Nevertheless, the action of the invading coalition went well beyond the intent and objectives of Security Council Resolution 1973 (2011). Manusama concludes, "The response to the crisis moved from an immediate and necessary protection of civilians towards regime change, illustrating that the UN collective security system does not appear to be capable of governing or regulating the use of force, even force which was initially taken under its authority, so that attaining a legally grounded UN collective security system increasingly seems as far away in 2011 as it did in 2003."[37]

Other Views

The powers of the Security Council under Chapter VII have been the subject of intense debate and little agreement. Many writers accept the validity of the arguments against these resolutions but insist that they be considered legitimate regardless. Many caution that authorised military action can be considered to be legitimate only under certain conditions and limits. This is not easy. The Charter does not contain any such qualification since it does not provide for delegating military action to member states. Payandeh notes, "The competences of the Security Council are formulated in a goal-oriented way with the focus on the maintenance of international peace and security, allowing for a strongly functional interpretation."[38] While the Charter gives certain powers to the Council and obliges states to obey its decisions, there is little agreement among experts on what the limits of those powers are under what Weston calls Article 42½.

Blokker points out that a resolution that does not specify the period of military action in effect gives a *carte blanche* to the permanent members since they can then veto any resolution terminating their operation. This happened in the case of Resolution 678 which resulted in the Security

Council effectively relinquishing its control. Blokker calls the practice a "half-way house" but says that it has developed to a point where it has become a constitutional development in which there is a "balance struck between rigidity and flexibility as twin requirements in the interpretation of constitutions of international organisations."[39]

Sarooshi says that it is on account of the Security Council not exercising command and control of the forces that commentators argue against such military action but there is the contrary view that "so long as a use of force can be characterized as a collective measure then it is lawful since it is being used to carry out the collective will of the Council on behalf of the United Nations."[40] He concludes, "In summary, the provisions of the Charter, in particular Articles 43, 46, and 47 of the Charter, do not prohibit a delegation by the Council of its Chapter VII powers to Member States. They only prescribe a way in which the Council can exercise these powers."[41]

Kirgis gives several justifications to establish the Charter-compatibility of the enforcement resolutions - Article 42 contemplates member states taking action on behalf of the Security Council, the Charter is a constitution that is capable of growing, it is an implied power under Article 42, it is consistent with the purpose of the article and it is a functional necessity for the Council's enforcement authority. However, perhaps not convinced with his own arguments, he concludes, "In final analysis, it is probably immaterial whether the Council relies on a specific article in chapter VII or on its own implied powers when it authorizes the use of armed force to preserve or restore peace...... there is no need for the Council to specify which of these sources it relies on in the particular case...."[42]

Quigley is more forthright in his characterisation of authorised enforcement action as a "trend toward privatization". He explains, "Instead of carrying out military actions itself, the Council hires the work out to individual states, typically to states that have expressed an interest in doing so and which, as a consequence, may have private aims to pursue." He regards this as a violation of the Charter, which being a treaty "cannot lawfully be interpreted by some of the parties to the detriment of another party." He cites the views of various judges of the ICJ who differ in their opinion on whether the Charter is a treaty or, like a constitution, acquires a character of its own. He notes that there is no unanimity among the judges on this. In any event, these are their individual opinions and the ICJ has not taken a stand on this.[43]

Manusama also maintains that "the legal basis and, thus, the legality of the authorising technique are obscure" and "substantial dangers are inherent in the authorization technique and there is a need to limit the discretion of states acting upon the authorization".[44]

The risks of misuse of such military action are also noted by Ferencz, "Unilateral national military might risks being abused for self-serving national purposes. Self-help without international controls is more likely to jeopardise world security than enhance it. An international military force under effective UN control is the best safeguard for world tranquillity."[45] He advises the setting up of new institutions and controls, "To avoid dangerous interventions in the future, new institutions or structures under international controls are necessary – imaginative improvisation is not good enough to cope with life and death on a regular basis."[46]

Grove points out that Article 43 specifically envisaged that all members of the UN – not just the permanent members – should make available troops to the Security Council. This would add to the credibility of the UN Force, a point made in the Agenda for Peace of 1992.[47]

There has never been any discussion in informal meetings of the Security Council on the operational details of military action under a resolution since the Western powers are aware that Russia and China would block such a resolution.[48] On the Libya issue in 2011, both Russia and China abstained because they believed that the resolution only provided for enforcing a no-fly zone to prevent Gaddafi's forces from using their air power against the rebels. However, the resolution was used by the West to carry out aerial attacks on Gaddafi's forces thereby giving tactical advantage to the rebel forces. One such operation enabled them to kill Gaddafi.

In its early years, the Security Council had shown some inclination to hold an investigation to confirm the existence of a security threat before considering action. In Spain in 1946, it set up a sub-committee to investigate the activities of the Franco regime and examine if it presented a threat to international peace and security. The same year it set up a commission to investigate the Greek civil war.[49]

In the late 1990s, following criticism by several states and legal experts, the Security Council started defining its delegation of authority more precisely – by enunciating the objectives more clearly, prescribing firmer time limits, imposing more frequent reporting requirements, and laying down guidelines of behaviour, like the requirement in Rwanda to act impartially. But none of these could compensate for the absence of command and control of the Security Council over the forces.

Schweigman identifies two possible limits to the Security Council's powers of delegating authority, the Charter and general international law. Under the Charter, the Council must respect "the right of self-determination, basic human rights, the principle of good faith and the core principles of international humanitarian law." On international law, Schweigman says that the Council is not *a priori* required to act in accordance with customary international law but it must abide by its peremptory norms, *jus cogens*. He accepts that the exact content of these norms is controversial but he includes in them "the outlawing of aggression and its corresponding right of self-defence; the prohibition of genocide; basic human rights such as the prohibition of apartheid, slavery and torture; and the core principles of international humanitarian law."[50]

Blokker too lays down a set of four safeguards - the power to be delegated must be within the authority of the Security Council, the implied power must be necessary for the organisation to perform its function, there should be certain explicit powers in the area concerned and the implied power should not violate the fundamental rules and principles of international law. Blokker points out that when France was given the authority to take action under Resolution 929 (1994) in Rwanda it was advised to operate "in an impartial way" because some members felt that France was partial to Hutus. Similarly, in the operation in Albania under Resolutions 1101 and 1114 authorised member states to conduct the operation in a neutral and impartial way.[51]

Sarooshi suggests three conditions that such resolutions must fulfil in order to be lawful - clear exposition of objectives, supervision by the Council and regular reporting to it. [52]

Wilson offers three limitations on the Security Council's powers of delegating authority for military action based on concepts of general international law such as "good faith, abuse of power and *jus cogens*".[53] These are - clearly stated objectives, fixed duration of the operation, and adequate scrutiny by the Security Council. He admits that most Security Council resolutions do not provide for these stipulations, though the more recent ones include some. He points out that some of the earlier resolutions did not even mention the term, use of force, and opted instead to use general words like "all necessary measures". He mentions that the Resolution 678 which authorised military action against Iraq in 1990 was so broad that it led to very wide and unintended interpretations. He admits though, "The provision of clear mandates does not provide an absolute guarantee that those exercising them will act strictly within their parameters."[54] This dilemma is faced by other experts who support the Charter-compatibility of authorised military action and unconvincingly addressed by them but they are loathe to declare as illegitimate a resolution that fails to meet these safeguards.

Endnotes

1   Comprehensive Review of the Whole Question of Peacekeeping Operations in All Their Aspects, UN Doc. A/55/305S/2000/809, 21 August 2000.

2   Corneliu Bjola, *Legitimising the Use of Force in International Politics: A Communicative Action Perspective.* European Journal of International Relations, London, 11.2 (Jun 2005), pp. 266-304.

3   Report to the President on the Charter of the UN. Hearings before the Committee on Foreign Relations, US Senate, 2 July 1945, pp. 62-63.

4   Bruno Simma. *The Charter of the United Nations – A Commentary.* (Munich: Verlag C.H. Beck, 1994), p. 651.

5   Simma, p. 652.

6   Oscar Schachter. *United Nations in the Gulf Conflict.* (85 American Journal of International Law, 452-473 (1991). p. 463.

7   ICJ, *Certain Expenses of the United Nations case*, 1962, p. 167.

8   ICJ *Certain Expenses case*, 1962, p.177.

9   Erika de Wet. *The Chapter VII Powers of the United Nations Security Council* (New York: Hart Publishing, 2004), pp. 260-261.

10 Niels Blokker. *Is the Authorisation Authorised? Powers and Practice of the UN Security Council to Authorise the Use of Force by 'Coalitions of the Able and the Willing'.* EJIL, 2000, vol. II, no.3, p. 551.

11 Blokker, p. 547.

12 Blokker, p. 568.

13   Higgins, p. 265.

14   Lindsay Moir. *Reappraising the Resort to Force: International Law – Jus ad Bellum and the War on Terror* (New York: Hart Publishing, 2010), p. 35.

15   Thomas Franck. *The United Nations as Guarantor of International Peace and Security.* Chapter in Christian Tomaschat (Ed.) *The United Nations at Fifty – A Legal Perspective.* (The Hague: Kluwer Law International, 1995), pp. 32-33.

16   Thomas Franck in Tomaschat (Ed.), p. 43.

17   Blokker, p. 551.

18   UNGA Resolution A/Res/60/1 of 24 October 2005, World Summit Outcome, 16 September 2005, para 79.

19   Hilaire McCoubrey and Nigel D. White. *International Law and Armed Conflict.* (USA: Dartmouth, 1992), p. 145.

20   Javier Pérez de Cuéllar. *Pilgrimage for Peace* (Hampshire, USA: MacMillan, 1997), pp. 250-252.

21   Gary Wilson. *The Legal, Military and Political Consequences of the "Coalition of the Willing" Approach to UN Military Enforcement Action.* (Journal of Conflict and Security Law, 2007, v.12), pp. 296-297.

22   GAOR, Fifth Session, First Committee, 354th Meeting, 9 October 1950, p.64.

23   Hans Kelsen. *Is the Acheson Plan Constitutional?* Western Political Quarterly, Vol. 3(4), 1 December 1950, p. 527.

24   Kelsen. *Is the Acheson Plan Constitutional?* p. 526.

25   Appeals Chamber of the International Tribunal for Yugoslavia, Decision on the Defence Motion for Interlocutory Appeal on Jurisdiction in *Prosecutor v. Dusko Tadic*, 2 October 1995, para 42.

26   Neil Fenton. *Understanding the UN Security Council – Coercion or Consent?* (Farnham, Surrey: Ashgate, 2004), p. 12.

27   Richard A. Falk. *Legal Order in a Violent World.* (Princeton University Press, 1968), p. 224.

28   Falk. *Legal Order in a Violent World,* p. 225.

29   W.M. Reisman in 'Sovereignty and Human Rights in Contemporary International Law'. (American Journal of International Law, Vol. 84, 1990), p. 872.

30   Schachter, p. 462.

31 Gary Wilson. *The United Nations and Collective Security.* (Routledge, 2014), pp. 130-131.

32 Jules Lobel and Michael Ratner. *Bypassing the Security Council: Ambiguous Authorizations to Use Force, Cease-Fires and the Iraqi Inspection Regime.* (The American Journal of International Law, Vol. 93, No. 1, Jan. 1999), p. 126.

33 Lobel and Ratner, p. 134.

34 Burns H. Weston. *Security Council Resolution 678 and Persian Gulf Decision Making: Precarious Legitimacy.* (The American Journal of International Law. Vol. 85, No. 3, Jul. 1991), p. 516.

35 Helmut Freudenschuss. *Art. 39 of the UN Charter Revisited: Threats to the Peace and Recent Practice of the UN Security Council.* (Austrian Journal of Public and International Law, 46, 1993), p. 34 and 39.

36 Letter of the Ministry of Foreign Affairs, 18 March 2003, *Kamerstukken II, 2002/03, 23 432, nr. 63.* Quoted by Kenneth M. Manusama, *Between a Rock and a Hard Place.* Chapter in I.F. Dekker & E. Hey (Eds.) *Agora: The Case of Iraq, Netherlands Yearbook of International Law, Vol.42.* (The Hague: Asser Press, 2012), p. 104.

37 Letter of the Ministry of Foreign Affairs, 18 March 2003, *Kamerstukken II, 2002/03, 23 432, nr. 63.* Cited by Kenneth M. Manusama, *Between a Rock and a Hard Place.* Chapter Dekker and Hey (Eds.), p. 228.

38 Mehrdad Payandeh. *The United Nations, Military Intervention, and Regime Change in Libya.* (Virginia Journal of International Law, Vol.52, 2012), p. 392.

39 Blokker, pp. 542 and 568.

40 Danesh Sarooshi. *The United Nations and the Development of Collective Security – The Delegation by the UN Security Council of its Chapter VII Powers* (Oxford: Clarendon Press, 1999), p. 145.

41 Sarooshi, p. 146.

42 Kirgis, pp. 520-521.

43 Quigley, p. 250 and 274.

44 Kenneth Manusama. *The United Nations Security Council in the Post-Cold War Era – Applying the Principle of Legality* (Leiden: Martinus Nijhoff, 2006), pp.238 and 263.

45 Benjamin B. Ferencz. *New Legal Foundations for Global Survival.* (New York: Oceana Publications. 1994), p. 129.

46   Ferencz, p. 139.

47   Eric Grove. *UN Armed Forces and the Military Staff Committee: A Look Back.* (International Security, Vol. 17, No. 4, Spring 1993), pp. 172-182.

48   This is based on the author's conversation with a Russian delegate in New York.

49   Nigel D. White. *Keeping the Peace – The United Nations and the Maintenance of International Peace and Security.* (Manchester University Press, 1997), p. 39.

50   David Schweigman. *The Authority of the Security Council under Chapter VII of the UN Charter (The Hague:* Kluwer Law International, 2001), pp 301-302.

51   Blokker, pp. 547-549.

52   Sarooshi, p. 155.

53   Wilson. *The United Nations and Collective Security,* p. 127.

54   Wilson. *The Legal, Military and Political Consequences of the "Coalition of the Willing" Approach to UN Military Enforcement Action,* p. 307.

13 Security Council and International Law

The Security Council's powers and actions often do not meet the tenets of international law. There is no judicial review of its resolutions. This failing is not lost on member states and has impacted its standing in world affairs and the attitude of the non-permanent members to it.

The United Nations, with the Security Council at its apex, was designed to be and has functioned as a political organisation. Its Charter was drafted neither as a constitution, balancing the powers and functions of different organs of government on the principle of the separation of powers, nor as a treaty, balancing the rights and obligations of the contracting parties. It made a subtle but significant departure from the Covenant of the League of Nations on the issue of the obligations of members on upholding and abiding by international law. The Covenant had provided for the "firm establishment of the understandings of international law as the actual rule of conduct among governments."[1] In the UN Charter, member states pledged to "fulfil in good faith the obligations assumed by them in accordance with the present Charter."[2] There was no explicit commitment in the Charter to abiding by the principles of international law as in the League's Covenant.

This was not an oversight. When settling international disputes by peaceful means the Security Council has to take into account the principles of "justice and international law" [Article 1(1)] but when enforcing international peace and security it is merely required "to act in accordance with the Purposes and Principles of the United Nations" [Article 24(2)]. The proceedings of the San Francisco Conference show that the big powers made the distinction deliberately to give themselves a free hand in the Security Council in dealing with threats to the new international order. In matters of peace and security, they were determined to avoid burdening themselves with the idealism of the League and its esoteric principles of justice and international law.

Schweigman tracks the progress of this provision at the San Francisco Conference, "An amendment that would have extended the obligation to act in conformity with the principles of justice and international law to measures taken by the Council pursuant to its responsibilities for the maintenance of international peace and security, was rejected by the major powers as curtailing the Council's freedom of (swift) action."[3] A committee at the San Francisco Conference discussed "a proposed insertion in the Charter of a statement of the principle that no state can evade the authority of international law or the obligations of the Charter". But this was objected to on the ground that "international law" was a "broad uncodified concept" and dropped.[4]

Nardin rues its impact, "The virtual abandonment of international law as the basis of association within the United Nations and its replacement by agreement to cooperate for common purposes marks one of the low points in the fortunes of the practical conception of international society in twentieth-century international thought."[5] This has affected the stature of the ICJ, whose lack of compulsory jurisdiction not only in adjudicating disputes but also in examining if a country's actions threaten international peace and security or if a member has violated its obligations under the Charter, has reduced it to a bystander in international disputes.

The Obligation to Obey the Security Council

Member states of the United Nations have pledged unquestioned obedience to the Security Council under the Charter. This authority of the Council flows from Article 25 of the Charter, which enjoins upon member states to "accept and carry out the decisions of the Security Council in accordance with the present Charter". A question is sometimes raised if the phrase "in accordance with the present Charter" applies to the decisions of the Security Council or to the obligation of the member states. In the former case, the states would only be obliged to accept and carry out the decisions of the Council taken in accordance with the Charter. The latter interpretation would merely reinforce the obligation of member states to obey the decisions of the Security Council. It is, however, generally accepted that the phrase applies to decisions of the Council and not to the obligation of members. Thus, to be binding, the decisions of the Council must be in accordance with the Charter. However, this gives rise to the problem that there is no provision in the Charter for a review of the legality of a Security Council decision in the Charter, either by the ICJ or the General Assembly. In its absence, a member state questioning a decision of the Security Council would have to base its arguments on its military prowess.

There is also a controversy about what constitutes a 'decision'. It is generally accepted that a decision is one that is taken by the Council under Chapter VII and is binding. There is, however, no consensus on whether an outcome of the Council under Chapter VI on the pacific settlement of disputes constitutes a decision. It is generally recognised that these are recommendatory. In 1947, on the issue of the Greek frontier, the Soviet Union maintained that all outcomes of the Council under Chapter VI were recommendatory. However, the US view is that outcomes to investigate, under Article 34 in Chapter VI, are decisions and are binding on member states.

The ICJ in its advisory opinion in the *Namibia case, 1971*, held that the text of the resolution has to be seen to decide if it is binding since the Charter does not confine this to Chapter VII. This is also borne out by the fact that at the San Francisco Conference, a Belgian proposal to limit the obligation of members under Article 25 to Chapter VII was not accepted. In fact, even though in Committee I of Commission III it received majority support of 14 to 13, it could not pass because it required two-thirds majority.[6]

The Security Council's decision-making is facilitated by the requirement of a simple majority, including for resolutions on enforcement action under Chapter VII. But the principle of unanimity among the permanent five makes the rest of the Council irrelevant when they are in agreement and helpless when they are not. Once it adopts a resolution all members of the UN are obliged to fall in line, including the member against whom it has been taken. This is a critical departure from traditional international law in which an international obligation depends on the consent of the state concerned.[7] This cardinal principle is accepted in the case of the permanent members on the ground of *realpolitik* but given short shrift for others.

The framers of the Charter also took care to ensure that a state could not use its obligations under other treaties to claim exoneration from its adherence to the Charter. Article 103 states that in the event of a conflict between obligations under the Charter and obligations under other international agreement, the obligations under the Charter shall prevail. A state cannot claim that its bilateral or regional agreement with a state precludes it from enforcing any economic or other sanction imposed by the Security Council.

Does the Security Council Make International Law?

The Security Council is believed to contribute to the development of international law through its decisions. The Council can be a valuable and rich source of customary international law through its actions, resolutions and debates. However, for this to happen it must compile a body of congruent resolutions and actions which can develop into international law over time. Experience, however, shows that while taking decisions the Security Council relies more on the prevailing interplay of power among the permanent five than on the principles of law and justice. There is no established procedure for dealing with complaints and past resolutions are not treated as binding precedents. The permanent five finalise the text of resolutions among them in informal meetings before bringing them to the Council. The records of the informal meetings are not made public.

In the 1990s, the Security Council started sprinkling its resolutions on terrorism with mandatory directives under Chapter VII to member states drafted like a legislative act. Phrases like "all States shall" deny flights operated by the Taliban rulers of Afghanistan and freeze their funds were included in Resolution 1267 (1999). This was in contrast to the earlier practice of calling upon or authorising states to take certain action. Soon after the 9/11 terrorist attacks in the US, the Security Council adopted a stronger resolution on the same lines. Resolution 1373 (2001) directed states to criminalise the financing of terror and incorporate other measures in their domestic laws and regulations. This refrain continued without reference to the article of the Charter under which it was being adopted.

Security Council resolutions rarely specify the article of the Charter under which they are being proposed or adopted, particularly those on military action. This leads to differences over their interpretation. All resolutions of the Security Council authorising military action have to be under Chapter VII and must be based on a determination of a threat to or a breach of international peace and security. However, the texts of these resolutions lack consistency. No resolution of the Security Council on military action has explicitly contained a reference to Article 42, which is the sole authority for it in the Charter. While 'threat' and 'breach' have been referred to in several resolutions, terms like 'disturbance' or 'endangerment' have also been used. The Council has followed the policy of simply stating that it is acting under Chapter VII.

Higgins explains that this practice emerges from the overriding concern of the Council to establish peace, "In the case of the Security Council – and to a lesser extent, the Assembly – the reference to specific legal authority is muted, in the sense that decisions are often demanded with some urgency. The prescription of law, rather than its application, thus becomes involved. This is especially true of the decisions made concerning peace and security, where the feeling may well be that, quite apart from traditional law on the subject concerned, it is essential to pacify the situation."[8] In the circumstances, Security Council resolutions do not offer a consistent set of precedents to be a guide for future decisions.

Judicial Review of Security Council Decisions

The judicial wing of the United Nations, the International Court of Justice, is the sixth and arguably its weakest organ. It has its own Statute, negotiated separately from the Charter in Washington and appended to it. Its jurisdiction is universal but not compulsory and is drawn from the voluntary acceptance by member states. Only 72 member states have accepted its compulsory jurisdiction, most with numerous reservations. Britain is the only permanent member of the Security Council to do so. Some multilateral treaties also empower the ICJ to deal with their interpretation and adjudication of disputes.

The reference to the ICJ in Chapter VI of the Charter on the pacific settlement of disputes is in Article 36, which merely provides that the Security Council should take into consideration that as "general rule" legal disputes should be referred by the parties to the ICJ. The requirement is made as a suggestion to the parties to the dispute, not to the Security Council. Brazil's ambassador regretted this in 1947, "If compulsory resort to the Court had been written into the Charter, a powerful instrument would be in our hands today for the promotion of the pacific settlement of disputes."[9]

The Charter also provides for the ICJ to give an advisory opinion on request to the United Nations. But the Security Council, in particular, has shown little inclination to do so. The ICJ has given advisory opinions in only twenty six cases and very few of these have been on substantive issues like the powers of the organs of the UN. Eleven cases pertained to administrative matters or questions relating to privileges and immunities, referred to it by the UN or its specialised agencies.

Does a state have the right to question the legality of a Security Council decision? The answer to this has to be ostensibly in the affirmative, for denying it would negate fundamental principles of constitutionalism and the rule of law. A democratic constitution defines the powers of the organs of government and provides for a judiciary to adjudicate disputes of jurisdiction. The UN has no such forum to determine if a Council decision is *ultra vires* of the Charter.

Decisions of the Security Council have been questioned by member states and others from time to time, including its authority to take them. These challenges have come from both from states against whom they have been taken and others. In 1993, Iraq protested against the Security Council's decision on UNSCOM and declared that it would not cooperate with it. In 1998, the Organisation of African Unity (OAU) and the League of Arab States declared that they would not cooperate with the full Security Council sanctions on Libya. North Korea has rejected the sanctions imposed on it as an infringement of its sovereignty.

The UN Charter does not contain any provision for its interpretation. This is left to each organ and is more often than not "the result of a bargaining process or an exercise of power than an attempt to apply Charter provisions by a process of reasoning based on accepted principles of interpretation."[10] At the San Francisco Conference, the sub-committee dealing with this issue felt that each organ should be left to interpret its own jurisdiction. It added an optimistic observation, "It is to be understood, of course, that if an interpretation made by any organ of the Organization or by a committee of jurists is not generally acceptable it will be without binding force."[11]

There was an animated discussion at the conference on Article 36 of the Charter on the jurisdiction of the ICJ. A majority of the members of the sub-committee dealing with this issue wanted the ICJ to be given compulsory jurisdiction. Belgium proposed that if a member state felt that a decision of the Security Council infringed its essential rights it could challenge it in the ICJ and if the Court upheld it the Council would have to reconsider the question or refer it to the General Assembly for a decision.[12]

This was one of the issues on which the big powers were determined not to cede ground regardless of the support among members. Senator Vandenberg warned that conferring compulsory jurisdiction on the ICJ would endanger American ratification of the Charter.[13] His threat was not baseless. Russell notes, "Senate reluctance to accept Court jurisdiction in the limited area of legal disputes under paragraph 36(2) went back to nationalistic fears arising out of misunderstanding of the Permanent Court of International Justice to 'intervene' in domestic affairs."[14] The Soviet Union was also equally vehemently opposed to compulsory jurisdiction.

In the face such pressure, the sub-committee adopted a text proposing optional jurisdiction by a majority of 31 votes to 14 with a curious statement, "The desire to establish compulsory jurisdiction for the Court prevailed among the majority of the Sub-committee. However, some of these delegates feared that insistence upon the realization of that ideal would only impair the possibility of obtaining general accord to the Statute of the Court, as well as to the Charter itself. It is in that spirit that the majority of the Sub-committee recommends the adoption of the solution described above."[15] It decided that the organs of the UN were free to submit such issues to the ICJ or seek its advisory opinion but there was no need to make a provision to this effect in the Charter. [16] It also unanimously adopted a resolution recommending that all member states accept the compulsory jurisdiction of the ICJ as soon as possible. Several delegations made statements that their vote did not indicate their views on the question of compulsory jurisdiction.

Many experts on the UN have advocated judicial review to strengthen the credibility of the Security Council. Claude counsels, "No harm would be done if it held the organisation closer to the stipulations of the Charter, particularly if it did this while maintaining a keen awareness of the necessity of creative adaptation to realise basic purposes, as the evidence suggests that the Court would do."[17] Conte also recommends judicial review, "The relevant authorising provisions of the Charter call for the Security Council to act in accordance with the Charter, and the World Court should, therefore, be disposed to measure that limitation."[18] Petculescu maintains that international judicial review would "guarantee both the respect of the UN legality and the efficient action of the organ principally responsible with the maintenance of world peace and security."[19]

The question that arises, however, is - how does the ICJ take up the challenge? Schweigman suggests that a member state can invoke the

General Assembly or any of the specialised agencies of the UN to seek the advisory opinion of the ICJ. Some have suggested that the ICJ should draw upon the US Supreme Court's decision in the *Madison v. Marbury case, 1803*, to introduce judicial review in the UN system. Some cite the judgments and advisory opinions of the Court turning down the plea of *litispendence* and the political question argument as evidence that it is already exercising judicial review. De Wet writes that in the *Namibia case* the ICJ has cautiously shown its willingness to review Security Council resolutions and its advisory opinion in the case was used by the international criminal tribunals of Rwanda and Yugoslavia to examine the legality of the Security Council resolutions establishing them.

If the ICJ were to exercise judicial review, how should it go about it? Schweigman believes that it cannot be expected to declare the Council's action illegal, but it can refer the decision back to the Council for a remedy.[20] Franck agrees that any review of Security Council resolutions by the ICJ would have to be advisory in nature, "Any judicial review by the ICJ of an action or decision of the Security Council could not but be in the nature of a non-binding opinion. Such an opinion, therefore, could only provide a basis for the Security Council to review its own decisions...."[21]

It would be advisable to treat these scholarly views with skepticism. Nowhere in the UN Charter or the ICJ's Statute is there provision for judicial review. The Court itself has been reticent, "Undoubtedly, the Court does not possess powers of judicial review or appeal in respect of the decisions taken by the United Nations organs concerned."[22] In the *Lockerbie case*, Judge Oda went to the extent of saying, "...under the positive law of the United Nations Charter a resolution of the Security Council may have binding force, irrespective of whether it is consonant with international law derived from other sources."[23] Justice Lachs, in the same case, stated, "While the Court has the vocation of applying international law as a universal law, operating both within and outside the United Nations, it is bound to respect, as a part of that law, the binding decisions of the Security Council."[24]

In the *Certain Expenses case,* the ICJ recognised the limitations to its powers, "In the legal systems of States, there is often some procedure for determining the validity of even a legislative or governmental act, but no analogous procedure is to be found in the structure of the United Nations. Proposals made during the drafting of the Charter to place the ultimate authority to interpret the Charter in the International Court of Justice were not accepted; the opinion which the Court is in course of rendering is an *advisory* opinion. As anticipated in 1945, therefore, each organ must, in the first place at least, determine its own jurisdiction."[25]

Freudenschuss asserts that judicial review would require an amendment of the Charter, "Measures designed to enhance the ICJ's role vis-à-vis the SC would require changes in the Charter which the Permanent Members are not prepared to accept."[26] Petculescu concedes that a significant number of scholars have rightly pointed out that no implied power of judicial review exists in the UN Charter. In any event, most experts concede that determinations made by the Security Council under Article 39 and decisions under Chapter VII will have to be treated as exceptions to the power of judicial review. Besides, the disdain shown by the permanent members for the ICJ does not bode well for it in the event of a confrontation.

Jurisdictions of the ICJ and the Security Council

While the ICJ has avoided confronting the Security Council by attempting to review its resolutions it has been anxious to protect its turf. There is no established practice between the Security Council and the ICJ on which organ will give way in case of *litispendence*, i.e. if the same matter is pending in the other organ. On some occasions, the Security Council has held back on a matter awaiting a decision in the ICJ, either out of caution or because it was bogged down by the veto. In the *Anglo-Iranian oil case*, it held back on its debate till such time as the ICJ had taken a decision on its jurisdiction in the matter. In the *Lockerbie case*, however, it went ahead and imposed sanctions on Libya, even though Libya had taken the matter to the ICJ where it was under consideration.

The ICJ has accepted cases even when they have been taken to the Security Council by only one of the disputing parties. It has maintained that it does not consider *litispendence* to be a hurdle but it has been reticent to confront the Security Council. In 1976, the *Aegean Continental Shelf case*, Greece brought a complaint against Turkey before the Security Council and also instituted proceedings in the ICJ. The Security Council adopted Resolution 395 (1976) appealing for peace and advising recourse to the ICJ. The ICJ judgment came two years later, well after the Security Council resolution. It took cognisance of the fact that the Security Council had also been seized of the dispute and had pronounced on it. It concluded, "Accordingly, it is not necessary for the Court to decide the question whether Article 41 of the Statute confers upon it the power to indicate interim measures of protection for the sole purpose of preventing the aggravation or extension of a dispute." The ICJ, thus, gave way to the Security Council and the question of its jurisdiction over a case pending in the Council was left open.

In 1979, when several hundred Iranians occupied the US Embassy in Tehran and took American diplomats and other personnel hostage, the US approached both the Security Council and the ICJ. The Security Council called for the immediate release of the hostages and asked the secretary-general to take all appropriate measures for this purpose.[27] In the ICJ, in what is called the *Iran Hostages case,* the US asked it to adjudge the seizure as violative of various international treaties and asked for reparations and the surrender by the Iranian government of those responsible. Iran refused to appear in the case. It asserted that the case should be heard in the context of the relations between the two countries over the preceding 25 years, during which the US had violated Iran's sovereignty. The ICJ ruled that it had jurisdiction in the case, even though the Security Council was also seized of it since such a restriction applied to the General Assembly, not the ICJ. It concluded, "It follows that neither the mandate given by the Security Council to the Secretary-General in resolutions 457(1979) and 461(1979), nor the setting up of the Commission by the Secretary-General can be considered as constituting any obstacle to the exercise of the court's jurisdiction in the present case."[28] However, in May 1981, the US withdrew its case following the release of the hostages through mediation. The court had not given its ruling till then.

In 1984, Nicaragua filed a case in the ICJ against the US for taking military action against it in its territorial waters. This time the US argued that the ICJ could not take up the case since it was pending in the Security Council, even though it had vetoed a resolution condemning its action and calling upon it to withdraw. The US argued that the UN Charter vests the Security Council with the primary responsibility of maintaining international peace and security and it contains no provision for issues relating to the use of force to be resolved by judicial means. The ICJ gave an interim order in which it cited the *Iran Hostages case* and asserted that the principle of *litispendence* did not preclude it from taking up the matter. It unanimously called on the US to stop all hostile action in Nicaraguan ports, particularly the laying of mines.[29]

However, in the *Lockerbie case*, the ICJ was reluctant to take on the Security Council and it stretched the case till Libya settled out of court. Libya had refused to extradite two Libyans accused in the bombing of a Pan Am flight over Lockerbie in Scotland and sought the ICJ's intervention to enable it to try them in Libya. The US and Britain challenged the ICJ's jurisdiction on the ground that it was a case of a threat to international peace and security in which the Security Council resolution took precedence. They got the Security Council to adopt Resolution 748 (1992) imposing sanctions on Libya. The Court declined to authorise any interim measures in view of the Security Council resolution. However, in 1998, it gave an interim ruling maintaining that it had jurisdiction since the Security Council resolutions had been adopted after Libya had filed its case before it. As the case dragged in court, Libya agreed to have it tried by Scottish judges sitting in a neutral court in the Netherlands. The case was delisted by the ICJ in 2003 at the joint request of the parties.

The Security Council itself has been reluctant to refer disputes to the ICJ, though in its early years it showed some willingness to do so. In 1947, it recommended to Britain and Albania to take their dispute over the damage to British ships in the Corfu channel in Albanian waters by mines to the ICJ. In the *Corfu Channel case*, 1947-49, the Court overruled Albania's arguments of lack of jurisdiction of the Court but it also held that Britain's mine-clearing actions in Albanian waters were violative of its sovereignty. The Greek complaint against Turkey for violations of its continental shelf in the Aegean Sea is the only other instance of a direct reference by the Security Council of disputes to the ICJ.

After the First World War, the administration of the German colony of South West Africa (later, Namibia) was handed over by the League of Nations to South Africa. South Africa continued to occupy the country after the Second World War and exploit its rich mineral wealth under the UN's mandate system. However, when the UN terminated its mandate and asked it to withdraw its forces it refused to do so. The Security Council adopted Resolution 276 (1970) condemning South Africa's presence in Namibia and declaring it illegal. It then sought the opinion of the ICJ on the legality of South Africa's occupation. In June 1971, the Court ruled that the presence of South Africa in South West Africa was illegal but South Africa refused to withdraw. The Security Council adopted Resolutions 309 (1972) and 319 (1972) following the advisory opinion and demanded that the UN take over the territory and administer it. But South Africa refused to honour the verdict and the Security Council chose not to take any further action.[30]

The ICJ has, however, upheld the General Assembly's initiative on peacekeeping missions. In the *Certain Expenses case,* it gave a supportive advisory opinion, "The functions and powers conferred by the Charter on the General Assembly are not confined to discussion, consideration, the initiation of studies and the making of recommendations; they are not merely hortatory."[31] The Court drew a distinction between coercive enforcement and other actions and held that only the former is the exclusive preserve of the Security Council. It maintained that peacekeeping is not coercive in nature and, therefore, falls within the joint competence of the Security Council and the General Assembly. It cited Article 11(2) under which the General Assembly is authorised to discuss matters relating to the maintenance of international peace and security brought before it by the Security Council or member state, or even a non-member, though it is required to refer to the Security Council any question on which 'action' is necessary. The court held that the 'action' referred to in this article is coercive enforcement action. This is one of the few instances of interpretation of the Charter by the ICJ, which marginally enhanced the power of the General Assembly and legitimised Hammarskjöld's Congo operation.

In the *Nicaragua case,* 1984-91, the ICJ also held that the rights and privileges of members and budgetary questions are areas in which it is the General Assembly that takes decisions and the Security Council's role is recommendatory.

However, all this does not confer any meaningful power on the ICJ. The Security Council can render meaningless any judgment of the court by refusing to implement it. In 1986, the US refused to accept a decision of the ICJ in a case brought against it by Nicaragua. It maintained that it had informed the ICJ two years earlier that it was withdrawing from the proceedings. The ICJ, nevertheless, went ahead with the case and delivered its judgment. Nicaragua took the non-compliance before the Security Council but the US vetoed it.

Oversight by the General Assembly

If judicial review of Security Council action is improbable, the possibility of oversight by the General Assembly is non-existent. Suggestions at the San Francisco Conference to give such powers to the General Assembly were rejected. They were dropped in order to ensure that the Security Council, a smaller and more compact body, could "act quickly and effectively."[32] The Charter bars the General Assembly from making a recommendation on an issue that is under consideration in the Security Council. Article 24(3) provides for annual and ad hoc reports from the Council to the Assembly but these cannot even remotely be considered to establish accountability of the Security Council to the General Assembly or limit its discretionary powers in any way. The General Assembly has no powers to review, examine or censor a decision of the Security Council.

Incompatibility with International Law

One of the tenets of international law is that it applies only to states that have voluntarily accepted it, except for certain peremptory norms, referred to as *jus cogens,* which are discussed below.[33] This principle is well established in the case of multilateral treaties which apply only to their states parties. Conforti and Focarelli maintain that only the principle of consensualism and its corollaries apply in the case of the functioning of the United Nations. They maintain that, "If acquiescence is not given, and the state explicitly denies the legality of the act, then, in the absence of any organ empowered to impose a different interpretation whereby the act is instead to be considered legally adopted, the dispute cannot but be allowed and the protesting state let to repudiate the effects of the act."[34] Can this also be said to apply to Security Council resolutions? It can be argued that member states have surrendered this right under Article 25 in which they agree to abide by the decisions of the Security Council. The Charter expects such compliance even by non-member states. Article 2(6) of the Charter empowers the UN to "ensure that states which are not members of the United Nations act in accordance with these Principles so far as may be necessary for the maintenance of international peace and security." In this spirit of empowerment, the Security Council resolutions are addressed to 'all states', not merely to member states. The near-universal membership of the UN has ensured that the legality of this provision has not been tested. The authority of the Security Council has not been challenged by states, which is understandable given its overwhelming political, military and legal clout. Instead, the challenge has come from what are dubbed "rogue" states or from non-state actors like terrorist organisations and crime syndicates.

Brierly wrote in 1958 that while certain principles of law like *pacta sunt servanda,* (agreements should be honoured), are applicable to international law, it has to be recognised that the basis of obligation in international law is *ex consensu* (based on consent). He reinforced his view with a quote from the English writer on the theory of law, Sir John Salmond, "The opinion which we shall adopt here is that the law of nations is essentially a species of conventional law - that it has its source in international agreement – that it consists of the rules which sovereign states have agreed to observe in their dealings with each other."[35] This principle of the basis of obligation in international law was subsequently accepted by several English judges. The Security Council's omnibus powers under Chapter VII can be said to be based on consent as it comes from their commitment under Article 25, but such unconditional submission stretches the limits of international law.

Then there is the principle of *nemo index in sua causa,* (one cannot be a judge in one's own cause) which is ignored in the Security Council's voting procedure. This principle is applied to all members, except the permanent five. Article 27(3) of the Charter requires member states to abstain from voting when they are parties to a dispute, but only in cases of peaceful settlement of disputes under Chapter VI and Article 52(3). It does not apply to decisions under Chapter VII. This issue too had been brought up in the San Francisco Conference by some countries but rejected by the big powers.

In the absence of any limits on the powers of the Security Council from within the Charter or other international agreements, some jurists have sought to build the principle that peremptory norms of general international law, called *jus cogens,* apply even to the Security Council, and its decisions are bound by them. The question that arises then is: what, if any, are these *jus cogens* or incontrovertible norms. There is no accepted definition of these and the norms suggested are such as would easily be accepted by any state, like not defending aggression, prohibition of genocide, protection of human rights and prohibition of torture. These norms are so general in nature and enjoy such universal acceptance that they will not impose any meaningful limit on the powers of the Security Council.

Articles 53 and 64 of the Vienna Convention on the Law of Treaties (1969) state that *jus cogens* apply to all treaties since they embody customary law, which includes the UN Charter. Orakhelashvili disputes the argument used by some that *jus cogens* does not apply to organs like the Security Council, "A Council resolution violating *jus cogens* would indeed be a derogation from *jus cogens* as it would be an attempt to use the

UN system for the establishment of a new legal regime through a resolution contrary to *jus cogens*." He cites the judgment of Judge Lauterpacht in the *Bosnia case* in which he said that *jus cogens* are binding also on the Security Council. He lists the prohibition of the use of force, especially the principle of proportionality, the principle of self-determination, fundamental human rights, and humanitarian law as constituents of *jus cogens* which bind the Security Council.[36] However, the enforcement of this view remains an issue that has not been addressed so far by either the Security Council or the International Court of Justice.

The Security Council's unfettered powers and undemocratic procedures challenge the basic tenets of international law. Its self-defined executive, legislative and judicial powers are difficult to reconcile with the principles of constitutionalism. Lauterpacht examined this conundrum and concluded that there are no legal principles that can resolve it, "We are faced here by a fundamental conflict between the principle that an illegal act is *null ab initio* and the principle that the mere assertion by an interested party that the act is unlawful should not be conclusively determinative of the question. There is no legal principle which can, by itself, resolve this conflict."[37] While international law in the form in which it exists at present has many lacunae and infirmities, the liberties taken with it in the UN Charter while endowing powers to the Security Council put it in direct conflict with the principles of justice and fair play.

The League's Covenant provided for greater checks and balance in the exercise of power by the Council. The Council was empowered in the case of a war or threat of war to "take any action that may be deemed wise and effectual to safeguard the peace of nations." In the case of a dispute that could "lead to a rupture", members were advised to submit the matter to arbitration, judicial settlement by the Permanent Court or enquiry by the Council. In case of an enquiry by the Council, it would try to settle the dispute, failing which it would vote on and publish a report with its recommendations. If the report were adopted unanimously, all members of the League would be obliged not to go to war with a party that had complied with the Council's recommendations. However, if adopted by a majority vote, each member was free to take such action as it deemed necessary. In the League's Covenant the power to act in case of a war rested not merely in the Council but also the Assembly, the Permanent Court, the Conference of Ambassadors and the Mixed Arbitral Tribunals. This left scope for overlapping jurisdictions but made for greater flexibility.

Mohammed Bedjaoui, a judge of the ICJ, was a strong advocate of judicial review of the actions of the organs of the UN for their conformity with the Charter, "Nobody should deny. . . that a member state had a right to challenge a decision and to have its revelations duly recorded." He asserted that an international organisation cannot seek to be above the law and then hope to be able to enforce it, "What it calls for is not so much release from the bondage of rules as a firmer anchorage in law."[38] He, however, admitted that "Judicial review of the legality of the act of international organs is still at a rudimentary and tentative stage. Its outlines are vague, its limits quickly reached." He concluded, "All the principal organs of the United Nations must respect not only the Charter but international law itself, if only because the founding states did not invest them with any function as international legislators or creators of new rules."[39]

Gharekhan drew a pithy conclusion after serving as India's ambassador to the UN and a stand-in for the secretary-general in the Security Council, "The Security Council also considers itself to be above the law."[40] He added, "Since there are no definitions of terms such as threats or breaches of peace, it is left to the members of the Council to decide how they ought to react in a given situation. What this means in practice is that the permanent members decide everything."[41]

Endnotes

1   Preamble to the Covenant of the League of Nations.

2   Article 2.2 of the UN Charter.

3   Schweigman, p. 29.

4   UNCIO Committee IV/2, Doc. 527, IV/2/27, 23 May 1945. (New York: UN Information Organization, 1945), p. 619.

5   Nardin, p. 110.

6   Doc 597 III/I/30 UNCIO Docs 393-395.

7   J.L. Brierly. *The Basis of Obligation in International Law* (Oxford: Clarendon Press, 1958), p. 10.

8   Rosalyn Higgins. *The Development of International Law through the Political Organs of the United Nations* (London: Oxford University Press, 1963), p. 5.

9   João Carlos Muniz, Statement at the second session of the UNGA, 16 September 1947, *The Voice of Brazil in the United Nations, 1946-1995* (Brasilia: Alexandre de Gusmão Foundation, 1995), p. 40

10 L.M. Goodrich, E. Hambro &A .S. Simon., *"Charter of the United Nations"* (New York: Columbia University Press, 1969), p. 15.

11 UNCIO DOC. 887, IV/2/39, 9 June 1945, p. 669.

12 UNCIO Vol. 3. Doc 2, G/7 (K) (1), 4 May 1945, p. 336.

13 Vandenberg, Jr. and Morris [Eds.]. p. 164.

14 Ruth B. Russell. *The United Nations and US Security Policy* (Washington, DC: Brookings Institution, 1968), p. 294.

15 UNCIO Vol. XIII. Commission IV – Judicial Organisation, Committee 1 – ICJ. Doc. 913, IV/1/74(1), 12 June 1945. (New York: UN Information Organization, 1945), p. 391-392.

16 UNCIO Committee IV/2 and IV/2/B, Doc. 843, IV/2/37, 7 June 1945 (New York: UN Information Organization, 1945), pp. 645-646. Also Annex II Doc. IV/2/39, 9 June, 1945, p. 669.

17 Inis Claude Jr. *Swords into Plowshares – The Problems and Progress of International Organization.* (New York: McGraw-Hill, 4th Ed. 1984), p.171.

18 Alex Conte. *Security in the 21st Century* (Farnham, Surrey: Ashgate, 2005), p. 185.

19 Ioana Petculescu. *The Review of the United Nations Security Decisions by the International Court of Justice.* (Netherlands International Law Review, LII, 2005), pp. 194-195.

20 Schweigman, p. 305.

21 Franck in Tomaschat (Ed.), p. 179.

22 ICJ: *Legal Consequences for States of the Continued Presence of South Africa in Namibia (South-West Africa) Notwithstanding Security Council Resolution 276, 1970-*1971.

23 Declaration of Judge Shigeru Oda in *Questions of Interpretation and Application of the 1971 Montreal Convention arising from the Aerial Incident at Lockerbie (Libyan Arab Jamahiriya v. United Kingdom).* ICJ, Order of 14 April 1992. (www.icj-cij/en/case/88/orders).

24 Separate Opinion of Judge Manfred Lachs in *Lockerbie case.* ICJ Order of 14 April 1992. (www.icj-cij/files/case-related/88/088-19920414-ORD-01-04-EN.pdf).

25 ICJ, *Certain Expenses of the United Nations (Article 17, paragraph 2 of the Charter)*, 1961-1962, p. 21.

26 Freudenschuss, p. 36.

27 UN Document, S/RES/457(1979).

28 ICJ, *US Diplomatic and Consular Staff in Tehran* (USA v. Iran), 1979-1981.

29 ICJ, *Military and Paramilitary Activities in and against Nicaragua* (USA v. Nicaragua), 1984-1991.

30 ICJ, *Legal Consequences of the Continued Presence of South Africa in Namibia, 1970-1971.*

31 ICJ, *Certain Expenses case*, 1962, p. 16

32 Statement of Morgenstierne, Norwegian President of Commission III, Doc 943 III/5, 11 UNCIO Docs, at 13.

33 Article 34 of the Vienna Convention on the Law of Treaties, 1969, states that a treaty "does not create either obligations or rights for a third State without its consent".

34 Benedetto Conforti and Carlo Focarelli. *The Law and Practice of the United Nations* (Leiden: Martinus Nijhoff Publishers, 2010), p. 425.

35 Brierly. *The Basis of Obligation in International Law*, p. 10.

36 Alexander Orakhelashvili. *The Impact of Peremptory Norms on the Interpretation and Application of United Nations Security Council Resolutions.* (European Journal of International Law, 2005, v. 16, No. 1), p. 63.

37 Elihu Lauterpacht. 'The Legal Effect of Illegal Acts of International Organizations'. Cambridge Essays in International Law: Essays in Honour of Lord McNair, 1965.

38 Mohammed Bedjaoui. *The New World Order and the Security Council – Testing the Legality of its Acts* (The Hague: Kluwer Academic Publishers, 1994), pp. 127-128.

39 Bedjaoui, p. 32.

40 Chinmaya R. Gharekhan, *The Horseshoe Table* (New Delhi: Pearson Longman, 2006), p. 4

41 Gharekhan, p. 3.

14   Impermanence of the Permanent Five

The United States is by far the most powerful player in the Security Council and, but for the brief period between 1970 and 1990, its main driving force. All Security Council resolutions authorising military action and imposing sanctions have been either sponsored by the United States or enjoyed its support. Britain and France have taken the lead on some. Russia and China have been content to react, either blocking or supporting grudgingly. Domestic politics determines the policies of all member states, but in the case of the United States its domestic politics often overshadows developments in the Security Council. Russia no longer enjoys the stature of the Soviet Union and is content with defending its national interests and its periphery. China follows a similar policy. Neither seeks to use the Security Council for pursuing global interests as the three Western powers do.

The five big powers claimed permanent membership of the Security Council so that they could provide security to all. However, all except the United States have undergone major internal changes, raising questions about the validity of their claim to permanent membership. There has also been little permanence in their policies, which has made the Security Council unpredictable and unreliable.

The United States

The US approach to dealing with the rest of the world has always been torn between unilateralism and multilateralism. Its isolation till the end of the nineteenth century, its religious zeal and contempt for what it considered the Old World diplomacy of secrecy and intrigue made it a reluctant participant in its affairs. Its unwavering belief in its own exceptionalism makes it an impatient negotiator, making for a difficult relationship with the United Nations. The United States feels a sense of propriety over the organisation it created and built into the world's first truly global body. The split in the ranks of the victors was the first disillusionment for its leaders, whose frustration turned into rage when the communist bloc made common cause with the newly independent countries of Asia and Africa and was joined by its traditional ally, Latin America. The end of the Cold War restored its interest in the United Nations but many of its leaders were uncomfortable with its slow pace of decision making and their inability to have their way all the time.

Enthusiasts of the United Nations in the United States face a dilemma in proving the fairness and effectiveness of the organisation to the world while reassuring leaders at home that it does not encroach on American sovereignty. Thomas G. Weiss declares that the United Nations serves American interests, "Pundits too often overlook how the UN system serves American interests and gives Washington cause to proceed with international acquiescence, if not jubilant support."[1] This approach overlooks the risk of undermining the stature and legitimacy of the United Nations in the perception of the other members.

In 1966, the US ambassador to the UN in 1960-61, James J. Wadsworth, examined the attacks on the UN by its critics in the US. He said that this criticism sprang from the numerous myths prevailing in the US about the UN: the UN is a nest of spies, its Military Staff Committee is permanently chaired by a Russian general, the UN secretary-general is a communist, communists prevent the UN from operating, the Russians stole US military secrets through the UN, the UN is anti-Christian, the UN can send US troops to war, etc.

Wadsworth then went on to demolish these myths. In the process he also inadvertently revealed the impotence of the UN and its subordination to the US, ".... the United Nations Military Staff Committee is set up by the Charter of the United Nations under the direction of the five permanent members of the Security Council. It consists of representatives of the five permanent members of the Security Council, and is, therefore, anti-Communist four to one. But further, this group has never conducted a United Nations military operation and has no immediately foreseeable function in this area; it had nothing whatever to do or say about the Korean operation, the UNEF operation in Palestine, or the ONUC operation in the Congo."[2]

Wadsworth called the Military Staff Committee an "appendix" within the UN body politic. He declared, "The Korean War was carried on by a special United Nations staff, headed both in New York and in Korea by a United States officer. No Soviet or other Communist personnel participated in any phase of the United Nations Korean operation; the United Nations Military Staff Committee was completely bypassed. The only military information given to the United Nations about the Korean War was decided upon and cleared by the United States Departments of Defence and State before being sent to New York for transmission to the international body."[3]

To emphasise the control the US had exercised till then on the UN, Wadsworth pointed out that the US had been on the winning side of General Assembly votes so often that it had become monotonous. He noted that the few occasions, such as on colonialism and nuclear testing, when the US was on the losing side carried "little stigma" and caused only "temporary upheaval".[4]

Referring to the possibility of the UN giving instructions to the US, Wadsworth affirmed, "There is nothing in the Charter that can compel the United States to do one single thing she considers to be against her best interests. The idea, somehow still widely held, that the United Nations has power to force obedience is utterly without foundation."[5]

Wadsworth did a head count of the number times the US and the Soviet Union confronted each other in the UN and concluded that on each occasion the Soviets had to bite the dust. They were on the winning side only when they sided with the West. He listed the West's victories: disarmament, nuclear testing, the Congo, Hungary, Lebanon, Laos, Korea, West New Guinea, Greece, Iran, and the opinion of the International Court of Justice on the responsibility of financing peacekeeping operations. He concluded, quite accurately, "All in all, the contest has been so one-sided that more than one impartial observer has felt it to be unhealthy."[6] This unusually candid assessment, designed to reassure American public opinion that the UN did not dilute their country's sovereignty and national interests, reveals the attitude of the US to the organisation. The US will cooperate with it so long as it does its bidding and serves its interests. Even on issues like decolonisation and nuclear testing, the US would not bow to world opinion.

Wadsworth wrote this in the days when the US commanded a comfortable majority in the General Assembly. Later, when the countries of Asia and African came to dominate it and the countries of Latin America joined hands with them, the US became hostile to the UN. During the Presidency of Ronald Reagan, the United States persistently called for reform of the UN, without going into specifics. It started withholding its contribution, which at the time stood at 25 percent of the UN budget. Pérez de Cuéllar notes in his memoirs that the US would vent its anger at the UN by withholding its contribution to it.[7] The US was furious over being repeatedly outvoted in the General Assembly on issues like Israel and Palestine, South Africa (during apartheid) and the UN budget. American diplomats would analyse the vote of countries in the General Assembly to put pressure on them individually. Realising that it could not have its way in the General Assembly it called for budgetary cuts, under the euphemism of 'reform'. However, as Pérez de Cuéllar noted in his memoir, despite his success in saving US$ 30 million, the US withheld its contribution, and its dues reached $ 500 million in 1986.[8]

Ironically, the collapse of the Soviet Union and the consequent unshackling of the UN became an added cause of American suspicion. The increase in multilateral cooperation in the 1990s in the new atmosphere saw the creation of such organisations as the World Trade Organization and the International Criminal Court. The European Union expanded the frontiers of international law by employing a large body of international civil servants and other elected or appointed experts to determine policies that were earlier considered to be in the sovereign domain of countries. The US saw this as a challenge to its constitutional principles of accountability and national sovereignty.

Europe's inability to address its internal problems in Bosnia and Kosovo, which compelled it to turn to the US and NATO, reinforced the US conviction that decision-sharing would be disastrous not only for its own security but also the world at large. The US would have to preserve its military preponderance and independence of action if it was to be effective. While the allies in western Europe could act as a drag on the US, the cacophony of the rabble-rousers in the United Nations was worse and would have to be kept at a safe distance when issues critical to America's interests and international peace and security were being decided.

The US supports making its military facilities available to the UN for the training of peacekeeping personnel but stops short of deploying its forces under the UN for peacekeeping duties or a stand-by rapid reaction force. The US fears that giving unquestioned assurance for peacekeeping will make the Security Council profligate in its operations. In its response to Boutros-Ghali's 'Agenda for Peace' the US stated that it would place its military capabilities at the disposal of the UN "in appropriate circumstances." There were no specifics on the nature of capabilities or circumstances.

Shortly after he took office in 1993, President Clinton had toyed with the idea of establishing a UN army. The thought was banished by General Powell, "As long as I am Chairman of the Joints Chiefs of Staff, I will not agree to commit American men and women to an unknown war, in an unknown land, for an unknown cause, under an unknown commander, for an unknown duration."[9] The new administration, however, continued to examine the possibility of creating a UN force, while shelving the idea of entering into an agreement with the UN under Article 43 on making US troops available to it. It considered the various arrangements under which the US provides troops to NATO, some under NATO command, some on call at short notice, some at longer notice and some which are unlikely to be sent to NATO.

However, the casualties suffered by US forces in Somalia led to the government coming under attack in Congress. Most leaders held the UN responsible. One such critic was the former national security adviser, Henry A. Kissinger, who referred to Clinton's enthusiasm for peacekeeping in an article for the Washington Post, "If these statements imply that international consensus is the prerequisite for the employment of American power, the result may be ineffective dithering, as has happened over Bosnia. If they mean that international machinery can commit US forces, the risk is American involvement in issues of no fundamental national interest, as is happening in Somalia."[10] After the Somalia fiasco, the draft proposals for cooperating with the UN in peacekeeping operations were quietly amended.

If Clinton chose to ignore the UN, his successor, George W. Bush, took his hostility to a new level. While Clinton was at best ambivalent and at worst indifferent to the UN, Bush was decidedly contemptuous of it. His aides mocked Clinton's occasional recourse to multilateralism. Condoleezza Rice accused Clinton of advocating "the belief that the support of many states – or even better, of institutions like the United Nations – is essential to the legitimate exercise of power."[11]

Bush and his aides believed that the UN had become obsolete because it had come to be dominated by small powers that did not share the high ideals of the organisation and most certainly not American principles. They accused these countries of opposing American interests and principles. Their antipathy may have remained just that and retreated into the traditional US isolationism of the pre-First World War period, but for the terrorist attack in September 2001. Bush is sometimes dismissed as not representing the mainstream of US foreign policy. His unilateralist and aggressive approach is contrasted with that of his father, George H.W. Bush, who not only took UN authorisation before invading Iraq in 1991 but also stopped once the primary objective of liberating Kuwait had been achieved. In their memoir, Bush and his National Security Adviser Brent Scowcroft write, "We also believed that the United States should not go it alone, that a multilateral approach was better... Building an international response led us immediately to the United Nations, which could provide a cloak of acceptability to our efforts and mobilize world opinion behind the principles we wished to project."

As can be seen from a closer look at the words and the views of Bush or Scowcroft discussed earlier in Chapter 9, this was not an endorsement of multilateralism. Rather, it reduced the Security Council to a convenient tool of US policy.[12]

The US continued to treat the UN as its sidekick in Iraq, to be called in to clean up the mess or take the blame when things went out of control. Not surprisingly, the UN got the short end of the stick. Its prestige suffered immeasurably when its compound in Baghdad suffered a terrorist attack by Iraqis on 19 August 2003 killing the UN Special Representative, Sergio Vieira de Mello, and 12 of his colleagues.

The US has found its constitutional separation of powers between the Presidency and the Congress to be a convenient escape route from international entanglements not to its liking. Patrick summed it up, "From the Senate's failure to pass the Treaty of Versailles (including the League Covenant) to its rejection of the Comprehensive Test Ban Treaty 80 years later, one finds multiple instances in which Congress has exercised its veto prerogatives by declining to assume obligations favoured by the White House."[13]

Changes in the presidency are also used to the same effect. The US refused to join the League of Nations because the Congress did not ratify it. In President Clinton's period, the US refused to ratify the Kyoto Protocol after signing it and rejected the Comprehensive Test Ban Treaty after voting for it in the General Assembly. President George W. Bush abrogated the Anti-Ballistic Missile Treaty with Russia, repudiated the International Criminal Court, blocked a verification protocol to the Biological Weapons Convention, and opposed a draft UN Convention to reduce illicit trafficking in small arms and light weapons. In 2017, President Donald Trump decided to withdraw from the Paris agreement on climate change, signed by his predecessor.

The United States has repeatedly chosen to act unilaterally against countries that have challenged its authority. After the First Gulf War, it refrained from attacking Iraq but bombed it on several occasions in retaliation against alleged terrorist attacks or repression of its minorities, the Kurds and Shias. These culminated in the invasion of Iraq in 2003. The United States also bombed targets in Sudan and Afghanistan in 1998 for alleged terrorist attacks. In 1999, it led a 10-week bombing campaign against Serbia for its repression in the province of Kosovo.

The US invoked Article 51 to justify its bombings of Iraq in 1993 for an alleged attempt to kill President Bush, the bombings of Sudan and Afghanistan in 1998 for terrorist attacks on US embassies and the bombing of Libya in 1986. It also took recourse to it to justify its invasions of Afghanistan in 2001 and Iraq in 2003. The US claimed that its use of force against Iraq in 1998 and its invasion of the country in 2003 were in enforcement of Security Council resolutions as was the bombing of Yugoslavia in 1999 over Kosovo.

This proclivity to resort to pre-emptive strikes under the right of self-defence was brought up by Secretary-General Kofi Annan in his address to the UNGA on 23 September 2003, "According to this argument, States are not obliged to wait until there is agreement in the Security Council. Instead, they reserve the right to act unilaterally or in *ad hoc* coalitions. This logic represents a fundamental challenge to the principles on which, however imperfectly, world peace and stability have rested for the last fifty-eight years." He cautioned that this could set precedents that would result in the proliferation of the use of force.[14] But such encumbrances are not palatable to any US administration. The countries attitude to the United Nations is summed up by President George W. Bush in his memoir, "I considered the UN to be cumbersome, bureaucratic, and inefficient."[15]

Soviet Union/Russian Federation

The Soviet Union saw the UN as an organisation intended to serve the limited objective of providing security. To Stalin, it was an alliance of the big powers for their security against the Axis powers, Germany and Japan. Stalin was dismissive of dreams of a world government as *bourgeois* ideas. He did not block western initiatives on Palestine, Kashmir, Indonesia and Italian colonies since he did not see any vital Soviet interests being affected. However, he became increasingly alarmed at the UN becoming a tool of US foreign policy. In February 1951, he said, "The United Nations Organisation is being turned into an instrument of war .... [It] is now not so much a world organisation as an organisation for the Americans, organisation acting on behalf of the American aggressors."[16]

In the early days of the UN, the Soviet Union argued the UN represented governments, not the people. Since communism associated the state with oppression, it advocated a role for the masses, the workers and hence the people in the United Nations. The Soviet Union claimed the right to speak on behalf of the workers of the world. The communists dreamed of the emergence of voluntary international commonwealth once the state withered away and, with it, all associations of states. Until then, they regarded the communist parties as the legitimate voice of the people of the world. Ironically, several decades later it was the West that endorsed the concept of civil society as the voice of the people and promoted it in the UN.

There was a congruence of views of the US and the Soviet Union on the need to maintain the dominance of the big powers in the UN, though their motives were different. The Soviet Union's concern was limited to ensuring that the UN did not operate against its interests. At the Moscow Conference in October 1943, the Soviet delegates talked of a "guiding nucleus" a concept similar to the "policeman" idea of President Roosevelt. Both countries believed in their great power status and held the conviction that this entitled them to special rights.[17] Once the principle of veto had been agreed upon, the Soviet Union was satisfied that the UN could not be used against it, as it had suspected the League of doing. It did not go into other issues in particular detail. At Yalta, the US secretary of state, James F. Byrnes, noted that Stalin was not greatly interested in the details of the UN organisation.

Stalin started with a positive attitude to the Security Council. In an interview to the Associated Press correspondent, Eddie Gilmore, on 10 March 1946, he said that it was "a serious instrument for the preservation of peace."[18] However, the Soviet Union soon found itself out-voted in the UN on almost every issue. Once the Cold War started the Soviet Union developed a deep animosity towards the United Nations. Its only allies were its satellite governments in East Europe, Ukraine, Byelorussia, Poland, Yugoslavia and Czechoslovakia, which had to be chastened periodically. They were of little help in the debates. After the takeover of China by Mao's Communist Party and the formation of the People's Republic of China, the Soviet Union insisted on it taking the seat of the Republic of China. This was opposed by the US. In 1956, Hans Morgenthau called the UN a grand alliance of countries opposed to the other grand alliance of the Soviets.

The Soviet Union was also disdainful of the emerging non-aligned movement of the newly independent countries in Asia and Africa. It drew a distinction between a communist party-led colonial struggle and a *bourgeois* one and maintained strict vigil in the Security Council on any criticism of the former. When the UN Commission found Yugoslavia, Bulgaria and Albania guilty of supporting the communist party of Greece in its civil war, it vetoed the outcome. However, on the Kashmir dispute, it abstained as it did on Indonesia, even though Indonesia itself had accepted it. It voted in favour of the resolution in the UNGA along with the European members on the partition of Palestine which led to the creation of Israel.

The Soviet Union took a dim view of what the West counted as successes of the UN. It maintained that the Iran affair of 1946 was resolved by direct negotiations. The Suez crisis was settled because of the Soviet threat of intervention. In Korea, the UN had acted under pressure from the US. Elsewhere the UN functioned as a rapporteur of events rather than a mediator.

The Soviet Union regretted its boycott of the Security Council in 1950 over Communist China's membership. It realised that while it could not have its way its presence was essential to prevent the Security Council from acting against its interests. After that, the Soviet Union remained in the Security Council despite threats of withdrawal. It tried to compete with the West by developing rival alliances. It formed the COMINFORM, a union of nine communist parties and also tried to form a World Peace Council. To counter NATO, it formed the Warsaw Pact.

Stalin's death in 1953 led to a struggle for succession in Moscow. Nikita Khrushchev, who came to power two years later, took a more active interest in the United Nations and pursued vigorously a policy of supporting the newly independent countries of Asia and Africa in order to turn the tables on the West. The position of the Soviet Union in the United Nations started changing with the enlargement of the General Assembly and the admission of the newly independent countries of Asia and Africa.

Khrushchev's coming to power coincided with the entry of sixteen new members in the United Nations, the first admissions after 1947. Then there was the Bandung Conference and the birth of Afro-Asian solidarity. Another 23 countries joined by 1961. The new members celebrated their majority in the General Assembly by adopting the Declaration on the Granting of Independence to Colonial Countries and Peoples in November 1960. The Soviet Union's support for decolonisation and the US alliance with European colonial powers made a dramatic turnaround in its fortunes in a very short period of time. The idea of the resolution came from the Soviet delegation and the text adopted was that of the twenty-six countries of Asia and Africa and based on the Bandung principles. The Europeans abstained. The US did likewise following an appeal from the British prime minister. Some Americans had wanted their country to support the resolution. But its Republican government identified itself with the interests of West Europe and continued to view the world through the prism of the Cold War divide. The countries of Asia and Africa turned towards the Soviet Union much to the indignation of the US. Eisenhower's brief attempt to distance himself from the aggressive colonialism of Britain and France in the Suez crisis was over.

The Soviet bloc supported Egypt and Sudan against Britain and Syria, Lebanon, Tunisia and Morocco against France. It endeared itself to India in 1957 by exercising its first veto on a resolution sponsored by Australia, Cuba, Britain and the United States on Kashmir.[19] A year later, the coming to power of Fidel Castro in Cuba gave another boost to the Soviet Union in the UN. Cuba was the first country in Latin America to break free from the hold of the United States. Articulate and vocal, Cuban diplomats delivered endless tirades against the US for its conspiracies against the Cuban revolution. The Soviet Union could not have asked for a better ally. The support of Asian and African countries in the General Assembly further increased its enthusiasm for the UN. It started using the General Assembly to embarrass the West. The convenient adoption of the Uniting for Peace resolution in the General Assembly to by-pass the Soviet veto in the Security Council now became a thing of the distant past for the West.

The transfer of the Soviet Union's seat to the Russian Federation is covered in Chapter 16. In its early years Russian Federation adhered sullenly to the western agenda. It moderated its policy on financing peacekeeping missions. It no longer insisted on these missions being financed by extra-budgetary sources and accepted part funding of the missions in Angola, El Salvador, Iraq/Kuwait and Western Sahara, between 1989 and 1992, from the UN's regular budget. It also sent troops to the former Yugoslavia and in smaller numbers to some other missions. However, murmurings started soon among its diplomats and in 1993 it blocked a British resolution on the UN mission in Cyprus (UNFICYP) because it sought to finance it partly from the regular budget. Russia reverted to its stand that such missions should be financed by voluntary contributions. Russia became uncomfortable about the expansion of NATO into Eastern Europe and what it considered its one-sided disarmament. However, in its considerably reduced stature and capacity, it narrowed its concern to protecting the interests of the people of Russian origin in the breakaway republics of the Soviet Union. It used its military to pull Abkhazia and South Ossetia out of Georgia and the blocked a Security Council resolution in 2009 extending the term of the UN mission there.

NATO's action in Libya in 2011 further hardened Russia's stand. It had abstained on the resolution on Libya on the understanding that it did not authorise military action. It refused to allow any resolution to go through on Syria, vetoing as many as 12 of them, six of them alone and the rest with China.

Russia maintains that there is no alternative to the UN today and although it recognises that there is the need for its reform it insists that it should be gradual and based on broad consensus. It retains its original conception of the Security Council as a body to keep big powers together and act jointly based on respect for national sovereignty. Russia accepts that the Security Council has the authority to outsource military action to member states as long it has the consent of the permanent five. In a speech at an international gathering in October 2017, President Vladimir Putin said that "this mechanism was designed and created in order to avoid direct confrontation of the most powerful states, as a guarantee against its arbitrariness and recklessness, so that no single country, even the most influential country, could give the appearance of legitimacy to its aggressive actions."[20]

People's Republic of China

The People's Republic of China has had by far the most chequered membership of the United Nations. While the inclusion of the Kuomintang regime of the Republic of China in the great powers had raised eyebrows then, the People's Republic, while not yet a member, earned an early distinction of being condemned by the United Nations as an aggressor in Korea. The issue of replacing the Republic of China with the People's Republic led to protracted and acrimonious debates in the UN and a brief boycott of the Security Council by the Soviet Union. The change, when it came after two decades, was an anti-climax, as was the new regime's performance in the next two.

The People's Republic of China has since grown in stature and has set at rest any doubts about its great power status and ambitions. It has built its image as a developing country standing side by side with the G-77 and gathered a small band of satellite states whose interests it protects staunchly. China has expanded its strategic sphere beyond its immediate neighbourhood with its economic heft and military muscle, but still prefers to let the Russian Federation take the lead on international issues beyond its periphery. The renewed bonding of the two former communist allies in their new *avatars* after the Western invasion of Libya in 2011 heralded a new balance of power in the Security Council. But despite its global ambitions, China preserves its diplomatic clout for its core interests – blocking Taiwan's international recognition and protecting its key allies, Pakistan, Sudan, Zimbabwe, Myanmar and North Korea.

In the years when the People's Republic of China was out of the UN, it feigned disinterest in it and accused it of ignoring such a large country in collusion with the 'Taiwan clique'. However, after 1969 it started seeking normal relations with countries and till the vote in the General Assembly in October 1971 "campaigned actively and effectively for its right to take its seat in the UN as the sole representative of China."[21] Its entry in the UN coincided with the second phase of the Security Council. It claimed to be a developing country, opposed to imperialism and aggression, but it would not always translate its rhetoric into a veto. Its delegates participated little in the debates and did not articulate their views in detail on any of the issues that animated developing countries, like the new international economic order or official development assistance. One observer of China's policy notes, "Such articulation of Chinese aspiration was often loaded with general declaratory principles but lacked details about tactics or strategies."[22] Its worldview and interests were still very limited, but it did not wish to identify itself totally with the *hoi polloi*. It exercised the veto only once, on Bangladesh's admission, in 1972. It would denounce the UN whenever it suited it and then not participate in the vote. It is difficult to avoid drawing the conclusion that China was biding its time and learning from the other permanent members about the role it would play when it caught up with them as a world power, as happened on the Israel-Syria issue two years after its joining the UN.

In October 1973, after the war in the Middle-East, the United States decided to broker talks between Israel and Syria outside the UN. The ten non-permanent members expressed outrage and in an unprecedented coming together tabled a resolution seeking a role for the Security Council in the talks. The resolution was adopted with the vote of the ten non-permanent members.[23] Four permanent members abstained. China professed sympathy for the non-permanent members but did not vote with them. Its ambassador, Huang Hua, declared solemnly, "The Chinese delegation is always firmly opposed to any attempt of the two superpowers to make behind the scene deals at the expense of the interests of the Arab and Palestine people."

In the third phase of the Security Council's history (1991-2011), while Russia was still recovering from the collapse of the Soviet Union and its own internal problems, China shed some of its hesitancy but remained unwilling to stand up to the other permanent members even when it disagreed with them. It would often leverage its veto to extract concessions, commercial or strategic from them. In the First Gulf War, China said that the use of the phrase "such measures commensurate to specific circumstances as may be necessary" did not authorise the use of force. In the case of Bosnia and Herzegovina, it said that the use of force would only complicate the situation and it could not agree to it for the delivery of humanitarian assistance under Resolution 770 (1992). But instead of vetoing the resolution it abstained, allowing it to be adopted.

Wuthnow describes China's diplomacy in the Security Council till the early 2000s as "measured and deferential" and its opposition often "primarily rhetorical". The US was confident during this period that China would not be a "spoiler" and block its resolutions.[24] But China did not always apply this principle uniformly. In 1981, it repeatedly blocked the re-election of Kurt Waldheim for an unprecedented third term, arguing for a person from the third world to be given the office. It later unsuccessfully supported Salim A. Salim of Tanzania.

On Somalia, it voted in favour of a resolution authorising military action to protect humanitarian relief operations.[25] On Haiti, it said that resolving such problems through military means did not conform to the principles enshrined in the Charter and lacked sufficient and convincing grounds.[26] In the discussion on Resolution 1973 (2011) on Libya, China said that it was against the use of force in international relations but it was abstaining on the resolution out of deference to the stand of the African Union and the views of the Arab League, which had demanded a no-fly zone on Libya.

China abstained in the enforcement resolutions against Iraq, Bosnia, Rwanda, Haiti, Albania, Kosovo and Libya. It supported Resolution 1080 (1996) on Zaire and 1125 (1997) on the Central African Republic but abstained on Resolution 1101 (1997) on Albania. Similarly, China abstained on Resolution 1244 (1999) on Kosovo. Both these were adopted by 14 votes in favour, with China abstaining.

China has exercised its veto alone on only three occasions. The first was to please its "all-weather friend", Pakistan, which did not want its breakaway eastern wing, East Pakistan, now an independent Bangladesh, to become a member of the United Nations. It vetoed the resolution in its first year in the UN.[27] Huang Hua accused India of not carrying out a "true withdrawal" of its troops from Bangladesh and of holding 90,000 Pakistani troops as prisoners of war in violation of the 1949 Geneva Convention. The resolution received 11 votes in favour. China's was the only vote against, while Guinea, Somalia and Sudan abstained. Thus, though reluctant to be alone, China does not hesitate to act on issues it considers to be of vital national interest.

The second Chinese veto was more egregious. In 1997, after years of negotiations, warring factions in Guatemala agreed to a ceasefire and UN monitoring. The resolution appointing a UN mission was supported by all members and received 14 votes in favour. But China vetoed it because the Guatemalan government had invited Taiwan to the signing ceremony of the peace agreement. The Chinese ambassador, Qin Huasun, declared that this was aimed at splitting China at the UN and giving Taiwan "a venue for secessionist activities against China", disregarding the "solemn warnings of the Chinese Government."[28]

China's third solo veto sought to take the high moral ground of exercising economy in UN expenses. In February 1999, the Security Council took up consideration of giving a six-month extension to its peacekeeping force in the Former Yugoslav Republic of Macedonia.[29] Macedonia had itself sought this extension and the resolution received 13 votes in favour. Russia abstained because its amendment seeking to reorient the mandate of the peacekeepers to the arms embargo had not been accepted. But China vetoed the extension on the ground that conditions in Macedonia had normalised and the Security Council could utilise its limited peacekeeping resources better in places like Africa. However, the real reason was that in the previous month Macedonia had established diplomatic relations with Taiwan.

In the fourth and current phase, China has aligned itself closely with Russia. It has exercised the veto eight times in tandem with Russia, six of them on Syria and one each on Zimbabwe and Myanmar. It has also been active in ensuring that no intrusive action is authorised against Iran or North Korea. It has gone along with sanctions against both, but there have been allegations of clandestine trade, particularly with North Korea. China has also protected Pakistan on the branding of terrorists like Masood Azhar.

However, China broke ranks with Russia on a draft resolution annulling the referendum being held by the latter in Crimea, with the intent of slicing it from Ukraine and annexing it. China called for a political settlement of the crisis in Ukraine but abstained on the resolution on the argument that it respected the territorial integrity and sovereignty of all states. Russia vetoed the resolution, which was supported by all the other 13 members.[30]

Britain and France

Britain and France were major colonial powers at the end of the Second World War by virtue of which they became permanent members of the Security Council. The loss of their empires made them turn to their European neighbours for greater trade and economic cooperation. The formation of the European Union in 1992 led to the further integration of its members, requiring coordination even of their foreign policies. Early in the 21st century, the members of the European Union decided to go for their own security arrangement distinct from but complementary to the United Nations and NATO. The European Security Strategy of December

2003 talked of the need for "effective multilateralism". The paper was updated in 2008 and still looked forward to a more active, capable and coherent EU foreign policy foreign and security policy. It even declared the EU to be a "global player". Britain and France retain their permanent seats but they oscillate between playing global powers and federating units of the EU.

Neither Britain nor France has exercised the veto since the Cold War ended. Nearly all the US vetoes since then have been to prevent censure of Israel, an issue on which the European Union takes a more detached view. Britain has the delicate task of preserving its 'special relationship' with the US but France takes more liberties. Britain's image as an independent global power took a hit in the Iraq war in 2003 when its prime minister, Tony Blair, initially insisted that a Security Council authorisation was essential for taking military action, but when it became evident that a resolution might not even secure majority support, he dropped the idea and toed the US line of unilateral action. France continues to dominate in the Security Council on issues relating to Francophone countries in Africa, where others fear to tread. It has undertaken authorised military action independently in Rwanda, Mali and the Central African Republic. Both Britain and France claim to support the idea of amending veto rules to prohibit them from being used against resolutions on mass atrocities. They have been in the forefront of the campaign to give new mandates to the Security Council. They champion gender issues, the environment, human rights, increased role for civil society organisations and the International Criminal Court. They have been the most ardent supporters of authorised military action and also been the most welcoming of Security Council reform.

Endnotes

1 Thomas G. Weiss. *What's Wrong with the United Nations and How to Fix It* (Malden, MA: Polity Press, 2009), p. 5.

2 James J. Wadsworth. The Glass House - The United Nations in Action (New York: Frederick A. Praeger Publishers, 1966), p. 161.

3 Wadsworth, pp. 161-162.

4 Wadsworth, p.165.

5 Wadsworth, p. 162.

6 Wadsworth, p. 164.

7 Cuéllar, p. 10.

8 Pérez de Cuéllar, p. 10.

9 Cited in Jeremy D. Rosner. *"Peacekeeping" – The New Tug of War: Congress, the Executive Branch, and National Security.* (Carnegie Foundation for International Peace, Washington, 1995). Chapter 3, 69, n. 14. Quoted in Durch (Ed.) *UN Peacekeeping, American Politics, and the Uncivil Wars of the 1990s* (London: *Macmillan, 1997), p. 43.*

10 Henry A. Kissinger. *Recipe for Chaos,* Washington Post, 8 September 1993, A 19. Quoted in William J. Durch (ed.) *UN Peacekeeping, American Politics, and the Uncivil Wars of the 1990s (*London: Macmillan, 1997), *p. 50.*

11 Condoleezza Rice. *"Campaign 2000: Promoting the National Interest"* Foreign Affairs 79, No. 1 (January/February 2000), pp 45-62.

12 Bush and Scowcroft, p. 356.

13 Stewart Patrick. *The Mission Determines the Coalition: The United States and Multilateral Cooperation after 9/11.* Chapter in Bruce D. Jones, Shepard Forman and Richard Gowan [Eds.], *Cooperating for Peace and Security.* (Cambridge University Press, 2009), p. 24.

14 Annan. *We the Peoples,* p. 98.

15 George W. Bush. *Decision Points* (Crown Publishers, 2010. Reprinted in India by Replika Press), p. 336.

16 Mazower p. 249.

17 Quoted in Dallin, p. 22.

18 Quoted in Dallin, p. 28.

19 Draft resolution S/3787 on 20 February 1957. The Soviet Union used its veto

on five more occasions for India, including one in 1961 on Goa and other Portuguese colonies in India.

20 Vladimir Putin. Speech at the 14th Annual Meeting of the Valdai International Discussion Club, Sochi, 19 October 2017. (http://en.kremlin.ru/events/president/news/55882).

21 Robert Boardman. *Post-Socialist World Orders – Russia, China and the UN System.* (New York, St. Martin's Press, 1994), p.123.

22 Suzanne Xiao Yang, *China in the UN Security Council Decision-making on Iraq* (Routledge, 2013), p. 38.

23 UN Document, S/RES/344(1973).

24 Joel Wuthnow. *Chinese Diplomacy and the UN Security Council – Beyond the Veto.* (Routledge, 2012), p. 22 and 30.

25 UN Document, S/RES/794(1992).

26 UN Document, S/RES/940(1994).

27 UN Document, S/10771, 25 August 1972.

28 Qin Huasun, Statement at 3730th meeting of UNSC, 10 January 1997, UN Document, S/PV.3982, p. 20.

29 UN Document S/1999/201, 25 February 1999. It proposed a 6-month extension to the UN Preventive Deployment Force (UNPREDEP).

30 UN Document, S/2014/189 of 15 March 2014.

15 Wars that Escaped Security Council Action

The Security Council is a political organ controlled by the permanent five and has frequently failed in its task of maintaining international peace and security in disputes in which they are involved. The exercise of the veto or its threat has been enough to keep the Security Council from coming to the rescue of the small countries invaded by the permanent five or their allies. Vietnam, Czechoslovakia, Namibia, Angola, Israel's Arab neighbours, Afghanistan, Kosovo and Iraq are some of the most striking examples. Civil wars are currently raging in Syria and Yemen but the Security Council is unable to take action.

The Security Council is pilloried for being all talk and little action. This reputation is well founded, but it is not a malfunction of the system. This is how the Charter designed it to be. The founders of the UN wanted unanimity among the permanent five for all action to be taken by the Council but their veto was not to be applicable on procedural resolutions. This was done to enable discussion to take place even if no action could eventually be taken.

Debates in the Security Council are thus reduced to exchanges of allegations in formal meetings and cold bargaining among the permanent five in camera. Formal speeches are endless harangues over agenda items, rules of procedure, voting methods, inviting the combating countries to participate in Council debates and so on. Debates in the General Assembly seek to influence other member states and win their support but in the Security Council, where the permanent five can kill a substantive resolution with their veto, they merely raise hopes to disappoint. For the greater part of the 1940s and 1950s, Soviet delegates resorted to filibustering by mastering the rules of procedure and holding up proceedings for hours. The debate on the Soviet invasion of Czechoslovakia concluded at four in the morning because of long speeches by the veteran Soviet ambassador, Jakob Malik, and other communist country representatives, while the US representative pleaded for an early vote. In 1956, when Britain and France were in the dock for their invasion of Egypt in the Suez war, they adopted the same tactic.

The UN Charter permits the use of force in only three situations - one each by member states, the Security Council and regional organisations. Member states are permitted to use force in self-defence under Article 51 but only until the Security Council takes the necessary measures. The Security Council is authorised to use military force under Article 42 if sanctions have proved to be inadequate or are likely to be. Regional organisations can do so under Article 53 but only with the authorisation of the Security Council. Any other use of force or the threat of it is prohibited under Article 2(4). The Security Council plays the pivotal role in all three options and unanimity among the permanent five is indispensable for all.

While Security Council records provide plenty of speeches, occasionally sharp but mostly repetitive, they have little to show by way of action, except during the two decades of *bonhomie* among the permanent five around the turn of the century. The Council was unable to stop wars in which the permanent five were parties or had an interest. The United Nations was designed as a system in which security would be provided by the permanent five. The Charter did not cater for security threats emanating from them.

The three founders, the US, Britain and the Soviet Union, had tried to avoid a post-war clash among them by demarcating their spheres of influence but their rush to grab territory became a seamless continuation of the war and acrimony and recriminations started even before the war was over. The Soviet Union pushed into East Europe and the Far East. The US built military alliances and bases around the Soviet Union to check its expansion. The two confronted each other around the world and indulged in proxy warfare. The Security Council was a bystander in these conflicts.

Some of the bigger wars and the part played by the Security Council in them are discussed here.

Vietnam War

Vietnam, a French colony occupied by Japan during the war, became the theatre of the most devastating war of this period. The communist party of Vietnam, led by Ho Chi Minh, fought the French when they tried to re-conquer the country after the Second World War and inflicted a major defeat on them at Dien Bien Phu in 1954. Peace talks were organised in Geneva and France agreed to withdraw from the north. The country was split between a communist north, supported by the Soviet Union and the People's Republic of China, and a capitalist south, supported by France and the United States. These talks were held outside the United Nations since the PRC and the Vietnamese factions were not members. The United Nations was also not part of the international supervision mechanism set up by the Geneva accord. France soon withdrew from Vietnam completely, leaving the south in the hands of the US, whose operations grew into a full-scale war by 1964-1965. The Security Council's involvement in the war remained peripheral. In 1964, it adopted unanimously a resolution deploring the violation of Cambodia's borders by South Vietnam and sent a commission to investigate.[1] In 1966, the US requested an urgent meeting of the Security Council to discuss the situation in Vietnam and even submitted a resolution calling for immediate talks in a Geneva-style conference. However, both the Soviet Union and France objected to the issue being brought before the Council since the other parties in the conflict were not members of the UN.

Secretary-General U Thant was convinced that the Security Council was not the correct forum to seek an end to the war. In March 1967 he presented a three-step proposal: (i) a general standstill truce, (ii) preliminary talks, and (iii) reconvening of the Geneva Conference.[2] His successor, Kurt Waldheim, was equally unwilling to have the Security Council intervene. The Security Council had no contribution to make to the peace talks that started in 1968 in Paris. The secretary-general was ostensibly facilitating it but France took the lead by offering its good offices.

The Security Council's lack of involvement in the Vietnam War has been bemoaned by many diplomats in New York. India's ambassador, Rikhi Jaipal, said, "No other war of national liberation had left such a big scar on the conscience of the United Nations, because, as an organization, the United Nations stood aside and did nothing. That was one local conflict which the United Nations did not even try to stop, and as a consequence, the United Nation has, if I may say so, developed a sort of guilt complex about Vietnam."³ In 1975, the US vetoed the applications of membership of North and South Vietnam on the plea that members had refused to admit South Korea which was a similarly divided country. The US ambassador said that he was willing to accept North Korea since the US believed in the universal membership of the UN. This was the first US veto on membership.

A peace accord was reached in Paris in 1973 providing for elections in both parts of Vietnam. It enabled the US to start withdrawing its troops, but South Vietnam was unable to stand up to the North, and its capital, Saigon (later, Ho Chi Minh City), fell in 1975 when the last of the US troops and personnel were evacuated. A united Vietnam became a member of the UN in 1977.

Soviet invasion of Czechoslovakia, 1968

The Soviet invasion of Hungary in 1956 has been dealt with in Chapter 8 in the context of the Suez War.

In October 1968, Czechoslovakia tried to wriggle out of the Soviet embrace and received the full treatment of its military might. This gave the Western countries an opportunity of payback for Vietnam. It also put the developing countries of Asia and Africa, which had been receiving the support of the Soviet Union, in a dilemma. Ambassador Jakob Malik of the Soviet Union, who had come back to represent his country in the UN after an interlude of 15 years, defended his country's action by claiming that the troops from socialist countries had entered Czechoslovakia at the request of its government in order to help it meet the threat to its socialist order and constitutional state system. The Council discussed a resolution condemning the Soviet invasion and calling for its withdrawal sponsored by eight countries: the US, UK, France, Brazil, Canada, Denmark, Paraguay and Senegal and supported by the Republic of China and Ethiopia. The acting ambassador of Czechoslovakia, Muzik, also condemned the invasion as illegal. Malik, in response to the US criticism of the invasion, launched into a tirade against it for its war crimes in Vietnam. The resolution received 10 votes in favour. The Soviet Union vetoed it. Hungary also voted against the resolution while India, Pakistan and Algeria abstained. India said that since its proposal to drop the 'condemnation' of the Soviet Union had not been accepted by the sponsors of the resolution, it had decided to abstain.⁴

South Africa's invasion of Namibia and Angola

Namibia had been conquered by Germany in 1884 and after its defeat in World War I was handed over to South Africa by the League of Nations as a 'mandate' territory, which continued under the United Nations. In October 1966, the General Assembly terminated the mandate but South Africa not only continued to occupy the country but also carried out large-scale arrests and deportation of its people. In 1968, the Security Council unanimously adopted a resolution declaring South Africa's administration in Namibia to be illegal. It called for setting up an interim authority under the UN and early elections and independence of the country.[5] The resolution, on which the Soviet Union abstained, was supported by the US but it linked it with the withdrawal of Cuban troops, who were fighting alongside the Namibian freedom fighters.

Britain and the US succeeded in avoiding a harsher resolution by eulogising the virtues of holding consultations which they said were both an obligation and a tradition in the Council. They urged members to maintain unity in the Council so as not to give any comfort to South Africa. Britain urged members to hold consultations "on the basis of hard facts and practical possibilities."[6] The Soviet Union accused the US, Britain and Germany of maintaining close political, military and commercial links with South Africa and encouraging its rulers to ignore the UN and world opinion. Elections were finally held in Namibia in 1988 when the Cold War started easing and the country became independent in 1990.

In 1961, Liberia raised the issue of the disturbances in Angola due to Portuguese repression. Britain opposed it saying that the incidents did not represent a threat to international peace and security. It even cited Article 24 of the Charter to say that the matter was under discussion in the General Assembly, so the Security Council could not take it up.

A resolution by Ceylon (later, Sri Lanka), Liberia and the United Arab Republic (Egypt) could not be adopted in the Security Council as there were only five votes in favour, even though both the Soviet Union and the US supported it. Six countries, Chile, China, Ecuador, France, Turkey and Britain abstained. The Afro-Asian countries were still not able to get their way in the Security Council, even on the odd occasion when the US supported them, although in the General Assembly they were now able to get resolutions adopted, such as the landmark anti-colonial one in 1960.

The issue came up again in the Security Council in 1975 when South Africa invaded Angola to prevent communist forces from seizing power following Portugal's withdrawal. South Africa accused the Soviet Union and Cuba of interfering in Angola and of threatening its territory from there. It withdrew its forces in a few months when it found the going difficult. The Security Council adopted a resolution condemning South Africa's "aggression" and calling upon it to pay compensation to Angola for the damage during the invasion. Nine countries voted for the resolution.[7] The US, Britain, France, Italy and Japan abstained. China did not participate in the vote. France declared that it had abstained because the resolution had used the term "aggression" to describe South Africa's "intervention". Japan said that it had abstained because of the legal implication of a part of the text under Chapter VII. The British ambassador, Lord Richard, said that the South African forces had withdrawn so there was no need for a resolution, "We take the view that it is not the Council's task to sit in judgment on what has happened in the past." He added that holding an inquest by the Council would also not be useful, "The Security Council is not a court of law, nor is it the appropriate forum to determine questions of restitution and compensation for damages." He quoted Article 36 to say that legal disputes should be referred by the parties to the International Court of Justice.[8]

The debate also witnessed a clash between former communist allies, the Soviet Union and China. China's Ambassador Huang Hua condemned the "two hegemonic powers" for creating spheres of influence. The Soviet ambassador, Kharlamov, countered this by accusing China of harbouring superpower designs and not being among the 94 countries that had recognized Angola. Huang Hua retorted, "The Soviet representative has slandered China as a superpower. This is a preposterous fabrication. China is a developing socialist country belonging to the third world. China does not have a single soldier or base abroad. . . It would be unfavourable to the people of China and the rest of the world if China should become a superpower."[9]

Arab-Israeli War, 1973

In October 1973, the war in the Middle-East once again dominated the Security Council. The proceedings in the Council on this occasion are illustrative of the marginalisation of the non-permanent members in cases where the permanent members have vital interests involved. The Council adopted routine resolutions calling upon the combating countries to withdraw their troops to pre-war positions. Then the United States decided to broker talks between Israel and Syria outside the United Nations. This led to an unprecedented coming together of the ten non-permanent members who tabled a resolution seeking a role for the Security Council in the talks. The resolution was adopted with the vote of the ten non-permanent members.[10] Four permanent members abstained while China did not vote. The US, Britain and France claimed that the Geneva conference was in line with Security Council Resolution 338 (1973) and assured that the secretary-general would preside over the first session and his representative would be there subsequently. The US ambassador, Bennett, said, "Every effort is being made to give this Council its rightful role in the proceedings."

The US ambassador said that the invitations to the Geneva conference were still being finalised and his country could not support a resolution at that time. He said that there would be full involvement of the Security Council and he assured that "the framework for the negotiations is to be found in the resolutions which have already been adopted by the Security Council" and "every effort is being made to give this Council its rightful role in the proceedings." He did not explain which resolutions had called for a conference to be held and why the process was not controlled by the Security Council.[11]

Moving the resolution on behalf of the ten non-permanent members Jeanne Martin Cisse of Guinea quoted Resolution 338 (1973) which stipulated that the Security Council, "decides that, immediately and concurrently with the ceasefire, negotiations start between the parties concerned under appropriate auspices aimed at establishing a just and duration peace in the Middle-East." She asserted that the "auspices" envisaged in the resolution were the United Nations, "for us the ten non-permanent members of the Security Council. . . and for all fifteen members of the Security Council the appropriate auspices were clearly those of the United Nations."[12]

The Geneva conference resulted in an agreement between Israel and Syria to disengage their troops and have a UN disengagement observer force stationed there. The US ambassador, John Scali, said, "We are pleased that the United States, through the efforts of Secretary Kissinger, was privileged to help bring about this agreement."[13] He thanked the Soviet Union for its cooperation. Having brokered the agreement the United States brought the issue back to the United Nations. Lord Richard announced in the Council, "Now is the time for the United Nations to play its part."[14] China and Iraq abstained in the vote on the resolution which authorised the setting up of a UN disengagement observer force on the plea that this would legitimise the status quo on the ground, which meant endorsing Israeli occupation. The other members of the Security Council showered encomiums on Henry Kissinger. The Security Council then put together a peacekeeping force to monitor the disengagement.

Soviet Union invasion of Afghanistan, 1979-1988

In the late 1970s, the Soviet Union got violently involved in the internal affairs of Afghanistan. In 1978, a pro-Moscow faction of the Communist Party under Nur Mohammed Taraki seized office but was unable to restore peace. The Soviet Union instigated his overthrow by Hafizullah Amin, but Amin proved to be difficult to manipulate and it eventually sent its troops into the country in December 1979 to overthrow and replace him with Babrak Karmal. The US seized the opportunity to mobilise an Islamic opposition to the Soviet invasion. In January 1980, 52 Islamic countries asked the Council president to convene a meeting of the Security Council. Bangladesh, the Philippines, Jamaica, Niger, Tunisia and Zambia moved a resolution deploring the armed intervention, without naming the Soviet Union, and calling for the withdrawal of all foreign troops from Afghanistan. The resolution received 13 votes in favour. East Germany voted against as did the Soviet Union. The Security Council found itself in a familiar position of being unable to take a stand in the face of opposition from a permanent member. [15]

The matter was then taken to the General Assembly under the 'uniting for peace' procedure and a resolution was adopted at an emergency special session on the lines of the vetoed Council resolution.[16] The Soviets rejected the resolution but accepted Pérez de Cuéllar as the "personal representative" of Secretary-General Kurt Waldheim. This designation was acceptable to the Soviets in preference to "special representative" because the latter would have implied acceptance of the General Assembly resolution they had rejected. When Pérez de Cuéllar became secretary general, Diego Cordovez of Ecuador replaced him.

The United States proceeded to organise a resistance to the Soviet invasion through Afghan rebels and Islamic religious warriors, called *mujahideen*. The war went badly for the Soviet Union and it eventually settled for talks in Geneva. The credit for the Geneva Accords of 8 April 1988 went both to the efforts of the UN secretary-general's representative and the bilateral talks between the US and the Soviet Union. After the signing of these accords, the Security Council stepped in and posted a UN Good Offices Mission in Afghanistan and Pakistan (UNGOMAP), which was disbanded in 1991 and replaced by the Office of Secretary-General in Afghanistan and Pakistan. The Soviet troops withdrew from Afghanistan.

NATO bombing of Kosovo, 1999

In 1998, the enclave of Kosovo, with its majority population of Albanian Muslims, rebelled against Serbia. By this time the international scene had started changing. Russia could no longer be trusted not to use the veto in the Security Council and China too could not be relied upon not to join hands with it. Serbian troops responded to the separatist rebellion with force. The US asked President Milosevic to withdraw his forces.

Britain brought two resolutions against Serbia in the Security Council declaring its actions to be a threat to international peace and security and threatening further action if peace was not restored.[17] Both resolutions were adopted. China abstained instead of voting against because there was no provision for military action in case of non-compliance. Russia went along with both as did the US, each for its own reasons. As was to be expected, Milosevic ignored them and Secretary-General Kofi Annan reported so to the Security Council, which adopted another resolution in demanding that Serbia cooperate with NATO and the OSCE.[18] Even this resolution did not contain any authorisation for military action and both Russia and China abstained.

The US held back initially on military action, not because of hesitation in using force, but because President Clinton was preoccupied with impeachment proceedings against him. Once he was free from it he turned his attention to Milosevic. After a few warnings, he declared that NATO was prepared to act to stop the killings of Kosovar Muslims. Despite the Serbian brutalities in Kosovo, on which the legitimacy of the intervention was stated to be premised, the US chose not to take military action on its own despite assurances to that effect by presidents Bush and Clinton. It turned to NATO and confined the action to aerial bombardment, which accentuated the viciousness of the Serbian action against the Kosovars. The authors of a biography of Milosevic wrote later, "The most sensible policy for the Western alliance would have been to move decisively in a major way to prevent the suffering and bloodshed. But this did not happen. President Clinton had ruled out a ground invasion."[19]

The final order for the NATO bombing came from its secretary-general, Javier Solana. NATO launched the bombing of Serbian army positions in Kosovo in February 1998. Russia condemned the bombing as a violation of international law. However, even before the bombing stopped, in June 1999, it had been persuaded to accept a role in the peace process. It participated in the G-8 summit in Bonn a month earlier where a roadmap for a political solution was worked out. It accepted the plan and even sent an envoy to Milosevic to persuade him to agree.

After 72 days of bombing, Serbia capitulated. Its troops withdrew and NATO forces moved in to keep the peace. UN peacekeepers were neither asked for nor sent. Shortly after the Serbian withdrawal, the Security Council adopted a resolution authorising member states and "relevant international organisations" to establish a security presence in Kosovo "with all necessary means" to fulfil its responsibilities.[20] This validated the presence of NATO troops and arguably the bombing *ex-post facto*. It sought to restore UN authority in Kosovo by requiring NATO secretary-general to report to the Security Council and the setting up of a UN interim administration in Kosovo.

China condemned the bombing, but, citing Serbia's acceptance of the terms and the cessation of the bombing, abstained on the resolution. Russia supported it. The Western countries accused Milosevic of bearing responsibility for the bombing by not withdrawing his troops earlier. There was no reprimand either from the Council or from the UN secretary-general for the bombing of Serbia without Security Council authorisation. In fact, Kofi Annan condoned it as a necessity. He wrote later in his memoir, "And so when NATO decided to act against Serbia without Security Council authorisation, I expressed regret but said that 'there are times when the use of force is legitimate in the pursuit of peace'."[21] He admitted though that no secretary-general before him had endorsed a military action without Security Council authorisation. This was the beginning of the idea, which later evolved into the concept of 'responsibility to protect', that interference in the internal affairs of a country was justified if it was for a humanitarian purpose.

Western countries were cautious in their justification of the bombing of Kosovo. Villani notes that even some NATO states believe that the Security Council never authorised or approved the military action against Yugoslavia.[22] They preferred to call it an exception rather than precedent-setting. An independent international commission on Kosovo, co-chaired by Richard Goldstone and Carl Tham, reported, "NATO and its supporters have wisely avoided staking out any doctrinal claims for its action whether prior to or after the war. Rather than defining the Kosovo intervention as a precedent, most NATO supporters among international jurists presented the intervention as an unfortunate but necessary and reasonable exception."[23] In 2004, an American professor, John M. Murphy, wrote, "...it is likely that Kosovo will increasingly be viewed as an aberration that came about because of the extraordinary circumstances existing at the time."[24] He was to be proved wrong within a year. The concept of the responsibility to protect had been germinating since the late 1990s and was to be applied again soon.

The conflict in Kosovo was an internal ethnic crisis of Serbia and the charters of both the UN and NATO recognise territorial integrity as the basis of maintaining international stability. However, NATO deemed that protecting civilians was consistent with the primary objective of the UN of maintaining international peace and security. UK Prime Minister Tony Blair declared in 1999, "Non-interference has long been considered an important principle of international order....... but the principle of non-interference must [now] be qualified in important respects."[25] Fraser concludes, "The Kosovo crisis and the Iraq War demonstrate clearly how the Security Council is just a mirror of the great powers at the conference table, and how the politics of the P5 essentially chart the direction of international law."[26]

NATO Intervention in Afghanistan, 2001

The attack on the World Trade Centre in New York and other landmarks in the US on 9 September 2001 provided the US with yet another provocation to show its disdain for the United Nations and brush aside multilateralism despite universal sympathy and support.

The Security Council met at an emergency session within three days of the attack, invoking the Charter's inherent right of "individual or collective self-defence" and authorising "all necessary steps" against the perpetrators, organisers and sponsors of the attacks.[27] The North Atlantic Council of NATO also met the same day and for the first time took recourse the treaty's collective defence provision embodied in Article 5 and offered its full support to the US.

However, the US chose to act on its own, unencumbered by the rules and procedures of either organisation. It preferred an *ad hoc* "coalition of the willing", which gave it full operational control. Other countries in the coalition were called upon to provide whatever assistance or operational support it assigned to them. Even towards the coalition the US adopted a supercilious attitude, which was summed up by Secretary of Defence, Donald Rumsfeld, in an interview to Larry King on the US television channel, CNN, on 5 December 2001, "The worst thing you can do is to allow a coalition to determine what your mission is."[28] This did not imply that the US was indifferent to the attitude of countries to its war effort. President Bush in an address to a joint session of Congress on 20 September 2001, thundered to the rest of world, "Either you are with us or you are with the terrorists."

The US did, however, turn to the Security Council for performing back-office work. It got the Council to set up a Counter Terrorism Committee, to which all states were obliged to report the steps being taken by them to eliminate sources of terrorist financing. A UN-mandated International Security Assistance Force was sent to Afghanistan but its operations were restricted to Kabul and its neighbourhood. In September 2003, when the US got embroiled in another war, this time in Iraq, it handed over control to NATO and placed ISAF under its command.

After its intervention in Afghanistan in 2001 the US developed a new and aggressive doctrine of pre-emption, taking the UN Charter's accepted principle of self-defence to a dangerous level. The National Security Strategy of the US of September 2002 summed up this doctrine as follows, "The United States will not use force in all cases to pre-empt emerging threats, nor should nations use pre-emption as a pretext for aggression. Yet in an age where the enemies of civilization openly and actively seek the world's most destructive technologies, the United States cannot remain idle while dangers gather."[29]

US-British Invasion of Iraq, 2003

The invasion of Iraq by the US and Britain in March 2003 is often called the Second Gulf War. Unlike the first though, this was carried out without the authority of the Security Council. In October 2002, the US President, George W. Bush, who had decided to oust President Saddam Hussein, got the US Congress to authorise him to use US armed forces. The US and Britain then lobbied hard in the Security Council to get a resolution authorising the use of force against Iraq for failing to destroy its weapons of mass destruction. France, Germany and Russia were reluctant to support because UN inspectors had been allowed in by Iraq a month earlier to inspect its possible weapon sites. The Iraqi government cooperated reluctantly and the inspectors were not able to lay their hands on any significant stores of weapons of mass destruction.

The US and Britain moved an artfully drafted Resolution 1441 (2002), with some ambivalent assurances, which was adopted unanimously by the Security Council. It declared that Iraq had been in breach of its disarmament obligations and warned it of "serious consequences" if it continued.

The US ambassador, John Negroponte, however, assured the Council, "As we have said on numerous occasions to Council members, this resolution contains no 'hidden trigger' and no 'automaticity' with respect to the use of force." He said that the matter would return to the Council if there was a further Iraqi breach. However, he also warned ominously, "If the Security Council fails to act decisively in the event of further Iraqi violations, this resolution does not constrain any Member State from acting to defend itself against the threat posed by Iraq or to enforce relevant United Nations resolutions and protect world peace and security."[30]

Britain ambassador, Jeremy Greenstock, reiterated the assurance given by Negroponte, "Let me be equally clear in response, as a co-sponsor with the United States of the text we have just adopted. There is no 'automaticity' in the resolution. If there is a further Iraqi breach of its disarmament obligations, the matter will return to the Council for discussion as required in paragraph 12. We would expect the Security Council then to meet its responsibilities." But while pressing for inspections, he expressed the conviction that Iraq had made a "fatal decision to conceal weapons of mass destruction."[31]

Later in the day, China, France and Russia made an unprecedented joint statement asserting that there was no automaticity in the use of force in the Security Council resolution as affirmed by the representatives of the US and Britain and in case of non-compliance by Iraq the matter would have to be reported to the Council by the inspectors. The statement added, "It will then be for the Council to take a position on the basis of that report."[32]

The US soon started pressing members of the Security Council to authorise military action but was not able to get the support of either France or Russia, nor could it muster the nine votes required. Meanwhile, the UN inspectors felt that they needed more time to determine if Iraq was cooperating fully or was hiding some weapons of mass destruction. The US produced numerous intelligence reports to establish Iraq's guilt and even had its highly respected General Colin Powell, now secretary of state, make a personal presentation to the Security Council vouching for the authenticity of the intelligence reports alleging hidden stores of weapons of mass destruction.

With Security Council authorisation not forthcoming, the United States decided to go ahead regardless. When questioned about the wisdom and legitimacy of by-passing the Security Council and creating its own military coalition US White House spokesman, Ari Fleischer, clarified his government's attitude to the Security Council, "The point I'm making here is that there are many ways to form international coalitions. The United Nations Security Council is but one of them."[33]

Various justifications have been given by the US and Britain on the legal validity of the invasion. Britain's attorney-general, Lord Goldsmith, claimed the continued applicability of ten-year-old Chapter VII resolutions, "Authority to use force against Iraq exists from the combined effect of Resolutions 678, 687 and 1441. All of these Resolutions were adopted under Chapter VII of the UN Charter which allows the use of force for the express purpose of restoring international peace and security. . . It is plain that Iraq has failed so to comply and, therefore, Iraq was at the time of Resolution 1441 and continues to be in material breach. Thus, the authority to use force under Resolution 678 has revived and so continues today."[34]

The invasion of Iraq lasted from March to May 2003. Most of the troops came from the US, though Britain also provided a substantial number. Poland and Australia chipped in with token contributions. Saddam Hussein's regime collapsed very quickly and he was taken prisoner later and executed. However, the country disintegrated into chaos and became a base for numerous terrorist groups. US forces continue to operate there, despite repeated assurances of withdrawal.

Civil Wars in Syria and Yemen

Both Russia and the United States have deployed troops in Syria without Security Council approval and exacerbated the local civil war. In 2011, large sections of the Sunni population in Syria, backed by Turkey, Qatar and Saudi Arabia, revolted against the Alawite president, Bashar al-Assad. Russia and Iran joined the struggle in support of Assad while the United

States backed the opposition groups. Iran made common cause with Assad as a fellow Shia and got the Hezbollah fighters from Lebanon to assist the Syrian army. The war took a vicious turn when the Islamic State from Iraq joined it to fight both the government and the moderate opposition. Syria's Kurdish minority also took advantage of the situation to assert its autonomy. President Assad used it to hit back at Turkey and unsettle its Kurdish population. The United States was caught between the moderate and extremist Islamic elements, supporting the former while attacking the latter.

Russia made Syria a test case for asserting its regional influence. It provided air support to the Syrian army and refused to accept any interference by the Security Council. It vetoed a dozen resolutions brought by the Western three. China supported it on half of them and abstained on the rest. Two of the resolutions were under Chapter VII – one sought to refer violations of international humanitarian law to the Prosecutor of the International Criminal Court and the other proposed sanctions for the use of chemical weapons.

The civil war between the Shia Houthis in northern Yemen and the government of President Abed Rabbo Mansour Hadi, a Sunni, began towards the end of 2014. It resulted in the flight of Hadi, first to Aden in the south and then to Saudi Arabia. Saudi Arabia deployed its troops against the Houthis, who were receiving support from Iran. The United States entered the fray to help Saudi Arabia. Russia agreed to the imposition of an arms embargo and assets freeze on the Houthis but vetoed a British resolution under Chapter VII demanding compliance with human rights and international humanitarian laws. China abstained.[35]

This is not an exhaustive list of wars in which the Security Council was unable to intervene because of the involvement of the permanent five, but it establishes the violations of international peace and security committed by the permanent five and their use of the veto to prevent it from fulfilling its Charter mandate. In Vietnam, Namibia and Angola, the right to self-determination and freedom was given short shrift. In Czechoslovakia, Afghanistan and Iraq, the military invasions went without a response from the Security Council. In Kosovo, the territorial integrity of Serbia was subordinated to human rights and humanitarian concerns without clarity on where to draw the line in parallel situations.

Endnotes

1   UN Document, S/RES/189 (1964), 4 June 1964.

2   Andrew W. Cordier and Max Harrelson. *Public Papers of the Secretaries-General of the United Nations, Vol. 7, U. Thant, 1965-1967.* (New York: Columbia University Press, 1976), p. 388.

3   Statement by India's ambassador, Rikhi Jaipal, at the 1836th meeting of the UNSC on 11 Aug 1975, SCOR 1975, p. 3.

4   UN Document, Draft resolution S/8761, 22 August 1968.

5   UNSC Resolution 245(1968).

6   Gladwyn Jebb, Statement at the 1399th meeting of the Security Council, 19 March 1968, SCOR 1968, para 59, p. 6.

7   UN Document, S/RES/387(1976), 31 March 1976.

8   Statement by the British ambassador, Lord Richard, at the 1906th meeting of the UNSC on 31 March 1976, SCOR 1976, p. 31.

9   Statement by the Chinese ambassador, Huang Hua, at the 1906th meeting of the UNSC on 31 March 1976, SCOR 1976, p.36.

10 UN Document, S/RES/344(1973).

11 Statements by the US ambassador, William Tapley Bennett, Jr., and the Chinese ambassador, Huang Hua, at the 1760th meeting of the UNSC on 15 Dec 1973, SCOR 1973, p. 3

12 Statement by the ambassador of Guinea, Jeanne Martin Cisse, at the 1760th meeting of the UNSC on 15 Dec 1973, SCOR 1973, p. 1.

13 Statement by US ambassador, John Scali, at the 1774th meeting of the UNSC on 31 May 1974, SCOR 1974, p. 8.

14 Statement by the British delegate, Richard, at the 1774th meeting of the UNSC on 31 May 1974, SCOR 1974, p. 6.

15 UN Document, UNSC draft resolution S/13729, 7-9 January 1980.

16 UN Document, General Assembly resolution ES-6/2.

17 UN Documents: S/RES/1160(1998) and S/RES/1199(1998).

18 UN Document: S/RES/1203(1998), 24 October 1998.

19 Dusko Doder and Louise Branson. *Milosevic – Portrait of a Tyrant* (New York: The Free Press, 1999), p. 260.

20 UN Document, S/RES/1244(1999), 10 June 1999. Para 7.

21   Annan. Interventions, p. 11.

22   U. Villani. *The Security Council's Authorization of Enforcement Action* (Max Planck Yearbook of UN Law, v. 6 2002), p. 548.

23   Quoted in John F. Murphy. *The United States and the Rule of Law in International Affairs* (Cambridge University Press, 2004), p. 180.

24   Murphy, p. 180.

25   Trudy Fraser. *Maintaining Peace and Security? The United Nations in a Changing World* (New York: Palgrave MacMillan, 2015), p. 116.

26   Trudy Fraser, p. 115.

27   UN Document, S/RES/1368 (2001), 12 September 2001.

28   http://www.defenselink.mil/transcripts/2001/t12062001_t1250sd.html.

29   The National Security Strategy of the United States of America, September 2002, p. 15. [https://www.state.gov].

30   John Negroponte, Statement at the 4644th meeting of the UNSC on 18 November 2002. UN Document S/PV.4644, p. 3.

31   Jeremy Greenstock, Statement at the 4644th meeting of the UNSC, 18 November 2002. UN Document S/PV.4644, p.5.

32   www.staff.city.ac.uk/p.willets/IRAQ/INDEX.HTM. Website of City University, London.

33   White House: "Press Briefing by Ari Fleischer, 10 March 2003. http://www.whitehouse.gov/new/releases/2003/03/20030310-4.html#7].

34   Statement of Lord Goldsmith on 17 March 2003 in response to a parliamentary question on the legal basis for the use of force against Iraq. Quoted in Murphy, p. 171.

35   UNSC draft resolution S/2018/156 of 26 February 2018. The resolution received 11 votes in favour. Bolivia voted against, along with Russia, while Kazakhstan joined China in abstaining.

16   Security Council Reform

Reform of the Security Council has been talked about since the inception of the United Nations but no change has taken place in it, other than a minor increase in its non-permanent members half a century ago. The veto has ensured that no change takes place in the powers of the permanent members or dilutes their position by the addition of more such members. Wide differences among members on whether reforms are needed in the Council, and if so what, have made it an elusive prospect. The G-4 – Brazil, India, Japan and Germany - have been pressing their case for permanent membership but there is little incentive for the permanent five to open the door to them or the other members of the UN to vote them in.

In his closing address to the San Francisco Conference, President Truman had expressed the hope that the UN Charter, like the US Constitution, would be expanded and improved with time. He said that with changing times the Charter would be re-adjusted but there would be no re-adjustment of peace or of war.[1] None of the speeches ventured to declare that the Charter would be final and unchangeable. The leader of the US delegation, Edward Stettinius said, "Let us act now in the sure knowledge that our work can be improved upon with time . . ."[2] In over seventy years the only change in the Charter has been a slight expansion in two of its councils – the Security Council and the Economic Social Council. The resistance to change from the permanent five has been so strong that even routine amendments necessitated by the passage of time, like the references to "enemy States", the abolition of the Trusteeship Council, which has finished its work, have not taken place. All these changes are held hostage to the complexities of the Security Council reform.

The demand for a revision of the UN Charter started in 1946 itself. At the centre of this effort was the most controversial feature of the Charter – the veto. Western countries became frustrated by the frequent use of the veto by the Soviet Union, even on issues like the membership of countries and toyed with the idea of amending the veto rule.

The framers of the Charter had recognised that it could not be cast in stone and had provided for a review conference after ten years. But the conference never took place. In 1955, when the General Assembly took up this discussion the Soviet Union boycotted it. It also abstained on a resolution calling for a conference on Charter revision. The other major powers were also not keen on it and the committee set up to study it delayed submitting its recommendation. The newly independent countries, however, looked to the review conference to increase their weight in the organisation. Prescient observers could sense a change in the membership of the United Nations. The British writer, Martin Wright, called the new countries the "Bandung Powers". He said that they had been able to turn the UN into an anti-colonial movement, a kind of a "Holy Alliance in reverse".[3] Another British writer felt that the Bandung countries "were entitled to a far bigger share of the world authority, the UN, than they had when it was founded."[4]

India's V.K. Krishna Menon expressed optimism about the review at the General Assembly a year before it was due. He said that the review would be a kind of an audit of the organisation.[5] When this did not take place, he waited a while and finally, on 17 October 1960, reminded the General Assembly of the report of Commission I of the San Francisco conference, under the presidency of a former Secretary of State for Foreign Affairs of the United Kingdom, Lord Halifax. The passage of the report he quoted was, "Taking cognizance of the facts that the Charter being prepared at San Francisco could not be perfect and that the delegates could not foresee all eventual developments in international affairs, Commission I recommends for inclusion in the Charter provisions for a special conference on the revision of the Charter...."[6]

Menon allayed any suspicion that India was seeking a review of the Charter to secure a permanent seat for itself in the Security Council. He said, ".......we are not in the least quarrelling with the position of the great Powers in the Security Council. That is not the purpose of this."[7] In September 1955, Nehru had scotched rumours of India being offered and turning down a permanent seat.[8] Menon quoted at length on the increase in the membership of the UN from various continents and their poor representation in the Security Council. He pointed out that India would be able to become a member of the Security Council only once every forty or so years, and an African country would not be able to get in at all.

Regional distribution of Non-Permanent Members

In 1946, the permanent five had reached an informal understanding, a 'gentleman's agreement', on the regional distribution of the non-permanent members. Although the terms of this agreement were never made public, a Soviet diplomat said that one seat each would be allotted to the British Commonwealth, the Middle East, West Europe and East Europe.[9] India challenged the propriety of this agreement and voiced its objection to the absence of any representation being given to Asia and Africa. India was later elected for the 1950-1951 term on the Commonwealth seat. Even for the others, the regional seats were distributed with flexibility. Yugoslavia (1950-1951) and (1956 – one-year term); Greece 1952-1953; and Turkey 1954-1955 took the East European seat even though they did not belong to the Soviet bloc.

Expansion of the Security Council, 1963-65

In 1956, when it became clear that the review conference would not take place, 16 Latin American countries and Spain jointly proposed in the General Assembly to expand the Security Council. They introduced a resolution proposing amendments to Articles 23 and 27 of the UN Charter to increase the non-permanent members by two and the number of affirmative votes required for a decision from seven to eight. This nominal increase in the Security Council membership from 11 to 13 was proportionate to the expansion of the General Assembly due to new members. The enlargement of the General Assembly had increased the ratio between its membership and that of the Security Council and also rendered obsolete the regional distribution agreement for non-permanent members.

This modest attempt did not disturb the power equation in the Council or question the veto system. The proposal was, however, blocked by the Soviet Union which insisted on resolving the issue of China's membership together with Council expansion. No action was taken on the Latin American resolution in the General Assembly sessions till 1960. While the West blamed the Soviets for blocking the aspirations of the new members of the UN, the Soviets held the West responsible by their refusal to admit the PRC.

In 1960, the Latin American countries, joined now by Africa and Asia, tabled a resolution sponsored by 39 countries in the Special Political Committee of the General Assembly. This was akin to the Latin American proposal of 1956. Put to vote, it did not receive the number of votes necessary for Charter amendment. Many countries, convinced of a Soviet veto, did not vote. The Soviets had by now put forward an additional demand. They expressed dissatisfaction with the composition of the Secretariat and called for a troika to replace the UN secretary-general.

Meanwhile, 24 Afro-Asian states and Yugoslavia got together in Belgrade in September 1961, the first such summit meeting since the Bandung Conference of 1955, to form what would soon become the non-aligned movement. The structure of the UN was one of the issues discussed. The conference rejected the Soviet troika proposal as an attempt to weaken the UN and declared that the expansion of the UN Security Council and China's membership were two separate and unconnected issues. It called for expanding the membership of the Security Council to bring it into "harmony with the needs of the Organization and with the expanded membership of the United Nations." The non-aligned countries were divided on the issue of membership of communist China and the declaration was subdued in its endorsement of it.

In December 1963, the Latin American and Afro-Asian states submitted separate proposals for Council expansion. For the Latin Americans, this was a resubmission of their earlier proposal. This time, 21 Latin American states proposed expansion from 11 to 13 with two additional non-permanent members. Three days later, 37 Afro-Asian states moved a resolution for 4 additional non-permanent members, taking the Council to 15. Both proposals were moved in the Special Political Committee of the General Assembly. The US, Britain and France remained opposed to any expansion.

However, by this time the differences between the Soviet Union and China, still unknown to the rest of the world, had started. China told the Afro-Asian states in September 1963 that the expansion of the Council and its membership were separate issues and should not be "bundled together." It took the view that a re-distribution of the non-permanent seats among different regions would be a better way of addressing the problem than expanding the Council.

The Latin American and Afro-Asian countries merged their two resolutions and brought a single resolution proposing expansion from 11 to 15 to the Special Political Affairs Committee. On 16 December 1963, the Committee adopted the resolution 96 to 11 with 4 abstentions. The US and Britain abstained, as did Portugal and South Africa. France, Cuba and the Eastern bloc countries voted against. The Republic of China (Taiwan) did not participate in the vote.

The resolution was then brought before the General Assembly which adopted it by 97 votes to 11 with 4 abstentions.[10] The resolution also provided for the following regional representation of the 10 non-permanent seats: Africa and Asia - 5, Latin America - 2, West Europe - 2, and East Europe - 1.

Attention now turned to the issue of ratification of the Charter amendment. The resolution provided for this to be done by 1965. By this time, however, the Soviet Union had decided that it would be counter-productive to block the proposal any further. It became the first among the permanent five to ratify it. By August 1965, the required two-thirds of the membership and all the permanent five had ratified the amendment, the first of the Charter, 20 years after it came into existence.

This expansion of the Security Council, however, did not end the periodic calls for a review conference. In 1969, Colombia put forward a proposal and in 1972, Romania succeeded in getting another for strengthening the UN placed on the agenda of the General Assembly. In 1974, following a veto by the US, Britain and France of a resolution imposing sanctions on South Africa, African countries demanded a review conference. Various ideas were put forward on Security Council reform, including an increase in permanent and non-permanent membership and restrictions on the use of the veto. One of the proposals suggested amending the Charter to incorporate peacekeeping operations, maintaining a standing peacekeeping force and enlarging the Military Staff Committee. All these proposals were shot down by the permanent members.

In 1979, India along with 15 other countries, including Japan and Nigeria, proposed the expansion of the Security Council from 15 to 19 in line with the increase in the membership of the General Assembly. The increase was to be with the addition of 4 non-permanent members.

Changes in the Permanent Five

Till the 1990s, the debate on reform focussed on increasing the non-permanent seats in the Security Council. But while the composition of the permanent five appears to have remained unchanged, all except the United States have undergone a transformation. The People's Republic of China, a pariah in its early years, has displaced the Republic of China and the Russian Federation has taken the seat of the dissolved Soviet Union. The United Kingdom and France continue in their original seats but are now without their global empires and as members of the European Union have to coordinate their policies within it. The US ambassador, John Bolton, declared this proudly, "In fact, only the United States has remained as it was in 1945, in our case actually expanding with the admission of Alaska and Hawaii as states, while the others declined or fragmented."[11]

The Entry of the People's Republic of China

In 1971, the US assented to the People's Republic replacing the Republic of China in the UN without an amendment to the Charter on the principle that it was due to a change in government. The question here was: which government represented China? The Communist party had been in effective control of mainland China since 1949 but the US refusal to recognise it had kept it out of the UN. This changed in 1971. On 15 July 1971, Nixon announced that he would visit the PRC the following year.

In October, the PRC's old ally, Albania, introduced a resolution in the General Assembly stating that it was the only lawful representative of China and should be admitted to the UN, and also given China's permanent seat in the Security Council.[12] The resolution was adopted by 76 votes against 35, with 17 abstentions and 3 members not voting. The US, Japan and Brazil voted against. India, Britain, France and the Soviet Union voted in favour. The PRC declared condescendingly that it accepted the offer since it did not wish to disappoint the countries that had voted for it. There was no follow-up resolution in the Security Council to reaffirm this momentous change, nor was Article 23 of the UN Charter amended to replace the Republic of China with the PRC. Besides, the affirmative votes secured by the resolution fell short of the two-thirds required for an amendment to the Charter.

Replacement of the USSR by the Russian Federation

The formal dissolution of the Soviet Union in December 1991 and its replacement, at the Alma Ata summit, by the Commonwealth of Independent States brought the first serious legal challenge to the composition of the Security Council. There had been some earlier questions of change in membership due either to a change in government or change in the territory of a country. Thus, in 1947, when Pakistan became a separate country, India continued to retain its seat. This was done on the principle that Pakistan had seceded from India and would have to apply for new membership.

The case of the Soviet Union was, however, different. The Russian Federation was a new state. The Alma Ata declaration of 11 heads of state of the republics of the former Soviet Union, who got together to form the Commonwealth of Independent States, stated that "with the establishment of the Commonwealth of Independent States, the Union of Soviet Socialist Republics ceases to exist." On the issue of the fulfilment of the international obligations of the former USSR, the declaration added, "Member states of the Commonwealth guarantee, in accordance with their constitutional procedures, the fulfilment of international obligations stemming from the treaties and agreements of the former USSR."[13]

However, the Western countries were keen to resolve this issue with the least resistance and complication. They supported Boris Yeltsin's intimation of 24 December 1991 to the secretary-general of the intention of the Russian Federation to take over the seat of the Soviet Union as much in the expectation of his amenability as "the fear.........to open the Pandora's Box of Charter revision".[14] They deemed the change to be a continuation of the international personality of the USSR in the Russian Federation. President Yeltsin obliged by getting the CIS republics to support the permanent membership of the Russian Federation in the Security Council. On 24 December 1991, President Yeltsin informed the UN secretary-general that "the membership of the Union of Socialist Republics in the UN, including the Security Council and other organs and organizations of the UN system, is being continued by the Russian Federation with the support of the countries of the Commonwealth of Independent States."[15]

This was immediately supported by Britain, the European Community and the US. Britain followed it up with the unprecedented summit meeting of the Security Council on 31 January 1992. The stated agenda of the meeting was to chalk out the program of action of the new revitalised Security Council, but it also implicitly endorsed the membership of the Russian Federation and heralded a new era of western domination. Thirteen heads of state or government met in New York, the permanent five, Australia, Belgium, Cape Verde, Ecuador, India, Japan, Morocco and Venezuela. Hungary and Zimbabwe were represented by their foreign ministers.

The Security Council summit went well beyond endorsing Russia's membership. Instead of taking up Council reform, which had become essential because of the disintegration of one of the permanent members, it set out on an ambitious theme, 'The Responsibility of the Security Council in the Maintenance of International Peace and Security.' It tasked Boutros-Ghali, to prepare a report on strengthening the UN and making its role in preventive diplomacy, peacemaking and peacekeeping more efficient. In the replacement of the Soviet Union by Russia, "the UN was presented with a *fait accompli*……..The formula used precluded any substantive discussion of the real issues involved."[16]

The memberships of both the People's Republic of China in 1971 and the Russian Federation in 1991 were momentous developments. They were achieved without any discussion in the Security Council. In the case of China, there was a perfunctory one in the General Assembly. The UN Charter was not amended. It continues to provide for membership of the older entities, one isolated and the other extinct.

Italy's proposal for EU seat

In September 1990, the Italian foreign minister, Gianni De Michelis, taking advantage of the Maastricht Treaty negotiations on the formation of the European Union, made a valiant attempt to persuade Britain and France to give up their permanent status and be replaced by a single seat for the proposed European Union.[17] The Italian proposal was essentially to pre-empt any further dilution of its position by Germany's ascent to a permanent seat, as was being sought by some. Italy also proposed the addition of Japan as a permanent member.

Britain and France, however, were able to stall this move. They successfully got an article inserted in the treaty, settling the issue in their favour, "Member States [of the EU] which are also members of the Security Council will act in concert and keep other member states fully informed. Member States which are permanent members of the Security

Council will, in the execution of their functions, ensure the defence of their positions and the interests of the European Union, without prejudice of their responsibilities under the provisions of the UN Charter."[18]

The Current Reform Process

In September 1991, a group of 10 countries, including India and Brazil, tried to build on the post-Cold War zeal for change by seeking a discussion in the General Assembly on Security Council reform. The proposal was defeated and shelved to the next session. The permanent five argued that since the Council was working well, there was no need to reform it.

Two new aspirants now started a clamour for a permanent seat in the Security Council, Germany and Japan. The vanquished Axis powers, against whom the United Nations had been formed during the Second World War, had become leading economic powers. They now felt confident to voice their demand formally. Germany and Japan had given significant financial support to the First Gulf War. By 1992 they had become the largest contributors to the UN's regular budget and to its peacekeeping operations, after the US.

While Germany and Japan felt that they deserved a permanent place in the Security Council because of their deep pockets, the non-aligned countries invoked the principle of democracy to demand reform. The NAM summit in Jakarta in September 1992 declared, ". . . the veto powers which guarantee an exclusive and eminent role for the permanent members of the Council are contrary to the aim of democratizing the United Nations and must, therefore, be reviewed."

India and 35 other non-aligned countries tabled a resolution in the General Assembly in September 1992 for taking up the "Question of equitable representation and increase in the membership of the Security Council." Japan decided to co-sponsor this resolution, which was adopted without a vote as Resolution 47/62. The issue of Security Council reform was thus placed on the agenda of the General Assembly.

In pursuance of this resolution in 1993, 80 states sent written comments while 74 others gave their views verbally expressing support for the idea of reform. Thus, the urgency of reform was established and the need was felt for working on finding acceptable solutions. For this, the General Assembly set up a working group in 1993 to consider all aspects of the question of Security Council reform. This 'Open-Ended Working

Group' has been working almost continuously since then. It has gone through numerous meetings and compiled the suggestions of members in an omnibus document to facilitate the negotiations. In 1997, a special panel under the chairmanship of Razali Ismail proposed changes including in the permanent category but was rejected by the middle-ranking rivals of the permanent seat candidates and by the indifference of the permanent five.

Opposition to the proposal for reform came, as could be expected, from the two smallest permanent members, Britain and France, whose claim to the status was the weakest. They had not only lost their empires but had also been overtaken by Germany and Japan as global economic powers. They had even diluted their national sovereignty by joining the European Union. Britain and France supported the principle of "operational efficiency" to block the demand for enlargement. Britain submitted to the secretary-general, "The first priority must be to safeguard the effective operation of the Council and its ability to fulfil its primary responsibility under the UN Charter."[19] France used the same argument. It maintained that a compact Council was essential for quick decision-making in order to respond to crises.

Russia and China were less vocal but they too opposed any expansion. In its submission to the secretary-general in 1993, Russia said, "The organization cannot afford to engage in an overhaul of machinery which not only is not broken but is in fact in good working order."[20] China accepted the need for expansion but said that it should be with the "universal acceptance of the Member States" in a "prudent and cautious manner" when the "time is ripe".[21]

The only permanent member to support the demand for reform was the United States. In its submission to the secretary-general, it said, "The United States supports permanent membership for Japan and Germany as well, fully recognizing that permanent membership entails assuming an active role in global peace and security activities."[22] However, while the US supported reform it had no inclination to do anything about it. Condoleezza Rice said, "We adopted the strategy of acknowledging the importance of reform and welcoming reasonable proposals, but we never acted on any of them."[23] Patrick and McDonald concede, "Enlargement would certainly complicate US tactics in negotiations, particularly in lining up votes for important resolutions."[24]

The US maintained that the existing permanent five should continue as should their veto. Taking the cue from the US, Britain and France softened their opposition to reform. They turned their argument to the need for participation in UN military operations for any aspiring permanent member. Both of them said that Germany and Japan could be considered for permanent membership only when they were fully involved in UN peacekeeping operations. This was a problem for both Germany and Japan whose post-war constitutions imposed by the victors were strongly pacifist and prohibited sending military forces abroad.

Japan decided quickly to address this. In June 1992, it adopted a law permitting its military force to participate in UN peacekeeping operations but without a Chapter VII mandate. German public opinion was more difficult to deal with. It continued to oppose the deployment of troops outside, even though its judiciary had ruled that its constitution did not prohibit participation in UN missions.

India based its claim on the size of its population and its democratic credentials, ". . . population represents both an expression of the principle of democracy and an element of power. With increasing emphasis on the principle of democracy at the national level, there is a need for extending this principle to the international level also. The present permanent members of the Security Council have a combined population of less than 1.75 billion. This leaves two-thirds of the world's population without representation in the permanent membership category."[25]

All non-aligned states were for expansion in the non-permanent members and increasing the total membership from 15 to about 26. However, differences cropped up among them on expansion in the permanent category, both on the countries to be included and on giving them the veto.

Latin America and Asia initially proposed a 'two plus three' formula: the two being Germany and Japan and the three being one each from Latin America, Africa and Asia. Africa, however, wanted its share to be increased to two and was willing to concede the same number to the other two regions. Thus, the 'two plus three' formula became 'two plus six.'

The new formula was not universally endorsed by the South. Countries unlikely to make to the short list of permanent members opposed any increase in this category. The regional rivals of the countries claiming permanent membership were the most vociferous in opposing them: Russia, Italy and Spain against Germany; Pakistan and China against India; Russia, South Korea and China against Japan; and Argentina and Mexico against Brazil. They argued that an increase in permanent seats would make the Council more undemocratic.

On the issue of the veto, members realised that it would be impossible to persuade the permanent members to give it up. They turned their endeavour towards restricting its use. Some proposed that routine issues like the admission of new members and election of secretary-general should not be subject to the veto. Some proposed that the veto should be applicable only to decisions taken under Chapter VII of the Charter. The Netherlands proposed that a minimum of two vetoes should be required to block a decision. This was supported by Africa. While the aspirants were split on the names and numbers of new permanent members, the permanent five were united in their defence of the veto.

One significant development during this period was the proposal put together in 1997 by the chairman of the working group, Razali Ismail, extracting elements from the numerous proposals before him. The Razali Plan, as it came to be called, suggested an increase in Council membership from 15 to 24, with 5 additional permanent members and 4 additional non-permanent ones. The distribution of the 5 permanent ones was to be: one each for the developing countries of Asia, Africa and Latin America and the Caribbean and 2 from the industrial countries (presumably, Japan and Germany). The 4 non-permanent members were to be from Africa, Asia, Latin America and the Caribbean, and East Europe. Nothing came of the plan, but it became a template for the proposal promoted by the G-4 in 2005.

World Summit, 2005

Two summit meetings, the Millennium Summit in 2000 and the World Summit in 2005, tried to give a fillip to the reform process. On 8 September 2000, global leaders meeting in New York adopted the UN Millennium Declaration, which among others called for intensified efforts for a comprehensive reform of the Security Council. The declaration adopted at the world summit in New York in 2005, attended by more than 170 world leaders to celebrate the 60th anniversary of the United Nations, included a section on reform of the Security Council, "We support early reform of the Security Council – an essential element of our overall effort to reform the United Nations – in order to make it more broadly representative, efficient and transparent and thus to further enhance its effectiveness and the legitimacy and implementation of its decisions."[26] They requested the General Assembly to review progress on the reform by the end of 2005. This gave a sense of urgency to the reform process but its eventual failure was a serious blow to it.

In November 2003, in preparation for the second summit, Secretary-General Kofi Annan set up a 16-member high-level panel to examine the issue of Council reform. The panel gave its report in December 2004. It stressed the need for strengthening the capacity of the Security Council to fulfil its responsibility for maintaining peace and security by increasing it to make it more representative. It recommended the inclusion of countries that contributed the most to the UN – financially, militarily and diplomatically. It suggested two possibilities: (i) creation of 6 new permanent seats, without the veto and 3 new non-permanent seats (ii) a new category of 8 seats with a 4-year renewable term, to be divided equally among the four regions: Africa, Asia and the Pacific, Europe and the Americas.

Kofi Annan presented his own report, "In Larger Freedom", in March 2005. He recommended three key changes: (i) expansion of the UNSC from 15 to 24, by the inclusion of additional non-permanent members, (ii) creation of a Peace Building Commission, to help rehabilitate countries recovering from civil war, and (iii) replacement of the Commission on Human Rights with a smaller, standing Human Rights Council.

Annan made Security Council reform the cornerstone of his program. He maintained that no reform of the UN could be complete without it. His push gave an impetus to the process. However, once the reform proposals reached the General Assembly more options were proposed by member states. India, Brazil, Germany and Japan got together to form the G-4 and promoted the idea of 6 new permanent seats: 2 to Asia, 2 to Africa and 1 each to Europe and Latin America and the Caribbean. In addition, they proposed 4 new non-permanent seats: one each to Asia, Africa, Eastern Europe and Latin America and the Caribbean. On the issue of the veto, they advocated keeping it in abeyance till a comprehensive review had been undertaken of the Council's procedures.

The African Union proposed a similar model of 6 new permanent seats but added one more non-permanent seat for itself, making it 5. It also insisted on the right of veto for the new permanent members. A third proposal came from the Uniting for Consensus group, also referred to as the Coffee Club, which rejected the idea of new permanent seats and advocated 10 new non-permanent members.

The permanent five stayed out of the fray, content to leave the others to fight among them. As was to be expected, the proposals came to nothing. Regional rivals of the G-4 accused them of trying to grab power for themselves in the name of representativeness. The smaller countries felt left out. The African countries were the most strident and uncompromising in their demand for two permanent seats with the veto and five non-permanent seats. But they were unable to agree on their two permanent members. South Africa, Nigeria and Egypt were unrelenting claimants while Kenya, Algeria and Tanzania played spoilers.

With the countries of Africa undecided on their support for the G-4 proposal, there was little chance of it getting the required two-thirds majority in the General Assembly. The G-4 realised that they had overestimated the enthusiasm of the member states for Security Council expansion and underestimated the resolve of the permanent five to block it. China remained openly opposed to Japan and worked behind the scenes against India. The US did not have a clear policy on the issue and swung in all directions on the inclusion of Germany and Japan as permanent members. The G-4 relented and dropped its resolution.

The Security Council reform process survived the 2005 World Summit fiasco, but it had run out of steam. Intergovernmental negotiations were revived and the General Assembly president started consultations through facilitators. Discussions still take place periodically, essentially to keep diplomats engaged.

The Reform Debate

While most countries agree on the need for UN reforms, there is no agreement on the content or even the organs and procedures of the UN that need reform. The G-4 countries have been unable to get Africa to agree on the two countries from the continent. They also disagree with Africa on the veto. The G-4 is willing to compromise on the veto by shelving it for an unspecified period. African countries, on the other hand, insist on the veto for all new permanent members. This insistence and their inability to agree on the two countries for the permanent seats have become the major stumbling blocks for the G-4. The Uniting for Consensus group is opposed to an increase in the permanent category, though it is willing to consider longer tenures for select countries. With so many ideas floating around, Security Council reform has not made any headway since the 1990s. Britain and France are the only permanent members, occasionally joined by the US, to pay lip service to it, safe in the assurance that it is unlikely to go through. Some critics attribute the support of Britain and France to their calculation that an expansion is better than reform because that would raise questions about their own permanent seats.

For the United States and the EU, UN reform means giving more powers to the organisation to regulate the internal affairs of member states on issues like human rights, humanitarian affairs and good governance. They are against any change in the old power-based decision-making structure of the Security Council. Bolton recorded his aversion to the democratisation of the Security Council following a talk on it by the Brazilian ambassador, Ronaldo Sardenberg, ".... his long lecture to me about 'democratizing' the Council seemed calculated to ensure we would continue opposing their efforts."[27] The permanent five argue that their share in the global GDP may have declined but not significantly so. One study shows that, if the PRC were treated as part of it in 1950, their share of both the global GDP and population has fallen by about ten percentage points from 52 percent to 42.67 percent in GDP and from 38.65 percent to 28.12 percent in population, between 1950 and 2010. However, their share of military spending has come down only marginally from 63 percent to 61 percent during the same period.[28] Thus, while the permanent five represent only a third of the world's population, they account for nearly two-thirds of its military spending. This remains their main claim to permanent membership.

The reform debate remains stuck between the pulls and pressures of representation and efficiency. It is widely recognised that legitimacy can only come from greater representativeness and democracy but that will further complicate and slow decision making. The permanent seat aspirants face the impossible challenge of satisfying the larger membership of the General Assembly without displeasing the permanent five. They have to demonstrate their independence and effectiveness without questioning the inequities of the international order. The reform process has not been able to find a way out of this conundrum.

Endnotes

1   UNCIO, Doc. 1200, P/18, 26 June 1945, Closing Plenary, 26 June 1945, p. 715.

2   UNCIO Doc. 8, G/5. 25 April 1945. Verbatim Minutes of the Opening Session, 25 April 1945, p. 127.

3   This was a reference to the reactionary nature of the Concert of Europe, which was aimed at preserving the post-Napoleonic European order. This was also an acknowledgement of the similar objectives in the founding of the United Nations.

4   Mazower, p. 260.

5   Reddy and Damodaran. p. 32. Statement of V.K. Krishna Menon in the UNGA on 6 October 1954.

6   Reddy and Damodaran. p. 218.

7   Reddy and Damodaran, p. 219.

8   Two reported offers, by the United States in 1950 and by the Soviet Union in 1955, have been talked about. The denial was made by Nehru in the Indian Parliament on 27 September 1955. [Firstpost, 18 June 2016]. https://www.firstpost.com/india/that-indias-first-pm-deprived-us-of-a-unsc-seat-is-standard-anti-nehru-rhetoric-heres-why-2840188.html

9   D. Lee, *"The Genesis of the Veto"*. International Organization 1(1), 1947, p.34.

10 General Assembly resolution, 1991 of 17 December 1963.

11 Bolton, p. 249.

12 UN Document, A/RES/2758 (XXVI), 25 October 1971.

13 Alma-Ata Declaration, 21 December 1991.

14 Reinhard Drifte, *Japan's Quest for a Permanent Security Council Seat – A Matter of Justice or Pride?* (MacMillan, 2000), p. 110.

15 Quoted in Dimitris Bourantonis, *The History and Politics of UN Security Council Reform* (Routledge, 2005), p. 40.

16 Bourantonis, p. 40.

17 O. Croci, *"Italian Security Policy in the 1990s"* cited by Bourantonis, p.35.

18 Treaty on European Union, 7 February 1992, Article J 5.4.

19 Report of the UN Secretary-General, *Question of Equitable Representation*

on and Increase in the Membership of the Security Council, 1993. (UN Doc A/48/264, 20 July 1993), p. 91.

20   Report of the UN Secretary-General, Question of Equitable Representation on and Increase in the Membership of the Security Council (UN Doc A/48/264, 20 July 1993), p. 82.

21   Report of the UN Secretary-General, Question of Equitable Representation on and Increase in the Membership of the Security Council (UN Doc A/48/264, 20 July 1993), pp. 18-19.

22   Report of the UN Secretary-General, Question of Equitable Representation on and Increase in the Membership of the Security Council (UN Doc A/48/264, 20 July 1993), p. 92.

23   Condoleezza Rice, No Higher Honour (London: Simon & Schuster, 2011), p. 442.

24   Stewart M. Patrick and Kara C. McDonald, UN Security Council Enlargement and US interests. (New York: Council on Foreign Relations, 2010), p. 18.

25   India's submission to the Secretary General's Report on the Question of Equitable Representation on and Increase in the Membership of the Security Council, 1993, pp.47-48.

26   UNGA Resolution A/Res/60/1 of 24 October 2005, World Summit Outcome, 16 September 2005, para 153.

27   Bolton, p. 254.

28   Bart M.J Szewczyk.Variable Multipolarity and UN Security Council Reform. (Harvard International Law Journal, Vol.53.2, Summer 2012), pp.459-460.

Conclusion

How has the Security Council fared in performing its Charter responsibilities? Has it fulfilled the expectations of those who drafted the Charter? How do the current members of the UN evaluate it?

The enemy States of the Second World War against whom the United Nations was formed joined it a long time back and have ceased to be a threat to world peace.[1] In this respect, the Security Council has been a resounding success. The real threat of a major war, however, has come from the permanent five themselves and successfully preventing it is often cited as the Council's most noteworthy success. Assessing the first fifteen years of the UN, Eichelberger wrote, "[T]he decisive factor for world peace has been the United Nations. It has made the difference between the uneasy peace in which the world had lived and a Third World War."[2] This, however, is not a success but a critical failing of the Security Council. It is an admission that the permanent five, the putative policemen of the world, have been and continue to be the gravest threat to global security. One can also question if averting a third world war can be attributed to the Security Council. The Council was not designed to act against the permanent five. Preventing the third world war has to be attributed to the fear of the United States and the Soviet Union of mutual destruction, though the Security Council can be said to have served as a safety-valve for venting their acrimony.

Hurd believes that the Security Council's objectives were limited and it should be evaluated accordingly. They were confined to providing "collective legitimation" which is valuable for states and the efforts they make to secure it reinforce its legitimacy.[3] The military dominance of the permanent five has remained unchanged over the decades and they will continue to use the Security Council to legitimise their power. So long as their dominance remains, the Council will survive and continue its humble existence.

How have the secretaries-general assessed the United Nations? Trygve Lie was proud of the Korea operation and regarded it as his biggest achievement. His resignation amidst criticism from both the Soviet Union and the United States, however, soured his achievements. Dag Hammarskjöld had an equally torrid time dealing with the superpowers and towards the end of his tenure, he said, "The world cannot live in the shadow of either a holy alliance or a holy war between the two superpowers. They need the UN as a rubber stamp to authenticate their decisions. When they are in a minority, they ignore the UN completely. Those who have any real interest in the UN are the small and medium States which are driven by a dream they have no means to realise."[4]

U Thant expressed similar sentiments, "The Big Powers use the machinery of the UN only when they feel that their own interests will be served. In most cases, they have bypassed the UN in the settlement of disputes within their own spheres of influence."[5] Kurt Waldheim too had strong words of reprimand, "The UN has not yet cut through the political habits and attitudes of earlier centuries. While its system on paper is impressive, it has not been able to cope effectively with international conflicts, and its capabilities in other areas on international cooperation have dwindled. The superpowers have a preference for settling their problems bilaterally and inevitably they tend towards a policy of spheres of influence."[6]

Boutros-Ghali echoed the views of his predecessors, "Following the end of the cold war, it was the fate of the United Nations - and mine as Secretary-General - to be deeply involved in the effort to create a post-cold war structure and to do so with the United States, the sole remaining superpower of the conflict. But instead of producing a new international partnership to face the 21st century, the United Nations emerged from these years seriously damaged, despite some success. A post-cold war international system remains unbuilt."[7]

Writing in 1991, soon after the first Gulf War, the veteran UN official, Brian Urquhart, noted that the United Nations had not yet been able to provide a system for peace and security but had been functioning as a last resort or safety net. He recommended that the Military Staff Committee should activate Article 43 and start working on possible agreements with member states on the provision of forces to the United Nations. He wrote, "The Charter envisaged the gradual conversion of the existing military set-up into a world-wide system of common and collective security. The Military Staff Committee was also supposed to advise and assist the Security Council on 'the regulation of armaments, and possible disarmament' (Article 47.1), a task closely related to the basic task of conversion."[8]

A useful measure of the success of the Security Council is its ability to provide security to non-permanent members. In this, it has often been ineffective, singularly so when the invader has been a permanent five or its ally. The Security Council's sanctions and authorised military action have targeted only non-permanent members. Several member states which have taken disputes to the Security Council with high expectations have been disillusioned with it. But as we have seen from the debates in the San Francisco Conference, this was the arrangement envisaged in the Charter. The Council was not expected to take on a permanent member.

Then there are the votaries of humanitarian intervention. They regard the delay in intervention in former Yugoslavia and Rwanda and the inability to intervene in Syria as major failures of the Security Council. This again is not part of the Security Council's original mandate and should not be blamed on it. Thus, if the Security Council were to be evaluated on the limited responsibilities assigned to it by the Charter it would not fare too badly.

The real failure of the Security Council has been its inability to keep up with the progress in other international organisations and organs of the UN, which have worked towards developing processes of inclusive decision-making and modified their mandates and working with the changing world. The Security Council remains mired in its archaic politics of power. The veto can be seen both as a critical flaw in the system, an ignominious compromise that reduces it to a dictatorship of the hegemons and as a safety valve that allows the system to release overload that would otherwise blow it up. Either way, it is not a crowning achievement. It is at best an unpleasant necessity, an aberration that deflates the high expectations of the admirers of the UN. The veto reduces the Security Council to a legitimisation of power and prevents its evolution on the lines of other institutions of globalisation in the contemporary world.

Franck sums up this view succinctly, "The once-rational justification for Big Five privilege has lost its persuasiveness. Collective security, the area in which big military powers were expected to bear the principal responsibility, has virtually disappeared from the UN's agenda, to be replaced by peacekeeping, an activity which the neutral states of Northern Europe and the third world have accepted primary responsibility."[9]

The Security Council is a political body, constituted by the governments of member states who act in their own national interest. International bodies often acquire an institutional character over time which enables them to rise above narrow national considerations. But the veto has hindered such organic evolution of the Council. Its two-tier structure has impaired the growth of a collective spirit. The refusal of the permanent five to place their troops under Security Council command and their lukewarm participation in peacekeeping operations reinforces the hierarchical structure.

The permanent membership of the five violates a basic principle of democracy. In a study of the degree of democracy in international organisations, Zweifel found serious deficits of democracy and accountability in most, except the European Union. He found the UN to be particularly deficient, ranking just above the Organisation of African Unity in a study of eleven international organisations.[10] Within the UN, the Security Council will easily outclass other organs in lack of democracy, transparency and accountability.

Part of the perceived success of the Security Council comes from the fact that non-permanent members continue to covet its membership. Saudi Arabia's refusal to join it after getting elected in 2013 is the only instance so far of a country spurning it. The Saudi Foreign Office issued a statement soon after the country's election that the Council's refusal to impose sanctions on Syria was "irrefutable evidence and proof of the inability of the Security Council to carry out its duties and responsibilities."[11]

Why do members of the United Nations seek the two-year membership to the Security Council even though they have little possibility of influencing its outcomes? Momentary international prestige is an obvious consideration, as is the prospect of a domestic dividend. There is a distinct rise in interest in the country's foreign policy, especially on security issues. The permanent five, in particular, scrutinise it to gauge the prospects of garnering its vote. Vreeland and Dreher identified instances of elected members getting foreign aid in return for favourable voting, "Trades are possible, and they happen. The governments of rich and powerful countries such as the United States and Japan care more about votes and discussions at the UNSC than they do about foreign aid, which amounts to a paltry sum in their overall budgets." The big powers value Security Council legitimisation of their policies and actions and have "an interest in buying insurance votes."[12]

The United Nations has survived all these years because of the reluctance of the Soviet Union (and the Russian Federation) to walk out of it and the grudging support of the United States. Both have held on to the organisation and held it together despite their tantrums and complaints.

This compact now runs the risk of getting unravelled. The rise of China throws a new challenge to the organisation. Although China has been a member since 1971 and has not so far done anything to upset its delicate arrangement, its commitment to the values of the UN and to multilateralism remains in doubt. Its emergence as a global power will be a critical test for the organisation.

It is the countries of Asia, Africa and Latin America which imbued the UN with the exalted ideals for which it is known today. The permanent five were late converts to them and very soon vitiated them with the intrusive concept of responsibility to protect. Instead of defining these new ideals in universal terms, embedded in international law, and creating an appropriate machinery for their realisation they fell back on the old practice of enforcing them through unilateral action.

In the absence of compulsory adjudication of disputes and a machinery to enforce verdicts, the Security Council's actions to maintain international peace and security become a reactionary preservation of the *status quo*. Western countries wish to expand the mandate of the Security Council to include intervention in the internal affairs of member states but they are unwilling to alter the structure and procedures of the Council. The brief experience with such interventionism has left all five permanent members dissatisfied but they do not wish to dilute their privileged position.

The reformists, on the other hand, have an impossible task. An increase in the permanent seats will make the Council more undemocratic. A larger Council will make debates longer and decision-making slower and increase the temptation for the permanent five to meet separately. Zifcak points out that reform to be meaningful must address the issue of the veto, but any attempt to do so is doomed to failure, "While the debate was framed by the question of whether the Council should be recast to contain US power in particular or that of the P-5 in general, any proposals having that effect were never likely to succeed."[13]

Suggestions like the veto being replaced by a "supermajority vote – of perhaps three-quarters of voting members" seem to be eminently reasonable and judicious.[14] But without US military support Security Council decisions would be impossible to enforce and a division among the major powers would run the risk of a major war. While outsourcing military action is flawed, equipping the Security Council with military capability without changing its decision-making procedures will be equally unacceptable to many non-permanent members.

The dilemma for the permanent five and the reformers has been aptly summed up by Chesterman, Johnstone and Malone in their voluminous work on the UN, "The United Nations therefore faces a quandary. Reform is difficult but vital. Resistance is strong from the P-5, though often not made public. And there is no generally acceptable scheme around which the wider UN membership can currently rally within the General Assembly. The cost of continuing with the current system could be greater marginalization of the body as international security migrates to other institutions or flexible coalitions."[15] The Security Council has survived by limiting its activities to peacekeeping operations and gentle sanctions. It will not meet the fate of the League's Council anytime soon since the permanent five are still the dominant military force in the world, but its relevance and legitimacy will continue to be questioned.

Is there a way forward, and if so, in what direction? This is a difficult question and beyond the scope of this book but since I have raised some basic issues about the Security Council I will conclude with some thoughts on the principles on which solutions can be based. If the Security Council wishes to acquire powers, like the right to intervene in the internal affairs of member states, it must set high standards of constitutionalism. The UN Charter can become the constitution of a brave new organisation only if the permanent five show foresight and flexibility and incorporate in it the basic principles of a democratic constitution.

A beginning can be made by examining the premises on which the two main organs of the UN are based: the equality of member states in the General Assembly and their inequality in the Security Council. Both concepts are outdated. All countries are not equal – they vary in size, natural resources, population, size of the economy, development and military strength. Large countries legitimately resent being equated with countries the size of small towns. Weighted voting is recognised in organisations like the International Monetary Fund and the European Union and should be looked at for the United Nations as well. In the Security Council, the permanent presence of the five violates the principles of constitutionalism and the veto has crippled it. Weighted voting can partially address the concerns of the permanent five and introducing the requirement of a super-majority for resolutions under Chapter VII will allay the concerns of others. A moderate increase in the size of the Council will improve regional representation.

The other requirement is judicial review, which was considered but dropped at the San Francisco Conference. A fresh look at UN reform on these lines is needed if it is to grow into the protector of international peace and security in the modern world. While solutions are not easy to find, ignoring the growing irrelevance of the Security Council will jeopardise the entire international order at a time when there is dire need of greater cooperation to address global problems.

Endnotes

1   Japan joined in 1956 and the two parts (East and West) of Germany in 1973.

2   Eichelberger, *UN – The First Fifteen Years,* p. 5.

3   Ian Hurd. *After Anarchy – Legitimacy and Power in the United Nations Security Council.* (Princeton University Press, 2007), p. 193.

4   Cited by Rikhi Jaipal in U.S. Bajpai (Ed.): Forty Years of the United Nations. (New Delhi: Lancer International, 1987), p. 12.

5   Cited by Rikhi Jaipal in U.S. Bajpai (Ed), p. 13.

6   Cited by Rikhi Jaipal in U.S. Bajpai (Ed.), p. 13.

7   Boutros-Ghali, pp. 336-337.

8   Brian Urquhart, *Learning from the Gulf.* In Frank Barnaby (Ed.), *Building a More Democratic United Nations.* (London: Frank Cass, 1991), p. 301.

9   Thomas Franck, *The Power of Legitimacy Among Nations*, (New York: Oxford University Press, 1990), p. 177.

10 Thomas D. Zweifel, *International Organizations and Democracy – Accountability, Politics and Power.* (Boulder, Colorado: Lynne Rienner Publications, 2006), p.13 and 176.

11   Robert E. Worth, New York Times, 18 October 2013.

12 James Raymond Vreeland and Axel Dreher, *The Political Economy of the United Nations Security Council.* (Cambridge University Press, 2014). p. 4 and 8.

13 Spencer Zifcak, *UN Reform – Heading North or South?* (Routledge, 2009). p. 37.

14 G. John Ikenberry and Anne-Marie Slaughter. *Forging a World of Liberty.* (Princeton University Press, 2006), p. 25.

15 Simon Chesterman, Ian Johnstone and David M. Malone, *Law and Practice of the United Nations, Documents and Commentary,*(New York: Oxford University Press, 2nd Edition, 2016), p. 649.

Secretaries-General of the United Nations

1.	Trygve Lie	Norway	February 1946 – April 1953
2.	Dag Hammarskjöld	Sweden	April 1953 – September 1961
3.	U Thant	Myanmar	November 1962 – December 1971
4.	Kurt Waldheim	Austria	January 1972 – December 1981
5.	Javier Pérez de Cuéllar	Peru	January 1982 – December 1991
6.	Boutros Boutros-Ghali	Egypt	January 1992 – December 1996
7.	Kofi Annan	Ghana	January 1997 – December 2006
8.	Ban Ki-Moon	South Korea	January 2007 – December 2016
9.	António Guterres	Portugal	January 2017 – To date

Bibliography

Acheson, Dean. *Present at the Creation: My Years in the State Department* (New York: W.W. Norton, 1969).

Albright, Madeleine. *Madam Secretary* (London: Pan MacMillan, 2004).

Alexandre de Gusmão Foundation, Brasilia.

Annan, Kofi. *Interventions – A Life in War and Peace* (London: Allen Lane, 2012).

Annan, Kofi. *We the Peoples, A UN for the 21ˢᵗ Century* (London: Paradigm Publishers, 2014).

Annual Reports of the UN Secretary-General on the work of the Organisation.

Bajpai, U.S. (Ed.). Forty Years of the UN (New Delhi: Lancer International, 1987).

Barnaby, Frank. *Building a More Democratic United Nations* (London: Frank Cass, 1991).

Bass, Gary Jonathan. *The Blood Telegram* (New York: Random House, 2013).

Bedjaoui, Mohammed. *The New World Order and the Security Council: Testing the Legality of its Acts* (Kluwer Academic Publishers, 1994).

Bjola, Corneliu. *Legitimising the Use of Force in International Politics.* European Journal of International Relations, London, 11.2 (Jun 2005), 206-304.

Blair, Tony. *A Journey* (London: Hutchinson, 2010).

Blokker, Niels. *Is the Authorisation Authorised? Powers and Practice of the UN Security Council to Authorise the Use of Force by 'Coalitions of the Able and the Willing'.* (European Journal of International Law,

Vol. 11, No.3, 2000. Pp. 541-568).

Boardman, Robert. *Post-Socialist World Orders – Russia, China and the UN System* (New York: St. Martin's Press, 1994).

Bolton, John. *Surrender is Not an Option* (New York: Threshold Editions, 2007).

Bosco, David L. *Five to Rule Them All: The UN Security Council and the Making of the Modern World* (New York: Oxford University Press, 2009).

Bourantonis, Dimitris. *The History and Politics of UN Security Council Reform* (Routledge, 2005).

Boutros-Ghali, Boutros. *Unvanquished: A US-UN Saga* (New York: Random House, 1999).

Bowett, D. W. *United Nations Forces: A Legal Study of United Nations Practice* (New York: Frederick A. Praeger, 1965).

Bradley, James. *The China Mirage* (New York: Little, Brown and Company, 2015).

Brierly, James Leslie, *The Basis of Obligation in International Law* (Oxford: Clarendon Press, 1958).

Brierly, James Leslie. *The Law of Nations – An Introduction to the Law of Peace* (New York: Oxford University Press, 1963).

Brownlie, Ian. *International Law and the Use of Force by States* (Oxford: Clarendon Press, 1963).

Bull, Hedley (Ed.).*Intervention in World Politics* (Oxford: Clarendon Press, 1984).

Bush, George B. *Decision Points.* (UK: Virgin Books, 2011. Reprinted in India by Replika Press).

Bush, George H.W. and Brent Scowcroft. *A World Transformed* (New York: Alfred A. Knopf, 1998).

Carr, E.H. *Twenty Years' Crisis (1919-1939): An Introduction to the Study of International Relations* (London, Macmillan, 1946).

Chesterman, Simon, Ian Johnstone and David Malone. *Law and Practice of the United Nations* (New York: Oxford University Press, 2016).

Chowdhury, Subrata Roy. *Military Alliances and Neutrality in War and Peace* (New Delhi: Orient Longmans, 1966).

Churchill, Winston. *The Second World War, Vol. IV - The Hinge of Fate* (New York: Houghton Miffin, 1950).

Claude, Inis L. *Swords into Plowshares: The Problems and Progress of International Organisation* (New York: McGraw-Hill, 4th Edition, 1984).

Claude, Inis L. *The Changing United Nations* (New York: Random House, 1969).

Claude, Inis L. *The Management of Power in the Changing United Nations.* International Organization, Vol.15, No. 2, (Spring 1961). Pp. 219-235. (Carnegie Endowment for International Peace).

Claude, Inis L. *The United Nations and the Use of Force.* (International Conciliation, March 1961, No. 532).

Conforti, Benedetto and Carlo Focarelli. *The Law and Practice of the United Nations* (Leiden: Martinus Nijhoff Publishers, 2010).

Conte, Alex. *Security in the 21ˢᵗ Century* (Farnham, Surrey: Ashgate, 2005).

Cordier, Andrew W. & Wilder Foote (Eds.). *Public Papers of the Secretaries-General of the United Nations, Vol. I: Trygve Lie, 1946-1953* (New York: Columbia University Press, 1969).

Cordier, Andrew W. and Max Harrelson. *Public Papers of the Secretaries-General of the United Nations, Vol. 7, U. Thant, 1965-1967* (New York: Columbia University Press, 1976).

Dallin, Alexander. *Soviet Union at the United Nations* (London: Methuen and Co. 1962)

De Cuéllar, Javier Pérez. *Pilgrimage for Peace* (New York: MacMillan, 1997).

De Wet, Erika. *The Chapter VII Powers of the United Nations Security Council* (New York: Hart Publishing, 2004).

Dekker, I.F. and E. Hey (Eds.). *Agora: The Case of Iraq, Netherlands Yearbook of International Law, Vol.42.* (Netherlands: Asser Press, 2012).

Doder, Dusko and Louise Branson. *Milosevic – Portrait of a Tyrant* (The Free Press, 1999).

Drifte, Reinhard. *Japan's Quest for a Permanent Security Council Seat: A Matter of Pride or Justice?* (New York: MacMillan, *2002).*

Dulles, John Foster. *War or Peace* (MacMillan, 1950).

Durch, William (Ed.). *UN Peacekeeping, American Politics, and the Uncivil Wars of the 1990s* (London: MacMillan Press, 1997)

Eichelberger, Clark M. *Organising for Peace: A Personal History of the Founding of the United Nations* (New York: Harper and Row, 1977).

Eichelberger, Clark M. *United Nations – The First Fifteen Years* (New York: Harper & Brothers, 1960).

Eitel, T. *The Escape and Parole of the Imprisoned God of War: An Overview of the Second Gulf War from the Perspective of International Law.* 35 GYIL (1992) n. 292.

Falk, Richard A. *Legal Order in a Violent World* (Princeton University Press, 1968).

Falk, Richard A. and Saul H. Mendlovitz (Eds.). *The Strategy of World Order, Volume III - The United Nations* (New York: World Law Fund, 1966).

Fassbender, Bardo, *UN Security Council Reform and the Right to Veto.* (The Hague: Kluwer Law International, 1998).

Fenton, Neil: *Understanding the UN Security Council – Coercion or Consent?* (Farnham, Surrey: Ashgate, 2004).

Ferencz, Benjamin B. *New Legal Foundations for Global Survival: Security Thoughts for the Security Council.* (New York: Oceana Publications, 1994).

Franck, T.M. *Who Killed Article 2(4)? Or: Changing Norms Governing the Use of Force by States,* (64 American Journal of International Law 809, 1970, pp. 809-837).

Franck, Thomas: *The Power of Legitimacy among Nations.* (New York: Oxford University Press, 1990).

Fraser, Trudy: *Maintaining Peace and Security? The United Nation in a*

Changing World. (New York: Palgrave Macmillan, 2015).

Freudenschuss, Helmut. *Article 39 of the UN Charter Revisited: Threats to the Peace and Recent Practice of the UN Security Council.* (Austrian Journal of Public and International Law, 46, 1993, pp. 1-39).

Gaiduk, Ilya V. *Divided Together – The United States and the Soviet Union in the United Nations.* (Stanford University Press, 2012).

Gazzini, Tarcisio and Tsagourias, Nicholas (Eds.): The Use of Force in International Law. (Farnham, Surrey: Ashgate, 2012)

Gharekhan, Chinmaya R. *The Horseshoe Table: An Inside View of the Security Council.* (New Delhi: Pearson Longman, New Delhi, 2006).

Goodrich, L.M., E. Hambro, and A.S. Simons, *Charter of the United Nations.* (Columbia University Press, 1969).

Grove, Eric. *UN Armed Forces and the Military Staff Committee.* (International Security, Vol. 17, no.4, Spring 1993, pp. 172-182).

Harbutt, Fraser J.: *The Iron Curtain –Churchill, America and the Origin of the Cold War.* (New York: Oxford University Press, 1986).

Harriman, W. Averell and Elie Abel, *Special Envoy to Churchill and Stalin, 1941-1946.* (New York: Random House, 1975).

Hellinger, Daniel and Dennis R. Judd, *The Democratic Façade.* (Brooks/ Cole Publishing, 1991)

Higgins, Rosalyn: *Problems and Process, International Law and How We Use It.* (Clarendon Press, Oxford, 1994).

Higgins, Rosalyn: *The Development of International Law through the Political Organs of the United Nations* (London: Oxford University Press, 1963).

Hilderbrand, Robert C. *Dumbarton Oaks: The Origins of the United Nations and the Search for Post-war Security.* (University of North Carolina Press, 1990).

Hiscocks, Richard. *The Security Council - A Study in Adolescence.* (New York: Free Press, 1973)

Hoopes, T. and D. Brinkley. *FDR and the Creation of the United Nations.* (Yale University Press, 1997).

Hughes, E.J. *Winston Churchill and the Formation of the United Nations Organization.* (Journal of Contemporary History 9:4, October 1974).

Hull, Cordell. *The Memoirs of Cordell Hull, Vol. II.* (New York: MacMillan, 1948).

Hurd, Ian and Bruce Cronin. *The UN Security Council and the Politics of International Authority.*(Routledge, 2008).

Hurd, Ian: *After Anarchy – Legitimacy and Power in the United Nations Security Council.* (Princeton University Press, 2007).

Ikenberry, G. John and Anne-Marie Slaughter. *Forging a World of Liberty.* (Princeton University Press, 2006).

Ikenberry, G. John. *After Victory: Institutions, Strategic Restraint, and the Rebuilding of Order after Major Wars.* (Princeton University Press, 2001)

International Court of Justice website (www.icj-cij.org).

Jaura, Ramesh. *Serious Doubts Whether Sanctions Against DPRK are effective.* (In-Depth News, International Press Syndicate).

JN (SG) Papers, Nehru Museum and Library, New Delhi.

Jolly, Richard; Emmerij, Louis; and Weiss, Thomas G. *UN Ideas that Changed the World.* (Indiana University Press, 2001)

Jones, Bruce D; Forman, Shepard and Gowan, Richard, *Cooperating for Peace and Security: E*volving Institutions and Arrangements in a Context of Changing US Security Policy. (Cambridge University Press, 2012)

Kaplan, Lawrence M. *NATO and the UN: A Peculiar Relationship.* (Columbia, Missouri: University of Missouri Press, 2010).

Kelsen, Hans. *Is the Acheson Plan Constitutional?* (Western Political Quarterly, Vol. 3(4), 1 December 1950. Pp. 512-527).

Kelsen, Hans: *Law of the United Nations.*(New York: Frederick A. Praeger,1950).

Kirgis, Frederic L. *The Security Council's First Fifty Years.* (89 American Journal of International Law, 506, 539 (1995).

Koh, Harry. *On American Exceptionalism.* (Stanford Law Review 55).

Krause, Joachim and Natalino Ronzitti, [Eds.] The EU, the UN and Collective Security (Routledge, 2012)

Lauterpacht, Elihu.*The Legal Effect of Illegal Acts of International Organisations – Cambridge Essays in International Law,* 1965.

Lauterpacht, Hersch, *The Function of Law in the International Community* (Clarendon Press, Oxford, 1933).

Lee, D. *The Genesis of the Veto.* (International Organisation Vol. 1.1, 1947).

Lie, Trygve, *In the Cause of Peace, Seven Years with the United Nations.* (New York: The Macmillan Company, 1954).

Lobel, Jules and Michael Ratner, *By-passing the Security Council: Ambiguous Authorisations to Use Force, Cease Fires and the Iraqi Inspection Regimes.* (Vol. 93 American Journal of International Law, 1999. Pp. 124-154).

Lowe, Vaughan; Adam Roberts, Jennifer Welsh, and Dominik Zaum, (Eds.), *The United Nations Security Council and War: The Evolution of Thought and Practice since 1945.* (Oxford University Press, 2008).

Luck, Edward C. *UN Security Council.* (Routledge 2006).

Mahbubani, Kishore. *The New Asian Hemisphere: The Irresistible Shift of Global Power to the East.* (Public Affairs, 2008)

Malone, David M. (Ed): *The UN Security Council – From the Cold War to the 21st Century.* (Lynne Rienner, 2004).

Manusama, Kenneth. *The United Nations Security Council in the Post-Cold War Era – Applying the Principle of Legality.* (Leiden: Martinus, Nijhoff, 2006).

Marquand, David. *The End of the West.* (Princeton University Press, 2012).

Mazower, Mark. *Governing the World – The History of an Idea.* (Allen Lane, 2012).

McCoubrey, H. and N.D. White. *International Law and Armed Conflict.* (Dartmouth, 1991).

Meisler, Stanley, *United Nations: The First Fifty Years.* (New York: The Atlantic Monthly Press, 1995).

Moir, Lindsay. *Reappraising the Resort to Force: International Law – Jus ad Bellum and the War on Terror.* (New York: Hart Publishing, 2010).

Moynihan, Daniel P. *A Dangerous Place.* (Allied Publishers, Bombay, 1978).

Murphy, John F.: The United States and the Rule of Law in International Affairs. (Cambridge University Press, 2004).

Narasimhan, C.V. *The United Nations – An Inside View.* (New Delhi: Vikas, 1988).

Nardin, Terry. *Law, Morality and the Relations of States.* (Princeton University Press, 1983).

Nehru, Jawaharlal. *India's Foreign Policy: Select Speeches.* (New Delhi: Publications Division, 1961).

Nobel Lectures. (www.nobelprize.org).

Orakhelashvili, A. *The Impact of Peremptory Norms on the Interpretation and Application of United Nations Security Council Resolutions.* (European Journal of International Law, 2005, v.16, No. 1. pp. 59-68).

Patrick, Stewart M. and Kara C. McDonald. *United Nations Security Council Enlargement and US Interests.* (New York: Council on Foreign Relations,2010).

Payandeh, M. *The United Nations, military intervention an regime change in Libya.* Virginia Journal of International Law and Politics, 2012, v. 52, pp. 355-404).

Petculescu, Ioana. *The Review of the United Nations Security Decisions by the International Court of Justice.* (Netherlands International Law Review, LII, 2005. Pp. 167-195).

Quigley, J. *The 'Privatisation' of Security Council Enforcement Action: A Threat to Multilateralism.* (Michigan Journal of International Law, Vol. 17.2, Winter 1996, pp. 249-283).

Reddy, E.S. & A.K. Damodaran, *Krishna Menon at the United Nations – India and the World.* (New Delhi: Sanchar Publishing House, 1994).

Reisman, W.M. *Sovereignty and Human Rights in Contemporary International Law.* Vol. 84 American Journal of International Law, (1990), pp. 866-876.

Repertoire of the Practice of the Security Council.

Repertoire of the Practice of the United Nations Organs.

Rice, Condoleezza. *Campaign 2000 – Promoting the National Interest.* (Foreign Affairs 79, No.1, Jan-Feb 2000).

Rice, Condoleezza. *No Higher Honour.* (London: Simon & Schuster, 2011).

Ruggie, John Gerard. *Constructing the World Polity: Essays on International Institutionalization.* (London: Routledge, 1998)

Russell, Ruth B. *The United Nations and US Security Policy* (Washington DC: Brookings Institution, 1968).

Sarooshi, Dan: *The United Nations and the Development of Collective Security Chapter VII Powers.* (Oxford: Clarendon Press, 1999).

Schachter, Oscar. *United Nations in the Gulf Conflict.* (American Journal of International Law, Vol. 85, 1991. Pp. 452-473).

Schlesinger, Stephen C. *Act of Creation: The Founding of the United Nations.* (Cambridge, MA, USA: Perseus Books, 2003).

Schweigman, David. *The Authority of the Security Council under Chapter VII of the UN Charter.* (The Hague: Kluwer Law International, 2001)

Seaman, Kate. *UN-Tied Nations – The United Nations, Peacekeeping and Global Governance.* (Farnham, Surrey: Ashgate 2014).

Simma, B. (Ed.): *The Charter of the United Nations, A Commentary.* (Munich: Verlag C. H. Beck, 1994).

Szewczyk, Bart M.J. *Variable Multipolarity and UN Security Council Reform.* (Harvard International Law Journal, Vol.53.2, Summer 2012). P. 449-504).

Thakur, R. *The United Nations, Peace and Security.* (Cambridge University Press, 2006).

Tomaschat, C. (Ed.). *The United Nations at Age Fifty – A Legal Perspective.*

(The Hague:Kluwer Law International,1995).

Ugarte, Bruno Stagno and Jared Genser. *The United Nations Security Council in the Age of Human Rights.* (Cambridge University Press, 2014).

UN Conference on International Organization (UN Information Organization).

UN General Assembly Official Records.

UN Security Council Official Records.

Urquhart, Brian. *A Life in Peace and War.* (New York: Harper & Row, 1987).

US Department of State, *Dumbarton Oaks Documents on International Organisation, Publication 2257 (1954).*

US National Archives. (https://archives.gov).

US State Department, *Tentative Proposals for a General International Organisation,* July 1944.

Vandenberg Jr., A.H. and Joe Alex Morris, [Eds.], *The Private Papers of Senator Vandenberg.* (Boston: Houghton Mifflin Co. 1952)

Vandenbosch, Amry and Willard N. Hogan, *Toward World Order* (New York: McGraw Hill, 1963).

Villani, U. *The Security Council's authorisation of enforcement action by regional organisations.* (Max Planck Yearbook of UN Law, 2002, v.6, pp.535-557).

Vreeland, James Raymond and Dreher, Axel: *The Political Economy of the United Nations Security Council – Money and Influence.* (Cambridge University Press, 2014).

Wadsworth, James J. *The Glass House - The United Nations in Action.* (New York: Frederick A. Praeger Publishers, 1966).

Weiss, Thomas G. (Ed.) *Collective Security in a Changing World.* (Boulder, Colorado: Lynne Rienner, 1993).

Weiss, Thomas G. *What's Wrong with the United Nations and How to Fix It.*(Malden, MA, USA: Polity Press, 2009).

Weston, Burns H. *Security Council Resolution 678 and the Persian Gulf Decision Making: Precarious Legitimacy.* (The American Journal of International Law, Vol. 85, No. 3 (July 1991). Pp. 516-535).

Whitaker, Urban G. Jr. *Power and Politics: A Text in International Law.* (New York: Harper & Row, 1964)

White, Nigel D. *Collective Security Law.* (London: Dartmouth Publishing, 2003).

White, Nigel D. *Keeping the Peace – The United Nations and the Maintenance of International Peace and Security.* (Manchester University Press,1997).

Wilson, G. *The Legal, Military and Political Consequences of the "Coalition of the Willing" Approach to UN Military Enforcement Action.* Journal of Conflict and Security Law, 2007, v.12, pp. 295-330).

Wilson, Gary. *The United Nations and Collective Security,* (Routledge, 2014).

Wuthnow, Joel. *Chinese Diplomacy and the UN Security Council – Beyond the Veto.* (Routledge, 2012).

Yang, Suzanne Xiao. *China in the UN Security Council Decision-making on Iraq.* (Routledge, 2013).

Yunker, James A. *Beyond Global Governance: Prospects for Global Government.* (International Journal on World Peace, Vol. XXVI No. 2 June 2009)

Zifcak, Spencer. *United Nations Reform: Heading North or South?* (Routledge, 2009)

Zweifel, Thomas D. *International Organisations and Democracy, Accountability, Politics and Power.* (Viva Books, 2007).

Index

Biden, Joseph R. 180
Bildt, Carl 146
Biological Weapons Convention 242
Black Sea 45
Blair, Tony 192
Blood, Archer 173
Bodin, Jean 11
Bolton, John 178, 276, 285
Borah, Senator William E. 32
Bosnia case 232
Bosnia and Herzegovina 139, 144–146
Boutros-Ghali 20, 84, 101, 131, 132,
    139, 144, 145, 147, 148, 149,
    150, 151, 159, 168, 184, 240,
    278, 289, 294, 295, 298
Brahimi, Lakhdar 84, 133, 197
Brazil 27, 33, 72, 82, 99, 100, 125, 151,
    152, 155, 222, 234, 257, 271,
    276, 279, 282, 283
    compulsory jurisdiction of ICJ 222
    Haiti, authorising military action
        152
    Libya, authorising military action
        155
    permanent seat in Security Coun-
        cil 42
    permanent seat in the League
        Council 29
    Rwanda, authorising military ac-
        tion 151
    Security Council reform 283–285
    UN military 82
Bretton Woods Conference 43
Brezhnev, Leonid 137
Brierly, James L. 21, 23, 24, 230, 233,
    235, 298, 299
Britain
    alliance with United States 42–44,
        87
    Bosnia 146
    Brussels Pact 88
    Chilcot Inquiry 210
    China's inclusion in P-5 41–42

compulsory jurisdiction of ICJ 219
Concert of Europe 26–28
decolonisation and self determina-
    tion 64, 183
Egypt, British forces in 105
exercise of veto in the Security
    Council 59
interference in Greece 73
Interim Committee of the General
    Assembly 97
Iraq, bombing of 143
    military action in Second
        Gulf War 158, 265, 306
Korean war 106-116
League of Nations 29, 30
Libya 71, 137, 139, 154, 155, 157,
    158, 164, 165, 180, 182, 190,
    195, 203, 210, 212, 216, 223,
    226, 228, 242, 246, 247, 249,
    307
maritime dispute with Albania 73,
    94, 96, 139, 153, 154, 156,
    157, 213, 228, 244, 249, 276
military action in Kosovo 93
military bases abroad 96
Military Staff Committee 65
NATO 88–89
Nehru's view on British foreign
    policy 117
non-interference in the internal
    affairs 162, 171, 175, 206
on rise of Hitler 35–36
Palestine 74–75
Poland 61
rapid reaction force in Bosnia 84
sanctions on South Rhodesia 118,
    161
sanctions, policy on 165
Security Council reform 169, 271
selection of the first secretary-
    general 72
selection of UN Headquarters 71
Suez crisis 123–125

Colombia 60, 125
Cominform 97, 98
Communist International 34, 37, 97
Comprehensive Test Ban Treaty
 (CTBT) 241, 242
Concert of Europe 2, 19, 25, 26, 27,
 30, 32, 36, 286
Congo, Democratic Republic of the ix,
 3, 126, 132, 134, 139, 152, 158,
 161
  authorised military action 139
  Congo Advisory Committee 127
  human rights 181
  peacekeeping operations in 122,
   126, 152
Congolese forces 130
Congress of Vienna 29
Connally, Tom 60
Conner, Joseph 150
Cordovez, Diego 261
Corfu Channel case 228
Costa Rica 79
Côte d'Ivoire 132, 134
Crimean War 28
Croatia 139
Cuba 124
Cyprus 246
Czechoslovakia 96

D

Dayal, Rajeshwar 128
Decolonisation 46, 183, 184, 238, 245
de Cuéllar, Pérez 132, 138, 142, 203,
 215, 239, 252, 261, 295
de Guiringaud, Louis 124
de Mello, Sergio Vieira 241
de Michelis, Gianni 278
Democracy 183
Denmark 125
Disarmament 85
Dixon, Pierson 123, 135
Dole, Bob 151

Dulles, John Foster 83, 100, 120, 205
Dumbarton Oaks 40, 47, 49, 51, 52,
 55, 65, 66, 188, 197, 206, 297,
 301

E

East Pakistan 173. *See also* Bangladesh
East Timor 132
Ecuador 95
Eden, Anthony 45, 72
Egypt 79
Eichelberger, Clark M. 45, 49, 50, 69,
 108, 119, 288, 294, 300
Eisenhower, Dwight D. 72
El Salvador 60, 131
Ethiopia 127
European Court of Justice 165, 166,
 167
European Union ix, 154, 157, 165,
 166, 169, 191, 239, 250, 251,
 276, 278, 279, 280, 286, 291, 293
Evatt, Herbert V. 56

F

Fidel Castro 245
Fiji 135
Finland 125
First Gulf War 141, 143, 157, 158, 175,
 242, 248, 279
First World War 10, 29
Fleischhauer, Carl-August 141
Formosa 103. *See also* Taiwan
Forrest Davis 44
Four-Nation Moscow Declaration 40
France
  Brussels Pact 88
  Concert of Europe 26
  Congo crisis 126
  division of Ottoman Empire 33
  dominance in Francophone Africa
   251

T

Z

About the Author

Dilip Sinha was head of India's UN affairs during its membership of the Security Council in the eventful period, 2011-2012. He was ambassador to the UN in Geneva, where he was elected Vice President of the UN Human Rights Council in 2014 and Vice Chairman of the South Centre. Sinha steered India's response to the crises in Libya and Syria in the Security Council and to Sri Lanka in the Human Rights Council.

During his diplomatic career, Sinha headed India's relations with Pakistan, Afghanistan, and Iran and served in Germany, Egypt, Pakistan, Brazil, Bangladesh, and Greece.

Dilip Sinha is now based in India where he writes and delivers talks.

www.ingramcontent.com/pod-product-compliance
Lightning Source LLC
Chambersburg PA
CBHW021126270326
41929CB00009B/1065